ITALIAN TEXTS AND STUDIES ON RELIGION AND SOCIETY

Edmondo Lupieri, *General Editor*

Italian religious history has been pivotal to the formation and growth of European and Western civilization and cultures. Unfortunately, many texts which are fundamental for the understanding of its importance have long remained inaccessible to non-Italian readers. Similarly, the exciting developments of Italian scholarship in the field of the studies of religion have not always come into the public eye outside of Italy. Particularly since the end of World War II there has been continuous expansion in the field, and currently Italian scholars are combining the old and solid Italian tradition of philological and historical studies with new and innovative ideas and methodologies.

Italian Texts and Studies on Religion and Society (ITSORS) is a new series. Its publications are all English translations of works originally published or composed in Italy. The main aim of ITSORS is to have readers in the English-speaking world become acquainted with Italian socio-religious history and with the best of Italian scholarly research on religion with socio-historical implications. For this reason ITSORS will have two branches: *Texts* and *Studies*.

Texts consist of classical works and are intended to be useful as sources for a better comprehension of important events in Western religious history. Many are not readily available or have never been translated into English. *Studies* comprise original works of the best contemporary Italian scholarship which offer methodological contributions to research and make inroads into seldom studied areas.

ITALIAN TEXTS
& STUDIES
ON RELIGION
& SOCIETY

BOOKS AVAILABLE

Odoric of Pordenone
The Travels of Friar Odoric
(Sponsored by the Chamber of Commerce of Pordenone, Italy)

Edmondo Lupieri
The Mandaeans: The Last Gnostics
(Sponsored by the Italian Ministry of Foreign Affairs)

THE MANDAEANS

The Last Gnostics

Edmondo Lupieri

Translated by

Charles Hindley

WILLIAM B. EERDMANS PUBLISHING COMPANY
GRAND RAPIDS, MICHIGAN / CAMBRIDGE, U.K.

Published with the aid of a grant from the Office of Cultural Cooperation and
Development of the Italian Ministry of Foreign Affairs.

First published 1993 in Italian under the title
I Mandei. Gli ultimi gnostici.
© 1993 Paideia Editrice.
English translation © 2002 Wm. B. Eerdmans Publishing Co.
All rights reserved

This edition published 2002 by Wm. B. Eerdmans Publishing Co.
255 Jefferson Ave. S.E., Grand Rapids, Michigan 49503 /
P.O. Box 163, Cambridge CB3 9PU U.K.

Printed in the United States of America

07 06 05 04 03 02   7 6 5 4 3 2 1

Library of Congress Cataloging-in-Publication Data

Lupieri, Edmondo.
[Mandei. English]
The Mandaeans: the last gnostics / Edmondo Lupieri.
p.   cm.   (Italian texts and studies on religion and society)
Includes index.
ISBN 0-8028-3924-X (cloth: alk. paper)
1. Mandaeans.   I. Title.   II. Series.

BT1405.L86   2002
299′.932 — dc21

2001051056

www.eerdmans.com

to Sigrid

Contents

CONTENTS

Preface to the Italian Edition

Who could imagine that the old gentleman seated before me, talking amiably with a marked Roman accent in his small but elegant jeweler's shop in the heart of Rome, was a Mandaean? Indeed, the doyen of the Mandaeans in Italy. He belongs to the family of the al-Khamisi, which in the past included priests and scribes whose names appear in Mandaean manuscripts. Like almost all Mandaeans who did not become priests, he does not know their ancient language. Nor has he ever had time to go to school, either in Iraq or in Italy. He well remembers that as a child, in their big house made of wood and clay, they kept a sacred book, the Sidra, the "book" par excellence, wrapped in a white cloth and placed in a niche in the wall; a book no one could read.

As a boy, his village, in southern Iraq, a two-day journey from Basra by boat, was still part of the Turkish Empire. He recalls the Turkish soldiers coming into his father's shop for a chat, while his father, a blacksmith and gunsmith, repaired a jammed muzzle-loading rifle or replaced the butt of a pistol. He also remembers their flight before the English arrived: wretched soldiers of an army in disarray, who exchanged their guns for a piece of bread. Four hid in their home and left once the danger had passed. While he is speaking, many Italian war stories come to mind that I had often heard and that are indeed very similar to his — of soldiers seeking civilian clothes, a place to sleep, or a piece of bread to keep hunger at bay. In his village there was no shooting; the English arrived (it was 1917) on "those very small yellow warships" (because there the canals are not very deep). Behind the cannon and army of His Majesty, there were the Indians, filling the bazaar with their things.

The Roman jeweler's face is deeply lined by time and by events as distant as his memories. "I believe I'm 84," he says thoughtfully, "or perhaps 83." And there is a sudden change in his voice and a sparkle in his eyes. There were no registry offices where he had been born, and the date given on his papers, on his arrival in Italy, is a rough indication. He arrived in Italy via Paris and Malta on May 5, 1938. "It was different then; Mussolini was in power. . . ." Then Tripoli, the return in 1941, the war, the Germans, the Americans. His are all stories familiar to anyone in Italy, and it is hard to believe that a Mandaean, over eighty, is telling me them. A Mandaean who knows Porta Portese and at the same time the Šaṭṭ al-'Arab. He had not wished to stay where he was, though. Once the English had left what is now Iraq, the situation rapidly worsened. There were persecutions, with bands of fanatics who roamed around destroying Mandaean churches (i.e., the huts used for their cult). He immediately makes a connection with present-day Italy: "Just like now, with those guys that go around shooting gypsies."[1] Here, despite the hardships after the war, it was possible to make a living, and the shop made him some money. He had even been able to think of marrying. He is convinced he has always been a Christian, as are all Mandaeans; on the insistence of Catholic priests, he had all four ceremonies performed together: baptism, confirmation, first communion, and marriage.

According to this gentleman, Mandaeanism is dead. There are no more Mandaeans, or at least no true Mandaeans. He has been back to Iraq twice but did not like Baghdad any more. It was so completely different from before. Everything had changed. "I can't make head or tail of it," he repeats to me many times over when he speaks of modern Iraq. When he was a child, despite the poverty, life was wonderful. There were popular feast days every year, when everyone stayed at home and it was forbidden to touch cats or dogs for fear of contamination. And the food was good. You could drink the river water, and a great deal of yogurt was eaten. Butter making was done by shaking the milk in gourds (there were no glass milk bottles in those days!). "And when you committed a sin, because this happens to everyone, you went to the priest, who told you how many baptisms you had to undergo, three or four, to take the sin away."

---

1. The reference is to a band that specialized in this kind of violence, among others.

I had been trying for a long time to get in touch with some Mandaeans living in the West. I had heard that there was a family of Mandaeans in France, but no one was able to tell me where they lived. A colleague at a German university knew of a Mandaean doctor who had once lived in Bochum, but they had lost track of him. Then I got a tip that seemed to come straight out of a book of fairy tales. In Rome, in a famous square, behind the column of a church, there was a very small shop. An old Mandaean jeweler worked there. Despite my doubts, I went there and found a young Italian florist who had never heard anyone say anything about an Iraqi jeweler. Luckily, a neighboring shopkeeper, whose ample twirling mustaches must have known the taste of many a battle, directed me to an Iraqi pizza cook. Anywhere in Italy but in Rome an Iraqi pizza cook would have been quite strange. Once located, the Iraqi pizza maker, amiable and polite, gave me the phone number of a Mandaean journalist who lived in Rome, as if this too were a normal occurrence. It would seem that there are two Mandaeans in the whole of Italy, both from Iraq, and both, by pure coincidence, from the same family of al-Khamisi. I had found the first, who was as amazed to hear someone ask him on the telephone whether he was a Mandaean, as I was to hear him reply that yes, indeed he was.

Mr. al-Khamisi had many things to talk about as well. He had studied anthropology in Baghdad, and for his fieldwork he had worked for some weeks in a small Mandaean village, in the marshes to the South. I therefore took advantage of his courtesy (and of that of his Italian wife), and, thanks to the accuracy of his memories and his specific knowledge, I was able to fill in some of the gaps in this book. Through him I met the elderly jeweler and also one of the two Mandaean families who, in exile from a country that had been devastated, were then to be found on Italian soil, awaiting to transfer to another Western nation. While I also wish to thank these Mandaeans for their patience with me, I fervently wish that their sacrosanct desire for a normal life would be granted, as well as that of a rapid return to their own homes. To Mr. al-Khamisi I am especially indebted since he has enabled me to make contact with the present-day and human side of Mandaeanism, and hence to get beyond an approach based just on book knowledge and oriented to the past. I am deeply convinced that it is precisely this human dimension of knowledge that justifies studies of a historic nature. In spite of people's geographical, linguistic, religious, or cultural origin (in the broadest sense of the latter), it is still possible to get to know each other because each is driven by a curiosity to learn about the culture of the other. At this point research means something. In its small way, one of the main aims of this book is to facilitate a meeting between different ideal worlds that through mutual ignorance risk clashing violently, especially in recent years. Though well aware of the limitations of a work of this kind, one has to begin somewhere.

I would like to thank the many people who have helped me put this book together: my colleagues in Oriental Studies at Turin University (especially my friend Fabrizio Pennacchietti, whose help, as always, has been invaluable) and the University of Udine; librarians and archivists, in particular, in Rome; all those who enabled me to make use of the Archivio di Propaganda Fide; the Augustine Fathers of Rome, who have now been friends of mine for many years; and Padre Antonio Fortes, O.C.D., the exquisite archivist of the Curia Generalizia dei Carmelitani Scalzi, in Rome.

Finally, I would like to give special thanks to my colleagues at the Dipartimento di scienze storiche e documentarie of the University of Udine and to its director, Pier Cesare Ioly Zorattini, since without the funds they provided, this book would not have been possible.

Preface to the American Edition

Sunday, June 13, 1999. A man dressed in a long, white robe, his long beard concealed by a kind of white scarf that covers his mouth, his long hair wrapped in a white turban, stands in the river, holding in his left hand a long, wooden stick. Other men, all dressed in white robes, some of them dripping with water, stand on the bank. Many other people are nearby, some praying, others chatting, some taking photos, others filming the scene. A young boy with his own white robe is "called to the waters" by the man in the river, who continues to recite an old litany in an Aramaic language. The boy answers in the same language, and then, for the first time in his life, he "enters the waters" for the ancient rite — his first baptism in the Name of the Life. On this sunny day other young people paddle in their canoes and kayaks. They glance quickly from the river at the small crowd and continue on their way.

In the ancient Aramaic prayer, many names are pronounced, including that of John the Baptist, but not that of Jesus. What we are observing, indeed, is not the ritual of some strange Oriental Christian sect. We are not in Mesopotamia, and the river is not the Tigris or the Euphrates. We are on the banks of the Charles River in Boston, Massachusetts, facing Harvard University, where the "First International Conference" on Mandaeanism is being held. The young boy who just "entered the waters" is an American Mandaean.

After having witnessed the above scene, I was assured of the usefulness of translating this book into English. The questions I attempted to answer in the 1993 Italian edition (Who are the Mandaeans? What is Mandaeanism?) have now become more important in Western culture. Hopefully, the West is awakening from its tendency to swallow other cultures without even knowing "who they *had been.*"

This introduction to Mandaeanism is written for Western people who ask serious questions about cultural diversity in their own world and who want scholarly but readable answers. The book is written by a European from a Western historical perspective. It relies on the preceding works of other Westerners, scholars, travelers, and missionaries. It is the first attempt to reconstruct the history of the European perception of Mandaeanism by collecting and discussing the documentary testimony concerning the Mandaeans from the Middle Ages to contemporary times. Many of these documentary texts are published here for the first time, since these letters and official reports have remained for centuries in Roman archives.

This book is also the first attempt to reconstruct a reliable and "internal" history of Mandaeanism, based on the historical information contained in the colophons of Mandaean manuscripts (usually scrolls). These colophons, found at the end of each manuscript, are a kind of extended "signature" in which the scribe identifies himself and explains why he copied the work. Colophons are rich personal records that contain otherwise unknown data concerning Mandaean life. Often more recent colophons reproduce "signatures" written by older scribes, and, although a complete publication and study of all the manuscript evidence is not yet available,[1] what is already published and translated allows us to travel back in time from signature to signature. In this way we reach the very first names, which are always the same, of the oldest Mandaean scribes, possibly the historical fathers of Mandaeanism. From them everything originates that we know of early Mandaean traditions, language, and culture.

The last part of the book is an anthology of Mandaean texts. Some of them appear for the first time in English translation. The goal of the collection is to allow the reader a first contact with a living cultural and religious tradition that was often obliged in the past to fight for its identity and survival in a world controlled by external and unfriendly powers. The texts I chose are necessarily small fragments of a vast literary production. They testify not only to the theological and speculative richness of an an-

1. Jorunn Jacobsen Buckley is presently preparing such a work.

cient Gnostic religious tradition but also, and especially, to its constant struggle and everyday competition with "the religions of the others."

My hope is that the living community of the Mandaeans, whether in Iraq, in Iran, or in the contemporary diaspora abroad (especially in Australia, Europe, and North America), will see this as an attempt, albeit incomplete, to present their historical traditions and cultural reality to their present-day neighbors. We who are now their neighbors are the descendants of those who were once foreigners in their region, and it would be unfortunate to continue ancient misunderstandings.

This book is intended for anyone interested in religion, not necessarily scholars or specialized researchers in the field. The bibliography has been updated and modified for the English public. It lists all the published (and translated) Mandaean texts and the most important scholarly tools that can be used for deepening the reader's knowledge of Mandaeanism. The footnotes are intended to support the understanding of the text without being pedantic. By "searching the Web" readers can find websites set up by Mandaeans themselves. In this way readers can establish contact with a living and growing cultural reality.

I would like to thank the many people who made possible this English edition, the translators and editors, and especially William B. Eerdmans, Jr., whose friendly and wise guidance accompanied each phase of the enterprise. I am grateful to the administration and my colleagues at the Center of Theological Inquiry, in Princeton, New Jersey, where I was able to complete the revision of this work. Very special thanks go to the Italian Ministry of Foreign Affairs and to the Italian Consul in Detroit, Gianluca Alberini. His activity in support of the Italian culture made it possible for this book to be accepted in a ministerial program for the diffusion of Italian culture and language abroad and to receive generous financial help. Finally, I wish to thank my family, my wife Linda and our daughters, whose understanding, patience, and support allow me to continue with my work.

Prologue

Imagine the consternation of the authorities in the Roman Curia when in June 1990 a delegation of Mandaeans on a visit to the Vatican expressed their wish to celebrate a solemn baptism in the Tiber. Sheik ʿAbdallāh al-Šayḫ Naǧm al-Šayḫ Nahrun and the seven men accompanying him had hoped to put on their immaculate white ritual robes, perform several full immersions in running water, and actually drink the water, exactly as Mandaean ritual requires. Unfortunately, they had to be dissuaded, given the currently unappealing nature of the Italian capital's sacred river.

In Baghdad it would have been different, at least in the past, though the question of the water's purity had arisen there too, not long before. In 1985 the Mandaeans inaugurated a walled baptismal pool with water flowing in from, and then back into, the Tigris — a clear sign of advancing modernity compared to pools dug out of the earth. What did not change, however, is the fact that for the ritual ablutions and consumption (and for practicing Mandaeans, for any and all consumption), piped water should not be used. Being gathered in tanks, piped, or run through aqueducts, in fact, "cuts" and "kills" the water. The only water that is "alive," and therefore fit to use, is water that flows freely. Only in this water proceeds "Life," the heavenly and spiritual reality that lies at the origin of all life on earth. Physical water gushing from the spring is still charged with the divine force that animates it, but it loses this force the moment its free flow is interrupted. There is also a second problem, involving the process of purification that water has to go through before being piped. This would in the normal course of events be the work of Iraqi Moslem technicians, and thus the "purified" water becomes a drink prepared by Moslems. For Mandaeans such water is contaminated, since neither food nor drink should be accepted from a Moslem (if forced to do so, they should afterward subject themselves to thoroughgoing purification).

Given that the water of the Tigris, especially in and around Baghdad, is not what it used to be, it has to be disinfected before entering the immersion pool. This has given rise to something of a modern legend. The product used to disinfect the water is not normal chlorine produced in a factory by Moslem hands but a special product purchased in the Vatican.[1] This is because contact with Christians and their things is not contaminating.

As we shall see below, there are clear historical reasons behind such a favorable view of Christians and Christianity. Since Mandaeanism and Catholic Christianity rediscovered one another in modern times, the Mandaeans have always looked to Rome for help against Islam. While the more ancient Mandaean texts bear witness to the existence of a very real hostility toward Christianity, the need to obtain or maintain a certain degree of tolerance from the Moslem authorities has brought the Mandaeans to seek a friendlier rapprochement with the missionaries, and thence Catholicism. At times the friendship of the "Father of the Christians," the missionary, has helped save individuals or even entire communities. The privileged relationship with Rome and with Italy has also been strengthened by a curious historical coincidence, for the first Westerner to have described the Mandaeans, in the late thirteenth century, was an Italian missionary, just as it was another Italian missionary who first devoted an entire book to them in the middle of the seventeenth century. Sheik ʿAbdallāh's visit to the Vatican is merely the latest instance of a time-honored historical trend that in other times and in other circumstances had already brought Mandaeans there.

The papal audience itself, as reported in the Osservatore Romano of June 9, 1990, and in a brief film made on that occasion, revolved around what Pope John Paul II called "the many points of contact between your religion and the Christian faith." The time is ripe for old barriers to be removed, in the name of seeking for what may unite. These are the carefully chosen words the Pope used to address the Mandaean sheik: "The great respect you have for John the Baptist and the honor in which you hold the

---

1. This is what I was told by a Mandaean in Europe in 1991.

person of Jesus, John the Baptist's cousin, is the reason why you are pleased to call us 'your cousins'. . . . In your tradition, just as in the Gospel, when Jesus was baptized by John the Baptist in the Jordan, the Holy Spirit descended on him in the form of a dove." It is hardly relevant today that the idea in Mandaeanism that John and Jesus were kin was derived from Islam, or that the presence of the Spirit in the form of a dove can be found in only one ancient Mandaean text, and in a violently anti-Christian context at that. Any modern Mandaean, not having read the religion's sacred texts (as knowledge of the classical Mandaean language and writings is reserved to a restricted circle of the knowledgeable), is certainly convinced that there are no insuperable barriers separating the Mandaeans from their "Christian cousins." In fact, Iraqi Mandaeans held as prisoners of war in Iran requested (and were granted) the possibility of taking part in the Sunday services of Christian prisoners.

In contrast to the signs of Mandaean openness toward the Western world and Christianity (at least on concrete, if not ideological, questions), in our culture there is widespread ignorance of Mandaeanism and its history. In reality, it is an absolutely exceptional religion, even in the vast and varied world of the history of religions. Mandaeanism is one of the few cases of a religious faith preserved by a small nucleus of believers who are socially discriminated against and immersed in a hostile ethno-religious context. As with any religion of the past, we should not of course harbor any illusions that the passing of nearly two millennia has not left an indelible mark on Mandaean beliefs. Its very survival has sometimes been very much at risk. The select and esoteric structure of the group, typical of Gnosticism, reserving knowledge of the religious texts and mysteries to a tiny minority, has exposed the group to constant danger through the biological extinction of the caste invested with its knowledge. That same structure, however, has allowed the majority to survive, or if necessary to camouflage itself in the surrounding religious world. With the exception of the need to avoid circumcision, which otherwise would exclude one permanently from the community, Mandaeanism offers its "normal" believers the chance to coexist with noncircumcising religions, as well as the secular world. As a result, at least over the last few decades, many Mandaeans have joined left-wing ideological movements, within the limits of what that term can or could mean in the Islamic world.

Given these premises, we can not give a straight answer to the question of what Mandaeanism is. On the one hand it is an esoteric religious knowledge, reserved for a chosen few and preserved through centuries of adversity in a collection of not easily accessible writings. On the other hand it is a community of believers with a bare minimum of theological ideas, and which, perhaps for this very reason, has been able in one way or another to perpetuate itself through the all too often tragic ebbs and flows of their history, but not without adaptation and transformation.

PART I

HISTORY

1. The Mandaeans

LIFE, CUSTOMS, AND RELIGIOUS RITUALS

Soon after the Shah of Persia had been chased out and power had passed to the Ayatollah Khomeini's revolutionaries, the Mandaeans of Iran, having enjoyed complete tranquility under the secular and pro-Western government of Reza Pahlevi, thought it wise to take a precautionary measure in defense of their right to religious freedom under the new regime. In a delegation headed by the highest Mandaean authorities, they went to confer with Ayatollah Ṭāleqānī.[1]

Contrary to what people in the West usually think, Islam is not in itself an intolerant religion, and the line of conduct followed by governments drawing their inspiration from Islam depends on the decisions of those in power. The Koran, however, does grant special status (Ahl al-Kitāb) to the "people of the book," in other words to those groups who can demonstrate that they possess inspired religious texts. The Koran names three religions or ethnic groups that should benefit from this right: Jews, Christians, and the mysterious Sabaeans *(ṣābi'ūn)*. If we bear in mind that the age of Muhammed is certainly not famous for having fostered mutual understanding between peoples, his restriction of forced conversion to "pagans" and his goal of establishing a *modus vivendi* with the "religions of the book" demonstrate considerable open-mindedness, or at the very least a remark-

---

1. Ayatollah Ṭāleqānī was at that time an influential member of the Iranian parliament. The anecdote is taken from R. Macuch, *Neumandäische Chrestomathie mit grammatischer Skizze, Kommentierter Übersetzung und Glossar,* Porta Linguarum Orientalium, n.s. 18 (Wiesbaden: Harrassowitz, 1989), p. 17.

3

ably pragmatic instinct. He thus guaranteed Islam's very survival in its earliest years, when it was still a minority religion and had to find a way to accept non-Islamic neighbors, and be accepted by them. This may also help us to understand how some Islamic principalities of the past (Sicily, e.g., or the Iberian Peninsula) came to be islands of tolerance, enjoying the highest levels of civilization, where Jews, Christians, and Moslems alike could fill top posts in public administration or reach eminence in university culture.

So it was with feelings of hope mixed with uncertainty that our Mandaeans, their leaders and their books, went to confer with the Ayatollah.[2] What they heard froze their hearts. There was one concession: they would all be given the chance to convert to Islam.

Memories of past tragic times must have come to mind, for as late as the nineteenth century whole villages had been forced into apostasy and forcibly circumcised, men and women, elderly and adolescents.[3] Luckily, nothing of that nature happened again, but only a short while after the encounter described above, war broke out between Iran and Iraq. For eight years the lands of the Mandaeans were overrun by war, their villages were destroyed, and they were driven into forced evacuation. Shortly after the war ended, and there was hope of establishing some equilibrium among nonbelligerents, the Iraqi invasion of Kuwait and subsequent massive intervention by American, European, Arab, and other allied forces brought about further, enormous destruction. Finally, in southern Iraq, where there should still have been many Mandaean communities, the Iraqi regular army, faithful to Saddam Hussein, violently suppressed a secessionist rebellion that aimed (at least in the version provided by the Western press) to found a Shiite Islamic republic along Iranian lines. It is hard to tell if things really stood that way, but, if that was the case, a rebel victory would probably have placed the surviving Iraqi Mandaeans, tolerated by the secular Baathist government of Saddam Hussein, in a similar appalling dilemma to the one their Iranian co-brethren in faith had been presented with a decade earlier.[4]

---

2. Literally, "Sign of God."

3. The Turks do not impose circumcision on children. Even though clitoridectomy, improperly called circumcision of women, is prohibited nearly everywhere, it is still practiced on a large scale in Africa (even in modern countries with "secular" governments like Egypt's). Regarding the area that interests us here, there is explicit Mandaean testimony up to the second half of the nineteenth century.

4. Several years ago an Iraqi acquaintance of mine, a Catholic priest, told me that

Yet just who are the Mandaeans, and how many of them are there? There is no easy answer, partly because the terminology itself is ambiguous. Like the term "Jewish," and unlike the terms "Christian" and "Moslem," "Mandaean" means both someone who belongs to a particular ethnic group and one who adheres to a particular religious belief. Hence, if a family of Mandaeans converts to another religion (whether willingly or not), though not abandoning their ethnic identity, no one really considers them Mandaeans any longer, neither the believers in their old faith, nor those of the new one. Once they have abandoned their specific religious identity they cease to exist as a separate ethnic group. Furthermore, there is always some question as to just how willing members of minority ethnic and religious groups are to declare themselves such when faced with an official government questionnaire in countries with political regimes that are not of the Western democratic type. It is often more convenient to try to keep a low profile. It is therefore impossible to give even a rough estimate of how many ethnic Mandaeans there are. In religious terms, we know that prior to the violent upheavals of the recent wars there were about twenty thousand people in Iran and Iraq, taken together, who declared themselves to be practicing Mandaeans. They were concentrated along the Šaṭṭ al-ʿArab and the rivers that converge on it, the Tigris and Euphrates in southern Iraq, and the Karun (the ancient ʿUlai) in Iranian Kuzistan. There are significant Mandaean communities in the principal Iraqi cities, in Baghdad (where the largest one is to be found), and to the north as far as Mossul.[5] There is also a Mandaean diaspora. Some isolated families live in Europe, while there are a few hundred in Canada, Australia, and the United States, where there are at least two Mandaean cultural centers (Mandaean Houses), one in Los Angeles and the other in New York. The Mandaeans of the diaspora do not have their own priesthood, but this does not mean that they have been completely absorbed by the surrounding cultures. The last Mandaean manuscript to be copied out on American soil (at least the last one officially recorded) bears the date "New York, 10 November 1987." The scribe is a Mandaean from Persia who emigrated to America some thirty years ago. According to the scholar who mentions

---

only with the last Baathist revolution of Saddam Hussein had the national electric system reached his village (of Christians). The end of certain forms of discrimination can help to explain the support received by Saddam Hussein by the religious minorities of the country.

5. On this point I have had the direct testimony of an Iraqi colleague from Mossul, Dr. Ayar al-Abbar, whom I wish to thank.

this work, and from whose book I learned of this manuscript, its last words are in broken English and read, "to remembrd of me in usa mandic" ("in memory of me, a Mandaean in the U.S.A.").

As far as the Mandaeans who remained in their traditional home-lands are concerned, throughout the entire period for which we have reli-able accounts, from the seventeenth through the first half of the twentieth century, it would appear that they have always or primarily pursued four or five specific occupations. The more wealthy, belonging for the most part to the families of the priesthood, are goldsmiths. Since practicing Moslems are forbidden to work gold directly, it is only natural that in Islamic coun-tries the work of a jeweler should be carried out by members of a religious minority. Others are blacksmiths, carpenters (also known for their ability as boat builders), and finally shepherds and farmers. This last group does not appear to be very numerous, working mostly on date palm planta-tions. Following the accounts of some Western scholars, up to and through the nineteenth century the Mandaeans in Iraq owned their own houses but not the land, which at best they rented. With the two world wars and the rise to power of officially secular regimes in both Iran and Iraq, a period of transformation and acculturation began for the Mandaeans, along with the rest of the population. This brought about a degree of crisis and the partial collapse of the traditional socio-religious structures, which had luckily been recorded for us through the detailed fieldwork carried out by an extraordinary figure, Ethel S. Stevens. Also known as Lady Drower (her husband was an English diplomat), she spent much of her life in Iraq[6] in close contact with the Mandaean communities there, forming deep friend-ships with some of the Mandaean priests. More than anyone else, she is re-sponsible for the rediscovery and preservation of Mandaean culture in the West, thanks to her testimony, to her photographs and scholarship, and also to the numerous manuscripts she brought back to Great Britain (fifty-four in all, some of them containing previously unknown works), all of which are now housed in Oxford.

To that world, as portrayed by Lady Drower at the very limits of sur-vival, we shall thus be referring, describing a "Mandaean society" that per-haps by now no longer really exists.[7]

6. More precisely from 1921, the beginning of the British mandate, to 1947.
7. Except perhaps in a few particularly isolated villages. Recently, however, there has been a lively renewal of interest in their own traditions, even among the young and accultur-

The Mandaeans, then, lived along the rivers of Lower Mesopotamia in their own villages or in distinct areas of the larger urban agglomerations in straw and mud huts. In the eyes of the Western traveler they cannot have seemed any different from their Arab neighbors, except for apparently quite negligible differences in the style and color of the clothes and turbans that some of them wore. Westerners and Mandaeans have often viewed each other with mutual suspicion. Heinrich Petermann, a German professor who spent three months in an Iraqi village in 1854 in order to take daily lessons in the Mandaean language from a Mandaean priest, a certain Iahia (John), left us an amusing description of the tricks he used to keep Iahia from finding out what his true interests were. Petermann knew classical Mandaean perfectly well, but under the pretext of refining his knowledge of the language so as not to rouse suspicion, he gathered traditions, legends, and interpretations of sacred texts, descriptions of ceremonies, and in short a distillation of the Mandaean culture of the period. In Petermann's eyes Iahia was an untrustworthy Arab to be deceived, greedy for money, and none too clean either. Mandaean priests never shave their heads, and their hair is gathered in a long braid inside a turban. Petermann knew he had inherited a number of bothersome insects from Iahia's braid. However, when Iahia invited Petermann to his home he did not even let him in the house but hosted him on a comfortable divan in the courtyard. His excuse was that his home was too humble, but Petermann was sure that he did not want a European to see the women of the house. The Mandaean and the German remained foreigners from two separate worlds, united only by the interests of the occasion. It is also worth noting that Iahia, who left us some Mandaean texts written in his own hand, never even mentions Heinrich Petermann when recounting his own life.

---

ated Mandaeans. In Iraq there is also apparently a growing number of new priests. We also have information of books written by Mandaean priests in Iran, even toward the end of the 1980s, describing the principal elements of Mandaeanism in Persian. This means that the Mandaean community in Iran still exists and is resisting the changed situations in that country. In big cities such as Baghdad, however, it is practically impossible to observe the precise rituals and norms regarding food and drink (as we saw in the Prologue, a genuinely practicing Mandaean cannot drink water from the tap or from a bottle, but only running water). Regarding specifically cultural questions, we are witnessing an attempt at a revival that cannot, however, re-create the past as such. Lady Drower had already observed that the younger Mandaeans going to state schools in Iraq refused to believe that the earth was flat, held on the immense shoulders of 'Ur, an enormous serpent-like sea monster of the abyss.

From his own perspective Petermann was right. In 1870 yet another German professor went to the same village seeking information about the Mandaean language and religion from the same Iahia. This time the professor received nothing but extortionate demands for money for lessons that were never even held. Given the way things were going, the professor decided to follow official channels and sought help from the local authorities. At that time southern Mesopotamia was part of the Ottoman Empire, and the Turkish dignitary responsible for the region was very willing to further the interests of scientific investigation. He offered to have the Mandaean beaten until he talked! At that point the European gave up, and Iahia never did talk. Thus, with the exception of Petermann, up until Lady Drower's work almost the only information we have about Mandaeanism comes from apostate Mandaeans, whose stories were collected by Catholic missionaries, or from missionaries, whose stories were presented to scholars and European travelers. This, however, allows us to compare data from different sources and to trace the various kinds of cultural contamination that have affected them. While conversing with a "dear sister in faith" (the way Lady Drower was defined by a Mandaean priest of Basra), an elderly believer would certainly describe the mysteries of his faith differently from a young apostate who had broken all ties with his family, village, and past. Despite the appearance of cultural uniformity with the surrounding world, there is indeed a great abundance of Mandaean mysteries.

The first of our many uncertainties regarding the Mandaeans concerns the name itself, for we cannot be at all sure what the word means. What at first sight seems the most obvious hypothesis is that the word the Mandaeans use to define themselves, *mandaiia*,[8] is directly related to *manda*, the equivalent of *madda*, meaning "knowledge." The term would therefore exactly correspond to the Greek "Gnostic," from "gnosis," also meaning "knowledge." Mandaean would mean Gnostic, and everything would seem to be fine. In reality, though, this is quite hypothetical, and there are at least two other possible explanations that appear more probable. The most sacred Mandaean ceremonies are performed inside a fenced-off area, called a *mandi*, the only building inside the *mandi* being a sort of temple called *manda* or *bimanda* (from *bit manda*, "house of the *manda*" or "house of knowledge"), or even *mandi* like the fence. The *mandaiia*, therefore, could be "those who use the *mandi/a*."

8. The plural form ending in *-ia* is pronounced as a short *e*.

This hypothesis seems all the stronger given that another ancient name for the Mandaeans was *mašknaiia,* "those of the *maškna,*" which again means "temple," or *mandi/a.* We also have information regarding a sect of Kantaeans, *kantaiia,* who are in some way linked to ancient Mandaeanism and whose name is derived from the name they gave to their sanctuary, or *kanta.*

The third hypothesis, finally, is supported through analogy with the names given to other religions, just as the term Christianity comes from Jesus Christ, held by Christians to be the savior. The principal redeeming figure in Mandaeanism is Manda d-Hiia, whose name means "Knowledge of (the) Life" or "Dwelling of (the) Life," where "Life" is the epithet referring to the supreme divinity. Just as Christians are those who believe in, or thanks to, Jesus Christ, so the Mandaeans would be those who believe in, or thanks to, Manda d-Hiia.

I cannot believe that *mandaiia* means "Gnostics," since the Mandaeans within their own group distinguish from others among themselves the *naṣuraiia,* or "those who possess *naṣiruta,*" profound knowledge of the secret religious mysteries of Mandaeanism. These are the real "Gnostics," while the *mandaiia* include all the Mandaeans, even ordinary believers. When asked, a modern Mandaean would answer that in the past all the Mandaeans were *naṣuraiia* but that there are only a few today: the elders, the wisest, the most erudite. In any case the *naṣuraiia* of today are not like the *naṣuraiia* of the past. Those of former times were infinitely powerful: they knew the secrets of the stars and of herbs, they could read the future in the stars and in magic cups, they lived in absolute purity and were invincible, and they were not touched by fire and were unmoved by even the sharpest of blades. Apart from the hyperbole surrounding the legends of their past, we have to conclude that the *naṣuraiia* make up a sort of caste of cultural elites within Mandaeanism, a caste that does not coincide with the priesthood. While we can expect priests to be *naṣuraiia,* that is, we can expect them to possess knowledge, by no means all *naṣuraiia* are automatically priests.

Things are complicated further by the apparent connection between the words *naṣurariia* and Nazoraeans and/or "Nazarenes," a name usually used to indicate members of Christian groups or sects in the entire area stretching from Palestine to India.[9] To confuse things even further, in a

9. Region where the *Mar Toma Nazrani* live, that is, the Saint Thomas Nazarenes — Christians.

rather ancient text the term *naṣuraiia* is used not in reference to the best or most ancient of the Mandaeans, but to their Christian antagonists. Just why the Mandaean "Gnostics" are called *naṣuraiia*, then, is still far from clear. Without being too fanciful, it seems fairly plausible that the Mandaeans derived the term from some Gnostic Christian group or sect that they had come into contact with during their formative period as an independent religious entity. There is, however, no certain proof of this, and it remains a hypothesis. The one thing that is certain, though, is the name that their Arab neighbors gave them: *ṣubba*, "baptizers," "those who immerse [themselves in water]."

Within the community of believers, called the *laupa*, there are the *ialupia*, who are not priests but know how to read and write the classical Mandaean language. They have access to the sacred texts and the knowledge those texts convey, which is the preserve of the *naṣuraiia*, and they can be thought of as *naṣuraiia* who are not priests. The latter are called *tarmidia*. Originally the term *tarmida* indicated "disciple," but it later came to mean the Mandaean priest. In each Mandaean village or community the *tarmida* is considered the highest religious and civil authority and is also recognized as such by the Islamic authorities. He enjoys the titles and prerogatives of a "king" *(malka)* and in current Arabic is referred to as *šayḫ*, "sheik." He pays particular attention to the norms of ritual purity regarding food, drink, and behavior in general. His own purity guarantees the effectiveness of the rituals he performs. Thus, for example, if one of his wives is menstruating or has not yet completed the purification rituals following childbirth (which last about forty days), he cannot officiate over religious ceremonies. Like other Mandaeans he wears a ritual robe, the *rasta*, made up of seven parts (an overshirt or smock, a pocket, trousers, a belt, a turban, a sort of stole, and a sash or external belt), all of them of cotton or white wool. To this he adds the so-called "crown," a sort of tubular ring of white silk or cotton that he uses to crown his head, the *šum iauar*, a golden ring worn on the little finger of the right hand with the divine names of Šum Iauar Ziua (Shem, Light, Splendor) engraved on it, and the *margna*, a ceremonial stick usually made of olive wood. A debatable comparison can be made between the latter item and the Christian bishop's pastoral staff. With the exception of the golden ring, which is worn from the moment of ordination until burial, all the other things are put on or taken off to the accompaniment of long prayers and blessings, the opening and closing rituals of every ceremony.

Above the priests are the *ganzibria,* the name being connected to *ginza,* "treasury." So, they are "treasurers," whom Catholic missionaries always considered equivalent to the Christian bishops, whose original Greek name was *episkopoi,* roughly meaning "inspectors." Both terms seem to refer to some original function of possibly administrative control over the community. The Mandaean word *ginza,* however, also means a "collection of books," a treasure in the form of a library, and it is also the name of the best-known and perhaps most important of the Mandaeans' sacred texts, the *Ginza. Ganzibra* could therefore mean the person entrusted with preserving the treasure of knowledge, in other words, the sacred texts.

It is said that in the past, heading the religious hierarchy was a *riš ama,* or "head *(riš)* of the people *(ama)."* According to some contemporary Mandaeans this position has not been filled since the beginning of the nineteenth century, and, according to some scholars, the current lack of a *riš ama* and the scarcity of *ganzibria* are signs of the decline of the Mandaeanism and of its perhaps inevitable collapse. In a letter from Basra addressed to the Holy Congregation *de propaganda Fide* and dated April 29, 1627, however, a Carmelite missionary, Basil of Saint Francis, while describing to the Roman cardinals who the Mandaeans were, claimed that there were only three *ganzibria* all together, all of whom resided in Hoveyzeh in Persia, and he even provided their names. He, therefore, was unaware of the existence of any *ganzibra* in Turkish territory, in what is now Iraq (where he had been living for four years at the time of the letter), and he had never once heard of a *riš ama.*[10] Since Father Basil, the founder

---

10. In the Mandaean priesthood Basil distinguishes between the "Fathers" (called "talamide," i.e., *tarmidia*) and the "Great Fathers" ("ganzeure," i.e., *ganzibria*) but does not know of other figures. Ignatius of Jesus, in his 1652 book, never speaks of *riš amia* but, while relating an event that had occurred at Hoveyzeh "thirty years before," says that in that Persian city "their priests and bishops and [to sum up] the chiefs or leaders of the people lived" *(commorantur eorum Sacerdotes, et Episcopi, ac Primates huius nationis).* The text seems to me to say that priests and bishops *are* the chiefs or leaders of the Mandaean nation, as the use of the plural (the leaders) would suggest; that does not fit very well with the idea of a monarchical institution. Also, a colophon of a liturgical text that has preserved precious information on the earliest contacts with Islam always uses the plural and indeed says that a certain Anuš bar Danqa went to speak to the new Islamic authorities "together with the *riš amia*" (plural). Likewise, in another text a redactor says he had visited all the *riš amia* to check up on their books. It would therefore appear that the term was originally a generic one and did not indicate a distinct position of responsibility. I tend to suspect that the Mandaeans began to speak of an individual as *riš ama* (often thinking of a past era) to op-

of the Carmelite mission in Basra, was usually quite well informed regarding the social and broadly political aspects of the Mandaeanism of his day, his silence seems to provide us with a chronological terminus for the absence of a *riš ama*, or at least proof that Mandaeanism is used to surviving with a priestly hierarchy of modest dimensions, at least at the higher levels. An interesting confirmation of this can be found in the accounts Nicolas Siouffi provided in the nineteenth century. Siouffi was a Syrian Christian who, having received a European education, entered the French diplomatic corps. As vice-consul in Mossul, in 1875 he gathered information from a young Mandaean called Adam who had been on the point of being ordained as a priest but had then abandoned Mandaeanism and become a Catholic. Among other things, Adam told Siouffi that there had only ever been two *riš amia,* one before and the other after John the Baptist. The most recent of these was a certain Adam Abulparaš (Adam Abu l-Farağ), a well-known figure in Mandaean and Arab folklore, and therefore outside of historical time.[11] As for the number of *ganzibria,* according to Adam there was only one in 1875, and in recent times the greatest number that he was aware of at any one time was four.

Lastly, we should remember that the *tarmidia* are assisted in religious functions by the *šualia,* or "youth who will become *tarmida*" (analogous to the Christian "seminary student"), and the *šganda* (or *ašganda*), a sort of "acolyte" or "deacon," not necessarily destined to become a *tarmida*

---

pose this figure to that of the patriarch of an Oriental Christian Church, if not of the Catholic Pope.

11. Adam says that he was active five hundred years before, but the same chronological distance, still in the past, was indicated also to a French traveler who passed through Basra in 1649. *Abulparaš* is therefore always active "five hundred years before" the Mandaean who speaks about him. The name indicates a human character, defender of the Mandaeans in a crisis situation, which is usually a Moslem persecution or a clash with the Jews (but in the account referred to by Lady Drower, the antagonist was a fire worshipper, i.e., a Zoroastrian). If to Siouffi's informant the institution of *riš amia* appears by then to be in the dim and distant past, twenty years before, Petermann's informant Iahia related that one of his ancestors had been *riš ama* around four hundred years earlier, and that he had received from his own father the name of that ancestor in the hope that he too would have become *riš ama.* It would therefore seem to be still theoretically possible that one could become a *riš ama,* although the position was vacant at that time (in 1854). A priest told Lady Drower (around 1930) that his own great-great-great-grandfather had been *riš ama,* and that the *riš amia* had always belonged to one family (not Iahia's!). Lady Drower drew the conclusion that there may not have been any *riš amia* for around eighty years.

(though they usually do go on to become one). The entire priestly class is hence organized hierarchically, at various levels corresponding to some extent to those of the Christian churches of the East. A certain family right usually holds true in the Mandaean religious hierarchy. In other words, the sons of priests usually become priests, and, at least in the case of the *ganzibria,* it is hoped that they should each be *malka br malka,* "a king son of a king."

We have no certain information regarding women in the priesthood, and it would seem that they are even excluded from the function of "sacrificer." No animal with blood, in fact, although pure and acceptable as food, can be simply killed and eaten.[12] There is a special ritual with which an animal is sacrificed. The animal must be entrusted to a priest or a layman called a *halala,* which refers to his state of purity. At the time of the sacrifice the sacrificer also justifies himself and the community for the ritual guilt incurred for having destroyed a life. As early as the first half of the seventeenth century Ignatius of Jesus, an Italian Carmelite missionary active in Basra, observed with some amazement that women were not allowed to wring a chicken's neck and put it in a pot but had to take it to a man who would sacrifice it by following what to Ignatius's Western eyes seemed a ridiculous ceremony. There is a legend, however, whose heroine, Miriai (Mary), is described in priestly clothing and attitude, and there is a prayer containing the names of *tarmidia* and *ganzibria* of the past that also mentions some female names. Lady Dower was assured that there had been women *tarmida* and *ganzibra,* the latter having only one limitation, that they should and could celebrate not more than one marriage.[13]

The ceremonial life of the Mandaeans requires the presence of a course of water because, as we mentioned in the Preface, flowing water is the only water considered "alive," while rainwater or water collected in a cistern is thought of as "cut" and, therefore, inappropriate for purification. Running water is called *iardna* and draws its vital power from the heavenly

12. In general, animals without blood (such as fish) are legitimate, as well as birds (but not predators that feed on impure flesh). Of quadrupeds all those with tails, and females, are forbidden. The only one allowed is the ram since sheep do not have tails in a strict sense but a bag of fat (very highly prized and used also as food in the sacred meals). For vegetables and derivatives of farm animals (eggs, milk [even of cows], butter, etc.), there are no problems.

13. On this subject see now Jorunn J. Buckley, "The Evidence for Women Priests in Mandaeism," *Journal of Near Eastern Studies* 59/2 (2000): 93-106.

Iardna, the river of light and life par excellence. Water from the Iardna of light is present in every course of water on earth in the ratio of one to nine; it is absent from "cut" water.

The word *iardna* must in some way be related to the name of the river Jordan, pronounced "Iarden" in Hebrew and "Iardena" in Aramaic. The problem is whether the Mandaean word *iardna* is derived directly from the historical Jordan,[14] the one that flows in Palestine, or whether both terms are derived from a common Semitic root meaning "to flow." In the first case the Mandaeans would have defined *iardna* as the living water because of speculation concerning the sacrality of the river Jordan, speculation that they must have been aware of. In the second case, the similarity of the terms may be the result of mere coincidence. Yet there are scholars today who consider the coincidence *iardna*–Jordan of great importance for the history of the origins of Mandaeanism. They argue that *iardna* originally meant "Jordan," whose sacredness was then extended to all running water, becoming "Jordans" to the extent that they participate in its life and holiness. Such an exaltation of the river Jordan would prove that Mandaeanism was influenced in its formative stages by (or was a direct heir to) a Palestinian sect that exalted the waters of the Jordan as the only water suitable for purification.

In any case, in any fair-sized community the place set aside for performing rituals is not just anywhere on the banks of a river but at the *mandi*, a sacred area marked off by a palisade of reeds and dried mud. The entrance is a simple interruption in the palisade, while a ditch allows flowing water *(iardna)* diverted from a river close by to enter the roughly rectangular "*iardna* pool" and then to return to the river in a second ditch. A few meters to the north of the pool (dug into the ground) and parallel to it, there is a rectangular hut made of wooden beams and reeds, entirely covered with dried mud. This is the *manda*. This sort of temple, entirely empty inside, is positioned in such a way that the long sides face the north and the south, while the shorter sides face east and west. On the southern side, facing the pool, there is a narrow opening in the middle running from the ground to the roof. This is the *manda*'s only opening. There are no doors or locks on either the *manda* or the palisade. The most important phases of most Mandaean ceremonies take place in the more or less rect-

14. A river that is at present known to the Mandaeans by its Arabic name: Šaṭṭ al-Urdunn.

angular area between the pool and the *manda*, and this area, like the interior of the *manda*, must be kept in a special state of purity. This is so important that if a nonpurified person or animal should even accidentally penetrate the area (clearly marked off by small furrows in the ground), the ceremony is interrupted and can begin again only after the polluted ground has been ritually purified. Even the animals to be sacrificed, which have their throats cut between the pool and the temple, are purified through triple immersion; and when a ram is sacrificed, special attention is taken to prevent the animal from soiling the sacred area. The poor beast is purged mechanically with a cane before being taken into the *manda*, and once it has been purified it is not allowed to touch the ground again. From that point on it is tied up and held over a mat of woven reeds. The sacred texts are read and the prayers said aloud within the sacred area or inside the *manda* itself, with the priests' backs turned to the pool. In this way prayers are said while facing north. This feature too is typical and has a specific meaning: the Mandaeans consider the North Star to be the throne of Abatur, the divine judge of all mortals.

Concerning Mandaean rituals, then, the ones that they are most famous for, and from which their Arabic name is derived *(ṣubba)*, are those concerning immersion in running water (or, at any rate, its use). The most important of these is the *maṣbuta*, "baptism," a solemn "immersion" in the presence of a priest. Sunday, which the Mandaeans call *habšaba*, "first [day] of the week," is a holy day, just as it is for Christians,[15] and practicing Mandaeans are expected to participate in the *maṣbuta* every Sunday. The ceremony lasts several hours, occupying nearly the entire morning. Preceded by the officiating *tarmida's* preparatory prayers, the ceremony takes place along a watercourse or near the *mandi's* immersion pool, and can be divided into two parts. The first part takes place in water: the person to be baptized first immerses himself or herself three times and is then immersed three times by the *tarmida*. He or she must drink the baptismal water three times from the *tarmida's* hand, and then a small crown of myrtle is placed on the head, followed by a laying on of hands by the *tarmida*. The second part of the ceremony takes place on the bank once all the baptisms have been performed. With their white gowns soaking with water the Mandaeans consume a special bread *(pihta)* that has been prepared beforehand, and they drink the most holy water *(mambuha)*, which has also

---

15. While for Moslems the day of prayer is Friday, and, for the Jews, Saturday.

been prepared by the priest in advance. They are then anointed with sesame oil by the priest, that is, "marked" on the forehead and the face (from ear to ear), with a gesture possibly related both to the Christian sign of the cross and to baptismal anointing (of the ears). Handshaking (called *kušta*, meaning "right" or "truth") takes place repeatedly during the ceremony, each of the gestures described above being separated by hymns and prayers of varying length, recited by the priest.

Solemn baptism has two specific functions: it reduces (although it does not eliminate) the quantity and quality of punishment in the next world for sinful or irregular behavior, and restores those who have been very seriously contaminated to a state of ritual purity. The general theory is: the more one is immersed in water for a purification ritual, the better. One can be contaminated in various ways, particularly through contact with corpses or with blood, but also from traveling in Muslim or foreign territory, or from being imprisoned. Contamination can also be the result of an infraction of a ceremonial ritual, of eating the meat of forbidden animals or animals slaughtered by non-Mandaeans, of eating fruit and vegetables bought at the bazaar and not ritually purified in running water, or of being bitten by certain animals. The purifying aspect is connected in particular to the baptism prescribed for newlyweds at the end of their first week of living together, or for women following periods of impurity due to menstruation or childbirth. In the latter case solemn baptism marking the end of ritual impurity takes place on the first Sunday after the thirtieth day following delivery of a son, and after the thirty-second day in the case of a daughter. There are, however, those who maintain that the ritual should take place after the fortieth and forty-second day, respectively.

The *mașbuta* can and should be repeated several times when dealing with a serious case of contamination — laymen guilty of theft, adultery, or murder — even though with the most serious cases there is some doubt among priests as to whether or not going through all the purifying acts can guarantee the offender's salvation in the next world. Regarding the priests themselves, some sins, such as adultery, are absolutely unforgivable. From 3 to 366 *mașbutiata* are required of *tarmidia* and *ganzibria* in cases of specific, serious contamination: for example, when occurring during the time of one's consecration, or for having celebrated a wedding in which it later turned out that the bride was not a virgin. One preliminary to any wedding is, therefore, verification of the virginity of the bride. Three women, neither related to one another nor relatives of the bride (one is usually the wife of the officiating *ganzibra*),[16] proclaim the results of their examination with shouts of joy. However, when the verdict is not what was expected, the scene is hardly a joyous one, especially for the girl. The *ganzibra* leaves in silence, and the wedding is put off. The groom can reject the bride and ask for the dowry to be returned. When it is already known in advance that the bride is not a virgin, as in the case of a marriage involving a widow (the only case where the Mandaeans consider the marriage of a nonvirgin woman to be acceptable), then the ceremony is performed by a *paisaq*. This is a *tarmida* who, for example, because of physical mutilation occurring after his ordination, is no longer considered worthy of performing priestly functions except for the marriages of nonvirgins. A certain irony in human affairs would have it that, given the scarcity of mutilated priests and the relative abundance of widows, as well as girls who either through their own carelessness or through unfortunate circumstances have lost their virginity without being married, the figure of the *paisaq* is quite sought after, even to the point that, as was explained to Lady Drower, there have been *tarmidia* that for financial reasons decided to give up their role in order to work exclusively as *paisaq*.

The *maṣbuta* is also performed on newborn children, though with some differences from the ritual described above. It is during this ceremony that the child's astrological name is pronounced and given. The name is "calculated" beforehand by the priest, who presents the parents with a short list of names from which to choose. In fact, every Mandaean has four names, but this is the most secret and important one. It will hardly ever be told to a stranger, though it is the name used always (and almost exclusively) in religious rituals. The other names are a family name (our surname), a sort of clan nickname, and a personal Arab name without any astrological value (the name used in everyday life), whose choice does not seem to pose any particular problems. The astrological name, called the "name of the sign of the zodiac," or "*maluaša* name," is calculated in the following manner: the twelve signs of the zodiac, from Aries to Pisces, are placed in a circle, and beginning from the sign corresponding to the month of the child's birth, the priest passes from sign to sign, for as

16. It was explained to Siouffi in these terms. Lady Drower speaks of two mature women, usually the wife and the mother of the officiating *ganzibra*. Ignatius of Jesus says that the wife of the priest officiating guarantees on oath the outcome of the examination, and that she is accompanied by "some other women."

many positions as there were hours in the day until the moment of birth,[17] to arrive at the sign of the zodiac under whose influence lay the hour of the day in which the birth occurred. The numerical value of this sign is what counts,[18] and the numerical value of the astrological name of the child's mother is subtracted from this. Once a certain number has been arrived at, a list of names corresponding to that number is compiled from the lists in the "Book of the Zodiac,"[19] and the parents choose the child's name from that list. The priest subtracts the numerical value of the mother's name because the complete astrological name is always accompanied by a matronymic; in rituals each person's name is followed by "son of X" where X is the mother. In this way the numerical value of the complete name is once again the value of the sign of the zodiac dominant at the time of birth.[20]

Usually, the Mandaeans wait for spring and summer to baptize a child, and in any case until it is a few months old, unless its life is in danger. An astrologically similar *halala,* that is, someone in a state of purity, whose *maluaša* name has the same numerical value as the child's name, holds the baby during most of the ceremony and is immersed with it. At the end of the ceremony the baby's diaper is checked. If it is dirty, then both the water and the priest have been contaminated. The ceremony is valid but must be repeated a few years afterwards (when given the child's age there is no longer the same risk), and the *tarmida* must baptize himself again before resuming his priestly duties. Should the child die during the ceremony, a small paste figurine is used to symbolically represent the child for the remainder of the ceremony. The figurine is then buried with the child. In this case the officiating priest is very seriously contaminated and cannot resume his functions until after an entire week of repeated daily baptisms performed by two other priests and a *ganzibra.*

For laymen the *maṣbuta* is performed on Sundays, with the exception of holidays falling on a fixed date, such as (though even here with

---

17. The Mandaeans count the twenty-four hours of the day starting from dawn, not from midnight as we do, nor from sunset as Jews and Moslems do.

18. The numerical value of the signs goes from one, Aries, to twelve, Pisces; to cover the twenty-four hours; the zodiac is gone around twice.

19. Called *Spar Maluašia.*

20. The numerical value of Mandaean names varies therefore from one to twelve. It should be noticed that in the entire calculation no importance is attached to the day of the month in which the baby is born.

some variations in ritual) the great holiday of *paruanaiia,* or of the *panǧa,* using its Persian name, meaning "five." The "five" are the five supernumerary days of the Mandaean calendar. The calendar is composed of twelve months of thirty days each, to which five days are added. Rather than being counted with the months, these days are included between the eighth and ninth months.

These days are considered lucky, full of joy and festivities. Even those who happen to die during these days are considered particularly fortunate, for the gates of heaven are open to their souls. On their voyage toward the realm of light they do not have to fear attacks from the forces of evil. During the days immediately preceding the "five," however, the forces of evil are rampant, and thus those days are particularly inauspicious. Even the *manda* must be reconsecrated through a particular ceremony lasting from twelve to eighteen hours, which characterizes the holidays of *paruanaiia.* Among other things, the rituals include the sacrifice of a gallinacean and a ram. In the course of these days the Mandaeans purify their temple and themselves, and also their tableware and kitchenware. Pots and pans are brought from the kitchens to the *mandi,* and the priest immerses them three times in the pool, pronouncing over each one the name of Life and the name of Manda d-Hiia.

As for the Mandaean year, it is composed of 365 days. Since there are no adjustments made to make it correspond to the actual solar year (the Mandaeans do not have a leap year or similar methods), their calendar appears to be behind ours by one day every four years.[21] Thus the first day of the year — that is, the first day of "the first month of winter"[22] — should fall (for the period 1988-91) on our July 25, though the data available to me do not allow for exact calculation. The first day of the year would have been October 14 in 1665; October 1 in 1678; August 26 in 1854; August 20 in 1875; and August 8 in 1935. These dates, however, cannot all be correct. They vary by a number of days depending on the date with which one chooses to start. July 25 was arrived at by taking Lady Drower's indication for 1935 as the starting point.

Apart from the *maṣbuta,* there are two other purification rituals that

21. I say "appears to be" since in our calendar to make the numbers fit only one end of century year out of four is bissextile, the one in which the first two numbers make up a multiple of four. Thus, 1700, 1800, and 1900 were not, whereas the year 2000 was.

22. The Mandaeans name their months according to the position they occupy in each of the four seasons into which the year is divided.

the Mandaean performs in running water without the *tarmida*. The first is the *rišama* (or *rušuma*), the daily ablution of all parts of the body. This should be performed just before dawn, with the head covered, after defecation (which is in turn preceded by washing and a prayer of purification), and before participation in any religious ceremony. There is also the *ṭamaša* (or *ṭumušta*), a self-immersion performed in cases of contamination or, on Sundays, when it is not possible to participate in the *maṣbuta*. The *ṭamaša* is a sort of mandatory first step to be carried out as soon as possible while awaiting a *maṣbuta* that has been advised or recommended. It is performed in various cases of contamination: after contact with a human corpse; after touching meat not butchered by a Mandaean; following contact with one's own blood (for any reason whatsoever, from a blood-letting to a nosebleed or a wound to, for women, menstruation or childbirth); after quarreling with someone; if one has been ill; after eating or drinking anything offered by someone who is not a Mandaean; after coming into contact with human sperm, one's own or, in the case of women, one's husband's, whether accidentally or following legitimate sexual intercourse;[23] and after coming into contact with a woman in a state of impurity (through childbirth or menstruation) or someone in a state of impurity who has not yet undergone purification. As we can see, in some cases a *maṣbuta* is always prescribed. At any rate, a Mandaean in a polluting state of impurity who is touched by a fellow Mandaean must warn his or her co-religionist so that he or she can perform the necessary *ṭamaša*. In the past this practice was particularly irksome for women, who, it would appear, were required to carry out their immersions at night and dressed,[24] immediately after contamination and in the company of other women, whether neighbors or relatives. Such customs not only suggest an idea of privacy very different from our own but also that the village should be situated as close as possible to a watercourse, without which it is practically impossible to observe the precepts of the religion. Entire communities of Mandaeans have been known to

23. These being the only legitimate cases for practicing Mandaeans since in different cases it is presumed that the man or woman in question does not even carry out the ritual ablutions.

24. So as not to be seen by indiscreet eyes. Also in the *maṣbuta,* carried out during the day and under the eyes of the whole community, the women wear a long black cloak over the ceremonial *rasta*, and they keep it on even during the immersions, so that their shape does not appear.

move following changes in the water supply, such as the diversion of a river or a drop in its volume.

Contamination is often caused by sexual activity or moments in the biological life of women characterized by the presence of blood. This attitude is and always has been perfectly normal in the Middle East, from earliest times. In Zoroastrian villages, for example, a hut was built at the edge of the village where the women would go and spend the entire period of their impurity. Among the Mandaeans, as with practicing Jews and Muslims, a menstruating woman is segregated in the home; physical contact with others is reduced to a minimum; and sexual relations with the husband are suspended. However, the woman is more dangerous at other moments of her life when contamination is unavoidable: during her first sexual intercourse and during childbirth. In fact, once the wedding ceremony is over, the bride and groom spend an entire week in the "wedding chamber," a sort of canopy made of curtains inside the house where they are to live. Food is brought to them from outside, and they only leave for their physiological needs and, at the end of their period of isolation, for their purification baths. Of the two it is the groom who runs the greater risk; prior to entering the wedding chamber where the bride is waiting for him, the officiating *ganzibra* gives the man the most powerful Mandaean talisman, the *skandula*. This is an iron ring with a round medallion, on which figures of the most dangerous animals are engraved, symbols of the forces of evil: a wasp or bee, a lion, a scorpion, and around them a snake whose head reaches round to its tail. An iron chain is attached to the ring, and there is a knife made of iron (without a wooden handle) at the end of the chain. The *skandula* is a talisman whose power is clearly apotropaic; when a dead person is buried, the medallion's image is pressed like a seal on to the earth of the burial ground, duly watered, and a magic triple circle is dug around the grave with the knife. This ceremony has two functions: to protect the dead person from evil spirits during the three days before the soul leaves the body and to protect the living from the dead, keeping him or her from leaving the grave. The Mandaean groom can only enter the wedding chamber with this ring on his finger and this knife in the sash of his ceremonial *rasta*. If for some reason the bride or groom should die during this week, there would be little hope of salvation, in spite of the numerous ceremonies that the family would certainly perform to help purify and protect his or her soul.

In the case of childbirth, it is the new mother, the woman who is giving or has just given birth, who runs the greatest risks. Even when everything appears to have gone well, there is a particular demon that attacks women on the third day after delivery, hitting them with violent fevers and leading them rapidly to delirium and death; obviously septicemia. Lacking knowledge of modern pharmacopoeia, the Mandaeans provide their women with the usual *skandula* before they give birth and keep them in isolation as much as possible. As the time of the delivery approaches, old rags are piled up inside the hut on one side of it, near one of the bound bundles of reeds that, in the absence of wooden poles, act as the supporting structure of the building. In delivery the woman kneels on these rags, leaning forward and holding on to the bound bundle of reeds, to which the wall, itself of reeds, is joined, trying to push the baby toward the midwife and the other women who are there to help. After delivery the rags are burned (by the most orthodox) or thrown into the river and replaced by others. The woman changes her clothing, and as soon as she regains her strength she is taken to the river for the first of a series of purification rituals. A circle of small cobblestones or unbaked bricks are placed around her bed, and after three days they are substituted with new ones. After seven days they are eliminated. The new mother lives inside this circle, whether it is visible or not, leaving it only for her bodily needs or for ablutions, each time armed with the *skandula* and accompanied either by her husband or by other women. The women of the house hand her food and drink on special dishes they do not touch, or that they touch only if their hands are protected by a piece of cloth. These dishes are carefully purified later through a triple ritual immersion in the *iardna*. The new mother's period of isolation, called the *ṣurta,* ends with her participation in the *maṣbuta* held on the first Sunday after the end of the ritual puerperium.

Wedding ceremonies too take place, or begin, on Sundays. Preceding the week described above, the ceremony lasts an entire day, sometimes two. It has to be presided over by a *ganzibra,* without whom the marriage cannot take place, joined by two priests and two preadolescent *šgandia,* and it entails a solemn preventive baptism for both newlyweds (a *maṣbuta* with the taking of *pihta* and the drinking of *mambuha*). This is performed for both bride and groom, but separately since men and women are baptized at different times. In this preparatory phase the bride is accompanied by her mother or by another woman of the family and never says a word; during the entire wedding ceremony she will hardly ever have occasion to speak. Once the purifications have been performed and it is certain that the woman is not due to menstruate for some time, a wedding procession sets out from the *mandi* to the *ganzibra*'s house[25] to verify the bride's virginity. The procession then continues with much singing and dancing to the groom's house. During the procession the bride is preceded by a young boy carrying a lighted lantern and by a young girl with a mirror always reflecting the image of the bride. She is also accompanied by lighted candles, pitchers of pure water, and branches of myrtle and pomegranate, all of these being propitious objects and gestures (referring to purity, light, life, and fertility) or apotropaic ones (the reflected image in the mirror is there to deflect the powers of evil). In the meantime the wedding hut, the *andiruna,* has been prepared in the courtyard of the groom's house. This is a sort of great cage made of reeds, with no walls, decorated with flowers and covered with a broad white veil, also loosely stitched (e.g., like a mosquito net). This is where most of the wedding ceremony proper takes place. The groom enters with the *ganzibra* and a man representing the bride, along with other participants. The bride, however, returns home. When a bride enters the house where she is to live for the first time, or when a wife enters a new home, one or two chickens or doves are traditionally sacrificed on the threshold. The blood is let over the woman's foot, and the victim or victims are then thrown into the river. Crossing the threshold, the bride enters the wedding chamber and waits on the wedding mat,[26] beyond the curtains that she will not cross again for another week. In the meantime the ceremony in the *andiruna* continues for several hours more, the central nucleus of the ceremony being a ritual meal for the dead. The Mandaeans are convinced that in every moment of the community's ritual life all of their forebears, from Adam to John the Baptist, through the great priests of the past and the closest relatives of those present, can and should be invited to a community meal. This is rather akin in significance to the mystical body of the church for Catholics. At this time of "communion" for the Mandaeans, various ritual foods are taken, *pihta* and *hamra* among them, the latter not being pure water (like the *mambuha*) but a sort of surrogate for wine. It is made, in fact, when there are no fresh grapes to be pressed, by soaking raisins and dates in water. They are then squeezed to

25. In the case described by Lady Drower.
26. The Mandaeans did not know the Western use of the bed until recent times but laid themselves down on a kind of sack or mattress, which was placed in direct contact with the earth.

obtain a sweet drink that in some way resembles wine. This has led in past centuries to the belief that the Mandaeans had some form of Eucharistic ritual with water and wine, similar to that of Christians.

At any rate, the ritual meal held on the occasion of a wedding is usually quite rich, but the sacredness of the foods means that they cannot be thrown away or used on other occasions. If there is anything left, it is distributed among the poor, and the final leftovers are thrown into the river. During the ceremony in the *andiruna*, the bride's substitute answers the *ganzibra*'s questions for her, officially accepting the groom on her behalf. The groom and the *ganzibra* together take hold of a kind of bread roll prepared by the *ganzibra* that contains a little of all the sacred foods (raisins, dates, almonds, etc.). This roll, which seems to be intentionally phallic in shape, is then broken into two parts. As it is being broken, the groom says, "The name of Life and the name of Manda d-Hiia are pronounced upon me," and then he eats the half left in his hand. The *ganzibra* gives the other half to the bride's substitute, who takes it to the bride, sprinkles her hands with water, and gives it to her saying, "Eat this, and do not eat anything else unless from me." In this case he is acting in the name of the groom.

During the ritual various symbolic acts are performed. The upper part of a stone milling wheel is placed first on the threshold of the *andiruna* and then on the threshold of the house, and each time a terra-cotta vase is broken on it.[27] A basket with articles of clothing belonging to both the bride and the groom is carried about, and finally a woman's green dress, a gift from the groom to the bride, is drawn out and wrapped around the groom's breast. The bride also receives two rings, one with an agate (red) for the little finger on her right hand, and the other with a turquoise stone (green) for the little finger of her left hand. The groom buys the rings, but it is one of the two priests who puts them on her hands after asking her (she is still behind the drape of the wedding chamber), in the presence of witnesses, if she really does want to marry the man in question. Finally, toward the end the officiating priests, the groom, and the bride's representative go into the house. The groom squats just outside the wedding chamber with his back to the drape, and the bride does the same from the inside, so that their backs touch each other, but in such a way that they are still divided by the curtain. The curtain is moved slightly to allow the

---

27. Breaking one or more terra-cotta vases during the wedding is a custom widespread in the Middle East and in Jewish communities.

ganzibra to place his hands on the heads of both bride and groom, and he brings their heads together so that they touch three times (though divided still by the curtain). A crown of myrtle covered with saffron is placed on the head of each.

Much incense is burned during the final part of the wedding, and then rose petals, powdered sugar, and almonds are thrown over those present in much the same way as we (in Italy) throw rice and wedding candies, called "confetti." The officiating priests, the groom, and the bride's representative enter the *andiruna* a final time, where the groom is in some way "deconsecrated" and declared impure. Armed with the *skandula* (the ring on the little finger of his right hand and the knife in his sash at his side), the groom now can and must enter the wedding chamber. The moment of their first sexual intercourse is not, however, imminent. Based on the horoscope of both bride and groom, the *ganzibra* calculates the propitious and inauspicious aspects of the hours following the ceremony. Usually a good moment is found within the first six hours after the wedding.

The ceremony for consecrating a *tarmida* is even richer and on a bigger scale than a wedding. A *ganzibra,* who is also the candidate's *(šualia)* teacher, at least seven *tarmidia,* and two *šgandia* lead and accompany the aspiring priest during the first part of the rituals, which lasts nine days and eight nights (starting on a Saturday morning and drawing to a close on the Sunday of the following week) without interruption. The period is chosen with care, to be sure that none of the wives, whether of the *šualia* or the officiating priests, are menstruating, about to give birth, or having a miscarriage during the ceremony. If that should happen, the ceremony would not be considered valid, and all those concerned would have to go through various purifying practices. The *ganzibra,* for example, would have to undergo 366 baptisms. If the wife responsible for the impurity happened to be his own, the 366 baptisms would still be insufficient to remove the stain completely, and he would be forever prevented from becoming *riš ama.* Once the proper week has been chosen, and after the preparatory rituals (a double baptism, the sacrifice of a ram, the verification of the physical perfection of the *šualia,* the washing of his legs by two women who have passed menopause), a straw hut is built in the southern part of the courtyard of the *ganzibra's* house. As in the wedding, this hut is called an *andiruna,* even though its shape is different. The opening, once again with no door, faces north, and a broad piece of blue cotton cloth (a color the Mandaeans are forbidden to wear) is hung over it. Ignatius of Jesus tells us that toward the beginning of the seventeenth century, before his arrival in Basra, a Portuguese bishop who had come by way of Goa had tried to convert the Mandaeans en masse. They had claimed they were ready to accept everything, including papal authority, but not the idea of being able to wear blue clothing, or of having to. Apparently it was precisely this point that caused the negotiations to fail. For whatever reason,[28] to the Mandaeans blue symbolizes the material aspect of this world, its imperfection and evil. The *andiruna* covered with a blue cloth, then, must represent the material world, perhaps the body of the *šualia,* or at any rate his tendency to fall into an impure state.

The *šualia,* in fact, is clothed as if he were a dying or dead man ready for burial. He is dressed in a new *rasta* with a gold coin sewn on the right and a silver one on the left. Gold symbolizes the sun and silver the moon, and their presence means that whoever wears that particular *rasta* must undertake the voyage through the heavens, controlled by evil planetary powers, to the higher light. Dressed as a dead man, then, the *šualia* must demonstrate to his teacher, to the priests, and to the people gathered to celebrate that he possesses the necessary knowledge and preparation. He will recite from memory an entire sacred book, prayers, and the ritual for the dead. Two *drapšia* will also have been put up in the courtyard. A *drapša,* or *drabša* (drape, flag, or standard), is a broad piece of white cloth, unfolded and hung from two wooden poles placed in the shape of a cross. This particular feature led Christian missionaries of past centuries to believe that the Mandaeans worshipped the cross, but the cross in this case is merely a stand for the cloth, whose whiteness is a visual representation of the light of the divine world.

While the *šualia* recites the texts there is a great deal of coming and going all around him. Priests follow the texts to make sure that the candidate commits no errors, while others prepare the sacred food, and men and women prepare the white ritual crowns that the officiating priests will

28. The bishop in question must be the Portuguese Augustinian De Gouvea, who will be mentioned again in ch. 2. To the Christian missionaries the Mandaeans explained their aversion to the color blue by saying that it was the color used by the Jews to contaminate the waters of the Jordan and keep John the Baptist from baptizing Jesus. According to a seventeenth-century French traveler, however, the reason lay in the fact that dog dung was used in producing blue dyes (indigo). Or, perhaps Ignatius of Jesus was right when he claimed that the Mandaeans' hatred of the color stemmed from the widespread use of it by the Turks in their clothing. Today the taboo seems to have disappeared completely.

wear. Once the texts have all been recited, another straw hut is quickly built under the guidance of the priests. This hut is in every respect similar to the *manda,* but without the mud stucco. It is built to the north of the courtyard, with its opening facing south, directly opposite that of the *andiruna*. The second hut is called a *škinta,* which means "dwelling," "house," or "temple," and is covered with a large sheet of white cloth.

With the arrival of dusk both the *šualia* and the *ganzibra* enter the *andiruna,* where they will pass the night in a waking vigil. This is a festival night for the whole village, and very few people will sleep, but the *šualia* in particular cannot and must not fall asleep. The next morning just before dawn he will leave the *andiruna,* and, after pausing halfway between the two huts to again recite a sacred text, he finally enters the *škinta*. Here the symbolism becomes quite clear; the candidate has passed from his former life into the new one. While he enters into the second hut the priests demolish the first one, for once the voyage has begun there is to be no turning back. The candidate then receives the symbols of the priesthood: ring, crown, and staff. For the rest of the week, until the morning of the following Sunday, the *šualia* will only come out of the *škinta* to perform purification rituals on himself or on food, or for his own physiological needs. During this entire period he will pray, recite sacred texts, discuss things with his teacher, and receive secret instruction. Three sacred names will be revealed to him each day, names so sacred that no one has ever written them in a book or pronounced them aloud. They are written in the sand by the *ganzibra,* and once the *šualia* has learned them, they are erased. Above all, though, the candidate must never fall asleep. He is allowed to nap occasionally for a few minutes at a time, but then one of the priests or the *ganzibra* wakes him immediately. Just as the high priest of Jerusalem was kept awake the night before Yom Kippur, the Mandaean candidate to the priesthood must not sleep. Both cases respond to the same fear: a nocturnal ejaculation could make the man who must approach divine things impure.

If in spite of all precautions, a nocturnal emission should contaminate the candidate, the consequences are not light. They range from postponing consecration for a year (if impurity strikes during the first night between Saturday and Sunday) to a series of baptisms. These decrease according to the day of the week in which the unfortunate event has occurred, from 366 to a minimum of 9. When this grueling week, also a tough physical test for the aspiring *tarmida,* finally draws to a close with a series of solemn baptisms, he is still not considered a priest. A sixty-day period of isolation and purification follows. Separated from his family and especially from his wife, he must undergo three complete purification immersions *(tamaša)* each day, try to avoid any potentially contaminating contact, follow a nearly exclusively vegetarian diet, and prepare his own bread by purifying the wheat seven times in water before milling it. If for some reason the near-priest is contaminated during this period, the number of days of impurity are added to the total so that the whole period is often prolonged far beyond the sixty-day minimum.[29] The conclusion takes place on the first Sunday after the end of isolation. With the *mandi* having been prepared and purified on Saturday, on Sunday the candidate must celebrate an entire *masiqta* from memory. This ceremony, which lasts on average eight hours, is a solemn meal held in honor of the dead. In the past it was considered the Mandaean "mass." The term *masiqta* means "elevation" and emphasizes the ceremony's role in aiding the soul in its rise toward eternal light. While the ritual is intended primarily for the dead, in many respects it can also be applied to living people, as in this case. The new priest both dedicates the ceremony to the *ganzibra* who acted as his teacher (who is very much alive, and actually present) and pronounces his name, not his own, at the particular point in the ritual where the name of the officiating priest has to be indicated. He is still not acting autonomously as the performer of ceremonies.

There are several phases to the ritual, including the sacrifice of a gallinacean (chicken, hen, dove, etc.), whose meat is placed with the other sacred foods: raisins, pomegranate seeds, pieces of coconut (of Indian origin), various nuts and almonds (some of Persian origin), and pieces of quince. The celebrating priest grinds and crushes sesame seeds and dates to prepare the *miša* or unguent, and prepares the ceremonial bread *(pihta)* and the wine surrogate *(hamra)*. He also prepares, blesses, and cooks sixty and then six *patiria*, tiny biscuits or bread rolls. He takes only very small, symbolic portions of the dove meat and *patiria* (we suppose that the six and sixty *patiria* represent the Mandaean community, perhaps the dead). Only at the very end is the candidate considered a true *tarmida*. Indeed,

---

29. According to Siouffi, not only is a day added for each day of impurity due to a nocturnal emission, but seven days are added each time that the mother or the wife (or one of the wives) of the candidate menstruates. This information is not confirmed, however, by Lady Drower.

once the *masiqta* is over, for the first time using his own name he celebrates the *pihta* and *mambuha* ceremony. A helper *(šganda)* wraps the body of the dove and the sixty-six *paṭiria* in a white cloth and buries them all in a sacred area of the *mandi* (not to the east of the *manda*). A new *tarmida* has entered the chosen ranks of the Mandaean priests.

The consecrating rituals of a *ganzibra* are shorter but no less elaborate. The ceremony can only take place, in fact, when a person who has led a blameless life is near death, either a man or a woman from a spotless priestly family or a married person with children (the Mandaeans say that a person without children has no place in the next world). A dying person, or *napaqa*, "one who leaves," is absolutely necessary for the ceremony called *ʿngirta*, meaning "message." The soul of this privileged "departing" person carries the "message" of the new *ganzibra* to the realm of light. He or she acts as a go-between in this direct communication with the other world. This intermediary action has its advantages for the departing soul as well, because it will thus certainly cross the heavens in triumph, overcoming the hazards placed along its path.

The ceremony takes place within the sacred inner area of the *mandi*, prepared and purified as if for its consecration. Here the rituals that accompany the death of a Mandaean are performed, rituals usually performed in the dying person's house. The dying man or woman is carried on a litter near the pool and is stripped and showered with abundant quantities of water from the *iardna* three times from head to foot. The person is then clothed in the funeral *rasta*, new, with gold and silver sewn on the right and the left, and a crown of myrtle is placed on his or her head. Lying back on a bed, his or her face looks toward the North Star.[30] Sesame and dates are crushed in an iron mortar and a particularly sacred oil is prepared; a few drops of the oil are placed in a phial, which the future *ganzibra* seals with his priest's ring and the imprint of one of his fingernails. He then takes the phial over to the dying person and places it in the pocket of the *rasta*'s overshirt or smock. This is the physical medium of the "message," of the "letter" sent to the other world. At this point a *šganda*[31] takes the right hand of the dying person into his own, ready to speak on his or

30. This position will not change since the dead are buried in such a way that, were they to stand up, they would be facing north.

31. In addition to the future *ganzibra*, a *ganzibra*, two *tarmidia*, and two *šgandia* also take part in the ceremony.

her behalf should it be necessary, in a brief ritual dialogue with the future *ganzibra*. "May the Truth[32] make you whole and raise you up," says the candidate. The dying person replies, "Seek and find. And speak and hear." The future *ganzibra* concludes, "I have brought it to you, and you bear it to Abatur."

The meaning of the dialogue is only slightly veiled by the symbolism. True salvation comes with physical death, which allows the soul to rise. At the end of one's earthly existence, the search has come to an end; the time for questions is over, and the time for answers has finally arrived. The heavens are open, and the human message can cross them in a voyage toward divinity; Abatur is the judge of all the dead.

When the dialogue is finished the *šganda* and the future *ganzibra* give each other their right hand, each of them kisses his own hand, and then both bring their foreheads near to each other in reverent salute. This is the solemn gesture of *kušta*. The future *ganzibra* dips the fingers of his right hand in the sacred oil and anoints the face of the dying person, from right to left, three times on the forehead and three times on the lips. With this gesture the ritual ends, and all that remains is to await the death of the *napaqa*.

After the *napaqa* dies, a funeral ritual is performed. This funeral ritual is no different from the usual ones, except for the fact that it takes place in part in the *mandi* and not in the dead person's home. Since the ceremony is rather long and cannot begin within less than three hours after death, unless the person died in the early morning it is necessary to wait until the dawn of the following day. The lamentations and manifestations of suffering that usually accompany burials in the Middle East are forbidden among the Mandaeans. Tears become a river difficult to cross, and hairs torn out become bonds holding back the dead person's soul. The rule holds all the more in this case, where otherworldly salvation is practically certain. The nocturnal vigil takes place in the *mandi,* with the entrance blocked to keep out any impure people or animals that may try to enter. A vase of water, a stone, and a lighted lamp, referred to as "water," "earth," and "light," are placed next to the corpse and are left at the place of death for three days. Early in the morning four men in a state of purity prepare a straw mat and wrap the body in it, arranging it on a litter specially made for the occasion of straw woven together with palm branches. In the mean-

32. *Kušta,* which also means "right" and is often hypostatized as an image of divinity.

time a *mandalta*[33] is built in the courtyard of the dead person's house by a priest or by a *halala*. This appears to be a sort of tomb, or substitute house for the soul, should it return. A long, narrow, small, and shallow hole is dug. Three bundles of short, stiff canes are tied and placed in a vertical position in the hole. All of them are tied to six long canes, three on each side, placed lengthwise over the hole in such a way as to hold the three bundles upright. The funeral procession stops near the *mandalta,* and the chief *halala* places some mud on the bundles of cane, sealing them with the *skandula,* as is done with a real tomb. The procession then continues to the burial. All of those participating must be barefoot, and women are excluded (in case there was one in a state of impurity, which would damage the departed). Once the tomb, without a name or other marks of recognition, has been sealed with the *skandula,* those present usually take part in a funeral banquet.

Three days of feasts begin at the future *ganzibra's* house. During this period the candidate can neither sleep nor contaminate himself, he cannot eat impure foods, and he cannot even eat meat. At dawn on the third day the seals on the tomb are broken, that is, the imprint of the ring of the *skandula* is removed, and the soul of the dead person leaves the body and begins its voyage.

More funeral ceremonies are held in the newly purified *mandi,* and a period of separation begins for the one who is very nearly a *ganzibra.* The period of separation is similar to that of a new priest and at minimum is forty-five days in length, the amount of time that it takes the soul to cross the heavens and appear before Abatur. Once this period is finished, together with any further additions due to eventual contamination, the *tarmida* who sent the "message" becomes a full-fledged *ganzibra.* The new *ganzibra* cannot leave his state of isolation, however, until he has performed the marriage of a priest. In theory, without such a ceremony the *ganzibra* would have to spend the rest of his life in isolation. Thanks, however, also to the practice of polygamy among the priesthood, this has apparently never happened.

The soul's rise through the heavens is in itself a dangerous voyage because the heavens are inhabited by demons or evil beings. The various heavens are the site of the "houses of punishment" or *maṭarata,* a sort of heavenly purgatory, in which those souls who do not have a pass consti-

33. It means "dwelling place" or "house of God" or "house of the spirit."

tuted by the purity of their lives (in Mandaean observance) are imprisoned for various lengths of time, for purification through suffering. This is why on the first, third, seventh, and forty-fifth days after death ritual meals take place in which the soul of the departed supposedly takes part, and from which it draws strength. In addition, meals for the dead are also held during holidays, such as *panǧa*, on anniversaries, during solemn ceremonies, and, in short, every time it is considered useful or opportune. There are three kinds of meals for the dead. The simplest, known as *laupa* or *laupania*,[34] which could be translated as "communion," is celebrated at home without priests. A number of pieces of flat bread are broken among those present, to accompany the food, mostly the sacred foods mentioned already. Other fresh food is also prepared, either vegetable or animal (fish, mutton, or various birds), depending on the family's resources. The second, more complex kind of meal is called *zidqa brika*, meaning "blessed offering," and usually requires the presence of at least one *tarmida*. This ceremony can include the sacrifice of an animal, such as a ram, whose fat is used in preparing the ritual foods. In some cases the priest impersonates a particular deceased person, and the ceremony varies depending on the case and the specific aims involved. The ritual can be complex, with several priests, and requires the preparation of five *paṭiria* and two *ṣaia*,[35] bread rolled into a phallic form, which we mentioned in connection with the wedding rituals. An offering (*kana d-zidqa*, "the whole of the offerings") is usually given to the priest as suffrage for the dead.

The third and most sacred form is the *masiqta*, which we have already seen. There are various versions of this ritual as well, according to circumstances, but it always includes the sacrifice of a dove and the preparation of 66 *paṭiria*, or a multiple thereof. In the case of a ceremony for the soul of someone who drowned, who burned to death, who was struck by lightning, or who fell from a palm tree, 528 *paṭiria* (66×8) are required. Finally, a *dukrana* (a ceremony whose name means "commemoration," or "remembrance" of the dead) can always be held, with or without a *masiqta* or *zidqa brika*. This ceremony requires recital of the prayer *abahatan qadmaiia*,[36] very well known among the Mandaeans, in which all of the deceased Mandaeans are called upon to be present in the community. Pro-

---

34. Plural of *laupa*, that is, "community."
35. Plural of *ṣa*.
36. The expression means "our fathers (who are) the first," that is, "our ancestors."

nouncing their names creates their presence, and it is in this way that the word "remembrance" should be understood in connection with commemoration. Lady Drower was not wrong when she remembered the way the words of Jesus ("in memory of me") are believed, at least among Catholics, to somehow bring about the real presence of the Man and God who died and was called back to life. Behind ceremonies that may seem very diverse, therefore, there could be a common cultural background, rooted in the Semitic world, or, perhaps, in the deepest desires of the human soul.

THE IDEAS

Gnosticism

Toward the end of the 1960s it was estimated that, worldwide, about seventy new Christian denominations were formed every day, mostly in the United States, and most of them in California, with a particularly high concentration in the area around San Francisco.

The times were different then. The teachings of Marx and Mao, filtered through Marcuse and with psychoanalysis added, ran through the universities and high schools of the entire Western world like a floodtide. In Europe, on the one hand, the restlessness of that time took on decidedly political overtones, generating converts to several very different persuasions and eventually opening the doors to terrorism. In the United States, on the other hand, a country that from the very beginning has been a home to religious nonconformity, perhaps the most visible result was an incredible flowering of more or less ephemeral, and more or less original, religious groups. Bearing in mind that in the past historical phenomena required much longer gestation periods, the two moments in the history of Christianity that I equate with what happened in California in the sixties and seventies would be Reformation Europe during the sixteenth century and Egypt during the second and third centuries. These three situations, separated from one another in space and time, have one feature in common: the lack of a central religious authority able to control society at all levels. What weight could excommunication by the Pope have in a country where the papal bulls had been publicly burned only a few decades earlier? What social significance could be attached to breaking off communion with a markedly minority Christian church in the Roman Hellenistic world, especially in Egypt, accustomed as it was to the most extravagant religious behavior then imaginable?

It was indeed in Egypt between the second and third centuries that the complex phenomenon we call Gnosticism found fertile terrain. In actual fact it was a heterogeneous group of churches, schools of thought, and conventicles that shared a common exaltation of a "knowledge"[37] that, communicated to the faithful by illumination, meant salvation. It has to be said at once, of course, that all cultured Christians at that time (according to the parameters of Hellenistic culture) were "Gnostics," the differences between them consisting in the content they each provided for the category "knowledge." Gnosticism, then, is the set of Gnostic doctrines declared to be heretical by the great Church, this Church being the one whose theology won out. Each proclaimed the orthodoxy of its own set of beliefs, declaring all who believed differently to be heretical. From a historical point of view, the "orthodox" church was the one that succeeded in imposing its own ideas, relegating the others to marginal positions in society and culture, or even managing to eliminate them altogether. It is in that peripheral religious world, which at times enjoyed a quite precarious existence, and which often survives only in the documents of its victorious adversaries, that we must seek out the cultural coordinates for collocating Mandaeanism historically.

Of course, the world was full of contradictions in those days too. An unprecedented level of economic well-being allowed a certain number of people access to traditional culture, but an enormous mass of slaves and wretched peasants made up the suffering base of the social pyramid. I do not know whether the roofs of Alexandria, the pearl of Egypt, glittered with gold like those of Rome, roofs that — they say — even instilled a moment of awe in the barbarians as they were about to ravish the eternal city. The wealth of the urban pagan world, however, did generate anger and resentment among the peasants of the Nile Delta. Their insurrections, put down in blood, are remembered only in the footnotes of history books — nor could it be otherwise, given the scarcity of material that the historians of the ancient world have left us on the subject. The massacre of a few thousand poor men and women and their families just didn't "make the news" and, in effect, had less influence on the course of history than, say, a failed palace coup. When, however, the resentment of the Egyptian plebe-

37. In Greek *gnōsis*.

ians was duly channeled into Christianity and directed against the symbols of pagan cultural power, which had been dominant until that time, tangible results followed. The unforgivable flames of the Sarapeum appeared to mark the definitive triumph of Christianity (A.D. 391), and the blood of Hypatia, the last woman philosopher of classical antiquity, stained the marble of her home and the smooth stones of Alexandria's streets (A.D. 415). Less than two hundred and fifty years after paganism was buried, however, the same spirit of rebellion in the Christian poor of Egypt opened the gates to Islam, seeking freedom from Byzantine domination.

The heterodox Gnostics saw the negative side of the world. It was impossible to believe that a good God, a God who loved man, would have imprisoned him in a body that by its very nature stinks, that needs to destroy countless lives, both animal and vegetable, just to feed itself, that is the seat of all vices and the very worst of instincts, and that, in the end, is destined to decay and rot and be food for worms. This anguished vision of humankind remained substantially inexplicable. Even the idea that humankind had been placed on earth as punishment for some sin, committed perhaps even in an earlier life, or by some ancestor, could not explain why all of creation was suffering. Do animals not suffer, and does the vine not weep when it is cut? Are the springs not the tears that accompany the earth's lament, unheard by most, but not by those who had the ears to hear it?

Ears to hear and eyes to see, this is the tragic ability of the Gnostic. Not everyone is like him, most people being no different from beasts, destined to dissolution. The bodies of some, though, house a soul, however imperfect. They understand some truth but not the whole truth. They tend toward what is good but can do no more than follow the teachings of the great Church. Only a few, the Gnostics in fact, harbor a spark of the divine spirit inside their souls, which makes them different from everyone else. They also lived in ignorance, but a savior, a messenger come down from the impenetrable heights of the world beyond the heavens, has given them knowledge of the truth. The God who created this world is an evil demon, but there is a greater God who loves his children and will now save them. Salvation, in fact, is immediate. When the Gnostic realizes he or she is one, the knowledge dawns at once that by his or her nature salvation has already, and inevitably, happened, because nothing can change the fate of the spiritual particle present in the Gnostic's soul. This not only elevates the Gnostic above everyone else (including their laws), but also above God the creator and *his* laws. The Gnostic is aware of his difference, but an

eventual sense of frustration is dissolved in an individualistic consciousness of freedom and superiority that has few parallels in ancient history
and that explains the sympathies that such Gnostic Prometheanism
aroused in more modern times, for instance, in Romanticism.

Since heterodox Gnostic knowledge is arrived at through illumination, each Gnostic could feel authorized to receive slightly more than others, and thence give rise to a new school, a new conventicle for dissecting
the truth with ever greater precision. This led to a considerable degree of
fragmentation in their teachings, so that it is quite impossible to find a
unified body of Gnostic thought, but only certain points upon which most
Gnostics would have agreed. First, the demiurge, the ignorant and evil
God that created this world, is the easily angered and anthropomorphic
God of the Jews, that is, Yahweh. As a consequence, the sacred book of the
Jews, commonly known now as the Old Testament, must be considered
false and full of lies, an instrument of propaganda and oppression, invented by Yahweh and his followers. All of sacred history is to be reread
and reinterpreted in a new light: the ancient enemies of Yahweh and his
people, from Cain to the Sodomites to the generation of the Flood, were
the true depositories of spiritual knowledge. The God of this world, in his
jealousy, tried every way to smother or appropriate such knowledge, destroying its every manifestation. He is indeed only the latest product of a
degenerative chain that brought about the dispersion of a luminous particle of divinity in the world of darkness and of matter. After much wandering about, the last fragment of light was embodied in Adam, while the
demiurge Yahweh was left without. Awareness of what he lacked, then, led
Yahweh to persecute humankind, to attempt to appropriate its spirit, or at
least to keep it entrapped in matter. According to some, he even invented
Eve so as to seduce Adam and thereby draw from him his spiritual seed,
imprisoning it forever in the chain of reproduction. In this perspective,
Adam did not sin in the garden when he ate the "fruit of the tree of *knowledge*"; if anything he was reaffirming a right that made him "like God." If
there was any sin, it was that of allowing himself to be seduced by Eve. All
of history, then, is the tragic scene of an utterly ruthless struggle by the
demiurge and his evil princes (in Greek, the *archons*) to keep the sparks of
divine light that had precipitated down divided and imprisoned in matter.
The Light, however, has prepared a plan for salvation, providing for the recovery of all that is consubstantial to it.

The spirit was supposedly passed on to Seth (and there were Gnostics who called themselves "Sethian"), and from Seth to his descendants, who were always a hidden and oppressed minority, at times even unaware of their legacy. The savior, or the series of saviors as some believed, comes to "reawaken" the Gnostics' dormant knowledge and thus save them. For the Christian Gnostics this bringer of revelation and savior is the heavenly Christ, a divine being, a direct emanation of the very heart of the divine, which entered into the earthly Jesus to save the Gnostics. Others went so far as to believe that the earthly Jesus was a negative, demonic reality, a creature the demiurge made for the purpose of trapping the heavenly messenger within it. The demiurge thought he could take over the divine Spirit in this way, binding it in the coils of the flesh, nailing it to the cross, and swallowing it in death. Christ, however, fooled everyone. In different ways, according to the teachings of the various Gnostic sects, he never really suffered the passion, nor was he ever actually killed. Leaving the body of Jesus before the passion, he let the demiurge's thugs destroy his bodily image while he looked on in another form, laughing his heart out. Just as the personal crisis of the individual Gnostic was overcome by developing a clear sense of superiority, the wretched end of Jesus too, irreconcilable for many people with their own idea of a messiah or savior, was salvaged through the mythical reversal of a historical event. The logical presupposition of this is to be found in the positions of early Christians — Paul, for instance, who saw Jesus' true messianic triumph in the cross — but what is characteristic of heterodox Gnosticism is the sharp opposition between Jesus and Christ or, better, the opposition between the two constituent elements of the "composite" Jesus-Christ. This phenomenon is known as the Gnostic Christological dichotomy.

The whole Gnostic vision of the world is based on the opposition of conflicting principles. The diversity and laceration perceived among men and within each Gnostic is projected into the world, into the cosmos, and even into the divine itself. Just as there is a division between good and evil on earth (ethical dualism), the forces of good and evil, of light and darkness, battle throughout the entire universe (cosmic dualism). Even divinity is divided. Many Gnostics temper their dualistic vision of the divine with the idea that in the beginning there was only one positive divine principle, the Light, which later degenerated through multiple emanations until the last of these got caught up in matter, conceived of as negativity, void, and absence. Other more radical positions, however, such as that of Mani, which can be dated to the middle of the third century, considered darkness an active principle. It had the same strength as the positive principle and was capable of attacking light and defeating it, in part devouring it, thus creating that mixture, that initial imbalance, which led to the origin of this world. This will cease only when the irreconcilable components of the cosmos, once again completely separated when the light that is dispersed and imprisoned in darkness has been recovered in all its parts, return to the enjoyment of an eternal equilibrium.

Mandaeanism

The religious ideas of the Mandaeans show some remarkable similarities to the ancient doctrines of the Gnostics, and they also share a similar mode of expression, through myth. In other words, we do not find philosophical reflections but stories. Characters belonging to the divine world or the realm of human legend, sometimes with a clear symbolism barely veiled behind their names, perform deeds in them whose interpretation is believed to provide the meaning of things. Unluckily for us, it is impossible to reconstruct a unified, coherent vision of certain important aspects of religious doctrine from the *corpus* of Mandaean literature. The concept of divinity, the nature of the world and its creation, the nature of humans (anthropology), or the soul and its functioning (psychology) all elude us. Indeed, the Mandaean texts are the fruit of the sedimentation of different teachings recorded centuries apart. The more ancient traditions seem clearly dualistic and are nearest to the ideal positions of classical Gnosticism. There are also texts, however, where the physical world is seen in a positive light, considered the direct creation of the highest, good divinity. These passages must have been redacted in periods of clear cultural dependence on Christianity, or perhaps on Islam. In the *Ginza*, for example, perhaps the best known of the Mandaic sacred books, we find at least seven different accounts of the origins of the cosmos, each with features that are most difficult to reconcile. Similarly Hirmiz bar Anhar, a learned layman *(ialupa)* of a priestly family, a great friend of Lady Drower's, and the most important of her sources, would frequently repeat that one must also love darkness and the powers of evil, creatures of God, since love was the power that holds the universe together. This is a position that may be felt to be very congenial, but it is not at all consistent with available Mandaean texts from the ancient world. It has its uses, of course, in that it demonstrates that Mandaeanism does not seem to have developed a theological orthodoxy capable of pushing dissident opinion aside.

In the more clearly dualistic texts there is a sharp contrast between light *(nhura)* and darkness *(hsuka)*. At the highest point of light we find a supreme being, often possessing the qualities of transcendence: Life, or Great Life, or First Life.[38] In texts that appear to be more recent, the same reality is called Mara d-Rabuta (Lord of Greatness), Malka d-Nhura (King of Light), and Mana (Powerful).[39] The realm of light is inhabited by a great number of intermediate celestial beings, the *'utria*[40] or *malkia*.[41] These were presented to the European missionaries and travelers of past centuries as "angels" because of their function as intermediaries and messengers between humans and the highest divinity. Alongside them there are many abstract or hypostatized realities that sometimes seem to take on individual consistency and features: Kušta, the "Truth" or "Right"; 'Aina, the "Spring"; and Sindirka, the "Palm Tree." There is also the *iardna* of light, the "river" or "flowing water" or the ubiquitous "Jordan," that sometimes goes by a proper name: Piriauis, or Praš Ziua, "Euphrates-Splendor." This can be thought of as a unit, or as an infinite whole of rivers of light, in which the celestial realities immerse themselves, perpetuating the perfect cult that pleases God in eternity, the celestial liturgy compared to which mere earthly ones are but wretched imitations. The entire realm of light is structured in a limitless number of "worlds of light" *(almia d-nhura)*, where the celestial "dwelling-places"[42] are to be found, the seat of the *'utria* and the blessed Mandaeans.

As far as the highest hierarchy of Light is concerned, from the First Light emanates the Second Light, whose proper name is Iušamin,[43] from

38. Hiia, or Hiia Rbia, or Hiia Qadmaiia. In Mandaean, abstract terms (such as "life") are indicated by a plural of a participle (so *hiia* = "the living"). Grammatically, therefore, the term is a plural, and the adjectives that refer to it are in agreement with the plural (*rbia* is the plural of *rba*, "great," and *qadmaiia* is the plural of *qadmaia*, "first").

39. *Mana* means originally "vase," "recipient," or "receptacle." The term then takes on the meaning of "spirit" or "spiritual element," also at an anthropological level. Every person possesses her own *mana*, which, depending on the text, is either confused with the soul or is distinct from it, sometimes being considered her "image" *(dmuta)* or heavenly double.

40. The plural of *'utra*, "wealth."

41. The plural of *malka*, "king."

42. Škinata, the plural of *škinta*, "temple," "house," and "dwelling place."

43. This would seem to derive from Iao (the secret name of Yahweh, present in numerous magic and Gnostic texts) *haš-šammayim*, that is (in Hebrew), "Iao of the heav-

this the Third Life, called Abatur,[44] and from this the Fourth Life, Ptahil.[45] The process is clearly degenerative, and Ptahil, the least perfect, is to be found at the edge of light, by this point in contact with darkness. The structure of the latter is by no means clear, nor is it presented in a consistent way, at least not according to the criteria of our own traditions of logic. There are waters of darkness, which in certain contexts appear to be a sort of primeval and eternal chaos. Out of them sometimes emerges a Lord or a King of Darkness, the exact opposite of the King of Light. More often the prominent figure is Ruha, the "Spirit," a female being, also called Ruha d-Qudša, "Spirit of Holiness," that is, the Holy Spirit of the Christians. From an incestuous relationship with her own brother Gap, Ruha generates 'Ur, an enormous monster in the form of a serpent whose coils wrap themselves into the dark fires of the abyss. The created world stands on him. From a new incestuous relationship, this time with 'Ur (and, according to some texts, also with Gap and with her own father, the King of Darkness), Ruha generates the Seven, that is, the planets; the Twelve, that is, the signs of the zodiac; and the Five, the so-called "furious." The latter are astral realities, but it is not clear who or what they really are.[46] I would note in passing that five is the difference between twelve and seven, and this might not be without significance, given the love of the Mandaeans for purely arithmetical speculations.

The best-known myth on the origin of creation narrates that Ptahil, on the orders of his father, Abatur, created the cosmos. Having descended from the light toward the waters of darkness, however, he showed himself incapable of carrying out the task entrusted to him. So he turned to Ruha, to the Seven, and to the Twelve, and with their help molded from the waters of darkness Tibil, the created world. According to another version, after having risked being swallowed up in the dark waters, Ptahil obtained a mantle of light from his father and with it, by beating the water, he solidified it, thus creating the world. In any case, his creative gesture was incor-

---

ens." His position in the Mandaean pantheon is ambiguous, but in general he is considered a positive divinity.

44. Of uncertain etymology; possibly related to *ab,* "father."

45. Of uncertain etymology; perhaps connected to a root *PTH,* meaning "to mold," "to open" (and that would refer to his activity as demiurge), to which the suffix *-il* was added. This is similar in every way to the Hebrew *-el,* which characterizes a number of angels' names (Raphael, Gabriel, Uriel, etc.).

46. According to a Mandaean informant, one of them would be the star Sirius.

rect and was considered a sin. His father was also involved in this, since he was responsible for having given him the order to create. Both are driven out of the world of light and, above the firmament (the outermost confines of the created world) but under the light, they created their own worlds, in which they dwell and reign sovereign. Underneath them, starting from the celestial vault, the cosmos is entrusted to the malevolent control of the Twelve and the Seven. These are the ancient Gods, astral and planetary, worshipped in the entire Mesopotamian area but now transformed into evil demons, a transformation that always happens with the gods of others by the religions that are or claim to be monotheistic (in the area: Judaism, Christianity, Zoroastrianism, Manichaeism, and Islam).

This does not take away from the fact that there are some Mandaean texts, though to tell the truth not so very many, that take a positive view of the planets and, most importantly, that the everyday life of the Mandaeans involves (or involved) them in constantly consulting the stars. Such a life provides the chance to cultivate astral cults, lived more or less subjectively by individual Mandaeans (as is shown in relatively recent times by the solar cult of Hirmiz, Lady Drower's informant); it also means that one of the main activities of priests consists of redacting horoscopes or predicting the future. There is therefore a kind of complicity between the Mandaean priestly hierarchy and those planets and signs of the zodiac that, no longer demons to be despised, become true divinities, whose favor can be entreated and obtained. An instrument of prime importance for understanding and bringing the astral divinities nearer to us is the *Spar Maluašia,* the "Book of the Signs of the Zodiac." This is a Mandaean manual of astrology, demonology, and pharmacopoeia, made up of various books, the first and longest actually called the "Book of the Zodiac."[47] This is followed by a "Book of the Stars," a "Book of the Moon," and numerous other texts, in which all that may be of use to an astrologer, an exorcist, or a healer may be found. The texts are of various origins and dates, often translated from Arabic and Persian. From a strictly astrological point of view, they are arranged following the classical tradition, with the zodiacal signs, the houses, and planetary influences.

The passages that help to prepare personal horoscopes are of extreme interest to us since they offer a sociological glimpse of an otherwise inaccessible Mandaean world. The average life span of a fortunate person

---

47. This takes up about a quarter of the entire collection.

is considered to be around 70 years, with a maximum of 102 years for a man and 98 for a woman, according to the "Book of the Stars."[48] According to the sex and the various astral influences, everything about the newborn child is predicted, from its health to its marriage,[49] from its relationships with its parents to its travels, and from its physical appearance to its financial fortunes. Its physical features are given in detail: it is specified whether or not the newborn will have its teeth widely spaced out or have long eyelashes. Beautiful women are plump, and ginger or reddish hair appears to be prized in both the sexes. Special attention was paid to "marks" (moles or blemishes) on the various parts of the body, including the genitals. For men, only in one case is it said that the newborn child, as an adult, will have "big genitals," whereas this is said several times for women, though from the context it is not clear whether this is a good thing or not. Only of women is inconstancy predicted, and only women are associated with witchcraft, whereas men are predicted to have honorable futures as astrologers, exorcists, or healers. Of some women the masculine virtues are celebrated: "her speech will be like that of a man"; "she will be like a lion"; or "she will administer the goods of her husband." There are cases where women acquire goods and property.

It is often said that children will bring bad luck and catastrophe to their families. When this is the case, the advice is to feed them with breast milk (directly from the breast) from more than one woman (up to a maximum of seven), not just from their own mothers. In certain cases, a baby's first milk absolutely must not come from its mother. The most feared ways of dying are sudden death or death while on a journey, that is, ways that do not allow for the performance of the Mandaean ritual for the dying. The greatest misfortune is to fall from a palm tree or be struck by lightning. With illnesses, there are detailed descriptions of where they are located, but their nature is left vaguely generic, and any kind of vision with affinities to Western science is totally lacking. The only exception appears to be venereal diseases (called "genital sickness"), of which it is said that men contract them from women but never vice versa. There is an awareness of a difference between illness and demonic possession, even if in both cases

48. According to this text, however, most women die at around the age of fifty.

49. Successful men in general have three wives, with a maximum of seven, whereas for women it is considered a sad and disastrous thing to have many husbands (at any rate, never more than three and always one after the other).

what determines the outcome is the hour or the day of the week, or the sign, or at any rate the astral influence, at the moment of the appearance of the first symptoms. In some cases the illness will heal by itself, or the devil will leave after a certain number of days; in others, nothing can be done.

In the majority of cases a cure is possible. A good half of the book consists of a heterogeneous manual of pharmacopoeia, with instructions for amulets and various charms or spells, ointments for massage, drops for the nose, and potions to drink. Sometimes it is sufficient to read a passage from the *Ginza*, or even from the Koran,[50] in order to chase a demon away; sometimes the amulet is more complicated: "take a wing of a bat and write with the blood of a hoopoe" (there follows a list of demon names to cast a spell upon). In other cases otter skins and cat blood are used. Besides a certain number of herbs, there is a bit of everything: horse and ox saliva, the blood of a monkey, of a bat, of little pigeons, of a black crow, of a tortoise, of a pig, of a goat, of a black ass, of a wolf with rabies, the blood of the possessed himself, the blood of someone injured or killed by a lion, the blood of a black dog or white cock, water in which the Torah has been immersed or that has been taken from a mosque, the hairs of monkeys, of a lion, of a dog, of the nose of a horse, or of a mongoose, a dog's tail, the tongue of a tortoise or a wolf, the kidneys of a monkey and of a female ass, eagle's eggs, the gall of a lion, of a wolf, of a white pigeon, of a roan stallion or piebald ass, of an eagle, of a scorpion, and the urine of goat and pig. One medication even prescribes the use of the "liquid of a bee's sting." Quite frequently little owls were used, sometimes whole, sometimes only their innards, and in one case the contents of the stomach of one of them. Sometimes "seven black hairs" appear, and to combat a quite tenacious demon, the "hair of seven negroes" is recommended (to hang up as an amulet) as well as the "blood of one of them" (for massage). The use of human placenta or the ashes of the bones of a corpse I found only once. Usually one or two ingredients seem to be enough for the preparation of an amulet or concoction, but against a demon that attacks on the Sabbath, seven are needed: horse saliva, monkey blood, mint juice, portulaca juice, pigeon blood, olive oil, and oil of sesame (the whole mixture is cooked, left to cool, and finally instilled into the nose). The number seven therefore would seem to have some importance attached to it, as when there is the request to collect "ashes from seven ovens." It needs to be pointed out, however, that from a Mandaean

---

50. This recommendation is evidently of Islamic origin.

perspective seven is far from being a perfect or lucky number; it is the constant symbol of negative realities, such as Judaism or the planets. In addition, these recipes sometimes mean the consumption of parts of animals considered impure, or contact with blood or contaminating liquids, something, in short, that no practicing Mandaean should be able to carry out. Yet, whatever the historical origins of the recipes, it is (or was) the priests who prepare and provide the medicines.

Miscellaneous texts appear in the rest of the book. We have indications concerning propitious and unlucky days of the month and of the moon. The seventeenth of each month is especially lucky, a day suitable for purification ceremonies, for arranging contracts and trading. Whoever falls sick is certain to heal after seventeen days, and the children born that day will have long lives. Sixteen is less lucky, especially for those who suffer from hemorrhages. The children born then will suffer from constipation. The thirtieth is suitable for having sex, but on the second advances to married women should be avoided, while on the third one should not wash one's head (the thirteenth is more suitable). Everything is indicated with exactness according to the days and the stars: from when to cut one's nails to when to change one's clothes, conduct business, travel, convene court cases, request favors from the powerful, sow, harvest, hunt, fish, build a raft, or enter a new house. We have horoscopes for various years, according to the sign and the day they start, with forecasts for the climate and for world politics (some of these seem to be from quite ancient times; given the attention paid to the "great king," they could be from the Sassanid era or at any rate from an age prior to Islam). Finally, there are many omens or portents concerning astronomical manifestations (such as eclipses, comets, or meteors) or meteorological events. The latter go from rainbows, almost always an ominous sign, to the form of the clouds, the ways the wind blows, or thunder or lightning in a clear sky. Earth tremors or noises from underground are not lacking, nor are little signs from everyday household life, such as a door that creaks or a rumbling pan or a light that suddenly blows out. In every case, however, what gives significance to the omen or portent is the astrological sign in whose hour or time the event occurred and, in particular, the position of the moon compared to the various signs of the zodiac. Observed in the skies or more usually found in the calendar, the constellations of the zodiac determine every aspect of human existence.

The domination of the stars over human activities has roots going back a very long way. Having created Tibil, in fact, Ptahil and his helpers create Adam. Here the Mandaean version of a well-known Gnostic myth makes its appearance. The first attempt leads to little more than an abortion. *adam pagria,* physical Adam, is virtually a body without life. In the world of light, having felt pity for him, they convince the inner Adam (*adam kasia* or Adakas) to allow himself to be imprisoned in his body. He is the first soul, thanks to whose presence the earthly Adam acquires life. Now, however, the soul (or spiritual element; the Mandaean texts do not make much distinction) has to be saved. So Manda d-Hiia, called also Bar Hiia (Son of Life) or Dmut Hiia (Image of Life), the main Mandaean figure of revealer, descends. He brings Adam knowledge of his true celestial nature, he teaches him baptism, and he makes him the first Mandaean. As can readily be seen, in this context the sin of Adam makes no sense at all. In fact, he does not sin.[51] His salvation does not derive from repentance but from the knowledge that the divinity has bestowed upon him. Also, the baptism that was taught to him, on the model of the celestial liturgies, serves to maintain or recover the purity lost through contact with the physical. In the Judaic and Christian legends, however, from which the Mandaean legends would actually seem to derive, the baptism of Adam (and Eve) had a clear penitential function, in that it was an instrument for divine forgiveness after sin.

Among the speculations concerning Adam is the Mandaean myth about the celestial Adam. This latter figure, also called Adakas, is the double of the other Adam and lives in another world, the double of the earthly world: Mšunia Kušta.[52] The term indicates a seat, a kind of paradise, situated somewhere in the north. Not present in the more ancient texts, it acquires ever increasing importance in the more recent ones, turning out in the end to be the conflation of a number of realities, perhaps originally separate from each other. It is in fact the seat of the blessed and the ʿutria and coincides with the realm of light (also placed north). There it is imagined that Adam and his descendants, and the Mandaeans of the past, all live. It sometimes seems that they all continue to live and reproduce inde-

51. Only in one text does his one episode of drunkenness appear, but this is perhaps a Mandaean distortion of the stories of Noah. In other texts we shall see that the Mandaean Adam cuts a sorry figure when he refuses to die. However, there is no trace of his sinning, such as that in the Judaic and Christian traditions.

52. Literally, "the enraptured/chosen of the Truth." This is a collective plural indicating both the souls of the blessed Mandaeans, their celestial images, and the realities of the world beyond.

pendently of the events that happen to humanity. Sometimes they are the blessed double of Mandaean humanity. Sometimes Mšunia Kušṭa is a noneternal anteroom of the world of light. Siouffi's account puts forward a description organized according to logical criteria that is not borne out in any known Mandaean texts. There are four worlds in all, two celestial or spiritual and two earthly. The first two are the world of light and the world of darkness; the others are Mšunia Kušṭa and Tibil. The world of darkness is another world beyond this one, in which Mandaean sinners and the good people from other religions are placed. Without joy and without pain, it appears to be rather like a Christian limbo. Mšunia Kušṭa is an invisible but earthly world, whereas only Tibil is both earthly and visible. Unfortunately it is difficult to tell how far this arrangement depends on the goodwill of Siouffi's informant, or perhaps on Siouffi himself, wishing to present his readers with an understandable (i.e., noncontradictory) picture of Mandaean beliefs.

However that may be, the celestial Adamites correspond to the earthly ones. Three of these — Abel (Hibil), Set (Šitil), and Enos (Anuš) — are 'utria, who can substitute or stand beside Manda d-Hiia in the function of revealer and savior. Whereas Šitil remains rather in the shadows, a large number of stories see Hibil, called Hibil Ziua ("Splendor"), and Anuš, called Anuš 'Utra, functioning as intermediaries between the divinity and humankind. As far as the female figures of biblical history are concerned, starting from Hauua (Eva), they are called "Drop (niṭupta)[53] or Cloud or Treasure (simat) of Life or of Light" and are judged positively. In actual fact, besides certain names rather little remains of the stories of the Bible as we know them. Compared to the original legends, the Mandaean legends turn out to have undergone a profound transformation, insofar as they are the (perhaps oral) reworkings of apocryphal Judaic or Christian stories, whose tenor already differed quite considerably from the canonical texts. For example, the figure of Cain and his story are completely absent, whereas a couple of times an otherwise unknown Adam son of Adam, Adam bar Adam, who was reputed to have been seduced by Ruha, makes his appearance. In this legend it may be possible to glimpse the final result of Gnostic interpolations about the seduction of Adam by Eve (providing bodily cover for the demiurge), or else about the seduction of Eve and/or Adam by archons, or at any rate some demonic being. In the Mandaean

---

53. In that "drop of sperm" means "spring of life."

stories, Ruha always has the function of seducer or deceiver, both when she appears as herself and as another to confuse her victim.

As far as the sons of Adam go, Set (Šitil) dies before his time. He in fact accepts dying in place of his old father,[54] who is too afraid and who through tricks and excuses manages to deceive the angel of death. These Mandaean stories are probably the development and fusion of Judaic and Christian legends about Adam, and above all about Abraham and Moses, who all refuse to die by inventing excuses and preparing subterfuges. Whereas in the Judaic or Christian apocrypha the protagonist in the end dies, for the Mandaeans the one who dies is Šitil. The latter thus becomes the first Mandaean to enter into celestial blessedness. Hibil (the biblical Abel), however, is born miraculously, leaving his mother intact and appearing suddenly at her side. This idea appears in relation to Melchizedek in an apocryphal text of Judaic origin called the "Second Book of Enoch," and the Mandaeans probably derived their story from the Judaic traditions.

Whatever the genesis of the legends about Hibil, the son of Adam, a dense mass of mythical material is connected with Hibil Ziua's descent into the underworld or world of darkness. This happens in a prehistoric phase of the events that sees the opposition of light and darkness, when the cosmos still did not exist. Hibil Ziua is at the same time a revealer and an instigator of a Gnostic type. In fact, with a voyage that lasts an incalculable number of years, he penetrates right into the heart of darkness to appropriate its powers. Having overcome staggering obstacles and conflict with ever more mysterious and terrifying characters, he finds himself faced with Krun (or Akrun), known as "the mountain of flesh," who tries to swallow him, but his armor of sharp-pointed copper lacerates Krun internally so that he has to be vomited out. Krun is forced even to concede to him a kind of magic pass or key that allows Hibil Ziua to reach the actual bottom of the abyss. There he finds the couple that were the progenitors of darkness, who possess the object of his search, a mirror capable of reflecting the image of the world of light. The typically Gnostic symbolism is obvious. The light recovers its own image (the reflecting mirror), which had been lost in darkness. The couple who were lords of darkness, however, also have a daughter, Ruha, who is given in marriage to Hibil Ziua. According to some versions, there is also a sister, Zahr'il, who also becomes his wife. However

54. According to the Mandaeans, Adam came to be a thousand years old, an age that both the Bible (Gen. 5:5) and a wide range of Judaic and Christian legends deny him.

that may be, Hibil Ziua undertakes the very long journey back up, with the magic pass, the mirror, and his consort (or consorts). Once having arrived at the edge of darkness, however, he abandons Ruha and returns into the light.[55] Yet Ruha is pregnant (it is not clear by whom), and at the end of her pregnancy gives birth to 'Ur. The latter grows very rapidly and wishes to meet the one he believes to be his father; behaving in a most unfatherly fashion, Hibil Ziua then throws him down into the abyss and covers him up with seven earths, one on top of the other.[56] This was the origin of the created world.

Inside this mythical structure, finally, other fragments of Gnostic myth on the descent of the heavenly savior are to be found. According to some passages, Hibil Ziua turns out to be a prisoner of darkness, from which he will be freed through a new divine intervention. In other passages he appears to have forgotten the purpose of his mission. In short, Hibil Ziua impersonates the so-called "savior to be saved," very much a part of Gnostic traditions. On this subject I would like to recall the "Song of the Pearl," a Gnostic poetic text according to which a prince, the son of the king of a far-off country, goes to Egypt (the biblical symbol of idolatry) to recover a precious pearl. Once having arrived there, however, like the prodigal son he squanders everything and forgets the purpose of his journey. His parents entrust an eagle with a message and a precious suit of clothes for the son, who comes to his senses and triumphantly brings to a close the mission that had been entrusted to him. It seems pretty clear that the son is the spirit of the Gnostic, lost in the coils of physical nature but then reawakened by illumination.

55. This is also quite usual behavior in Gnostic myths. Comparison could be made with the plot of the so-called "Book of the Gnostic Justin," in which Adonai abandons his wife Israel to join his own father in the light, of whose existence he previously knew nothing. The myth represents through images the Gnostics' need to abandon even those attractive or seductive realities of this world, so that they could turn wholly and without regret to the world of the spirit. Given the anti-Judaic character of many Gnostic sects, it is not exactly surprising that a Judaic name (Israel) represents seduction, femininity, and the deceiving beauty of this world.

56. Here, too, outside the metaphor, there is the Gnostic myth of matter's being unable to know Light, and matter's incoherent desire for knowledge has to be rejected and neutralized in order to safeguard the realm of the divinity. The divine truths cannot be contemplated through the eyes of the flesh, and passion has to be suffocated ruthlessly, crushing it down into the lowest depths of being. Only afterward, as a gift of blessedness and salvation, will the contemplation of God be possible.

As far as the personal spirit and soul are concerned, Mandaean terminology is not by any means precise, nor can it be said that Mandaean anthropology is a model of clarity. The soul, usually called *nišimta,* certainly exists, and it is personal, detaching itself from the body on the third day after death, facing the otherworldly judgment, and suffering the consequences for good or for evil. Some texts, however, speak of a personal spirit, called *ruha,* which in spite of its name does not seem to have any relation to Ruha (d-Qudša). Again, in others a personal *mana* appears, and the relation among the three terms *(ruha, mana,* and *nišimta)* is not clear at all. In addition, the ascension of the soul (or of the spiritual principle, whether *mana* or *ruha)* of the dead person toward the regions beyond the heavens is at one time imagined as a journey undertaken in solitude and at another as the meeting and the reunion or fusion with the "celestial double" of the dead person. This ascension is usually favored by the presence of a celestial helper, named *adiaura.*[57] This character is an ʿutra, sometimes remaining anonymous, sometimes one of the more famous of the revealers, even Manda d-Hiia in function of psychopomp.

Just as the experience of the individual cannot know the repeatability of reincarnation, so human history according to the Mandaeans is linear rather than cyclical. It is subdivided into four ages of decreasing duration for a total of 480,000 years, from Adam to the end of the world. The first three ages have already passed, and we are now living in the fourth and last, the shortest, that will end up destroyed "from the air." The texts do not specify clearly how this destruction will take place, but some contemporary witnesses refer to Mandaean worries about what can in some way be brought from the air: aerial bombardment, radiation, and pollution. The basic test of a prophecy that is worth its salt is its capacity to be adaptable to any situation. If this is the end, in the beginning each age had a human couple, either created or survivor, that then populated the world. The first age, which began with Adam and Eve, was destroyed by the sword and the plague. The second, which began with a surviving human couple (Ram and Rud, according to their Mandaean names, although there are no particular legends about them in the literature), was destroyed by fire. The third, also begun by a couple with Mandaean names (Šurbai and Šarhabʿil) and about whom we know nothing, ended with the waters of the flood, around which there is an interesting group of legends. The Mandaean idea

57. The term is of Persian origin.

of human history, therefore, consists of the insertion of the theory of the four ages of the world, a theory widespread in various forms in the ancient world, into the structure of the biblical story, a structure received in very peculiar ways in that it had already been filtered through legends that grew out of the biblical story. The Mandaean hero of the flood is Šum bar Nu (Shem the son of Noah), who also has a corresponding celestial figure of quite some importance, named Šum Iauar (Shem Light) or Šum Kušṭa (Shem Truth). The earthly Shem is the original ancestor of the Mandaeans, who thus show they have adapted for themselves a widespread legend in the Semitic world and one very much present in the biblical and Judaic traditions. Their racial exclusiveness, however, led them to conclude that other peoples cannot be of the same branch as Shem, that is, they cannot be sons of Nu and his legitimate wife (usually called Nuraita or Anhu-raita). Before the flood Nu had only had Šum and no one else by Nuraita. According to a story told to Lady Drower, at the time of the flood, after Noah, his wife, and his daughter-in-law had entered the ark, Shem arrived late. He clambered up onto the roof, and there remained the whole time, under the torrential rain, but fed miraculously by the divinity, who had planned the accident. Only afterward, when the flood was over, was he able to rejoin his wife (named Anhar).

This story probably originates in Judaic and Christian legends that deny the navigators in the flood any kind of sexual activity during their stay in the ark. Yet sexual abstinence is absolutely extraneous to the Mandaean mentality, and the narrative concerning Shem's misadventures at present take the form of an anecdote, without consequences of a specu-lative type. Once the flood was over, without rainbows or covenants with God, the two surviving males take up their respective conjugal habits once more. Whereas Shem and his wife found the chosen stock of Mandaeans, things do not go so smoothly for Noah. On this new adventure of his we do not have any written Mandaean evidence. The *Ginza* refers just to Shem, adding that Noah had two other children, Iam and Iapit. Elsewhere these children become four, with the (re)appearance of Ham. While Ham and Iapit are the Mandaic transcription of the biblical Ham and Japheth, compared to the Bible Iam is a novelty,[58] destined as he is to replace Shem,

---

58. His name appears to be constructed out of the fusion of the initial part of Iapit and the last part of Ham. The homophony with the noun that means "water" would seem to be a coincidence.

chosen by Mandaeans as their own founding father. From the stories orally transmitted we learn that the three are bastards: already in two of his letters (of 1624 and 1627) Basil of St. Francis was reporting that, according to the Mandaeans, the Negroes are not sons of Adam but of Noah and an evil spirit. The details appear in the reports of Siouffi and Lady Drower. When he left the ark, Noah wandered around a little to see how things stood after the flood, and at a certain point found himself face to face with his own wife, dressed to kill with her hair flowing loose. According to the Mandaean narrators, after the worries of interminable days and nights shut in an ark crammed full with animals, with scenes worthy of the apocalypse going on outside, poor Noah was unable to resist the urges of the flesh. It was the first time he had been able to breathe the fresh and presumably bracing air of the new world, and he was thus incapable of realizing that the woman who had wrapped herself around him was not his usual partner. According to Adam, Siouffi's informant, she was "a female of the evil angels"; though for Lady Drower's informant (an Iranian Mandaean priest), she was Ruha in person. The triplets were born as a result.

These are thus the three "bastard" progenitors of all the other peoples, who naturally turn out to be different from the pure and chosen stock of the Mandaeans. Yet who the "others" are is not entirely clear since their identification changes with the historical moment and possibly from questioner to questioner. Everyone seems to be in agreement over Ham, the progenitor of the Negroes or, in other words, the "slaves." As far as the other two go, Siouffi heard that Iamin (*sic*) was the progenitor of the "Turks" and Iapit of the "French"; it was explained to Lady Drower, however, that Iam had generated the whites, Abram, and the Jews, while Iapit was the ancestor of the gypsies. The contradiction is not as unresolvable as may appear at first sight. "French" is the general term for Europeans (i.e., the whites, descendants of Japheth) in use in many Middle Eastern countries. Before the end of Ottoman power in Mesopotamia, "Turks" indicates all those who recognized Islamic power. As in Italian villages along the Mediterranean coast, fear of the "Turks" did not allow the wretched inhabitants to distinguish between Berbers, Tripolitans, Egyptians, Arabs, (apostate) Europeans, or real Turks when the latter arrived from the sea armed to the teeth. Similarly for the Mandaeans in Ottoman territory, the "Turks" were virtually bundled together as Moslems, that is, as more or less all the Semitic stock in the area. A confirmation of this is to be had in the deformed name of their progenitor, who for Siouffi was not Iam but Iamin.

In certain Mandaean legends there is a Jewish character named Bnia Iamin, roughly the equivalent of Benjamin. The expression Bnia Iamin is the Mandaean transliteration of a Hebrew syntagma meaning "Sons of Iamin," which is always written with its component parts (Bnia and Iamin) separate, and at least once it is considered grammatically plural. This leads us to suppose that Bnia Iamin originally meant "Sons of Iamin" and is therefore a general name for the Jews, eventually becoming the proper noun for an eponymous character.

That the substitute of Shem, whether he goes under the name of Iam or Iamin, is the progenitor of the Semites is in its way confirmed by the information Lady Drower received. Her informant also had to find an original ancestor for the gypsies, for whom, with a kind of ethnographical consistency, he had recourse to Iapit. By doing this, however, he deprived the Europeans, perceived as ethnically different from the gypsies, of their own specific ancestor. Since Ham was the Negroes' forefather, the only original ancestor left was Iam, who thus not only procreated Abraham and the Jews, that is, the descendants of the biblical Shem, but also the "Whites."

The moral of the story is the same: the descendants of Šum, the Mandaeans themselves, are the only ones who are pure and genetically without sin. Adam in actual fact does not sin. Noah was the one who sinned, but his sin is of no concern to the Mandaeans. Adam's salvation does concern them, however, since for them alone is he a model, in that they alone are his worthy descendants. This salvation is protohistorical, or dates from prehistory. The savior and revealer already appeared at the beginning of time, and his return would not make much sense. Nevertheless, through the influence of Christianity, or rather as a polemical reaction to what the Mandaeans could learn of it, whether through direct contact or via Islam, some Mandaean texts await a return of Jesus at the end of time, and others suppose that Anuš 'Utra or Manda d-Hiia was around in Jerusalem at the time of Jesus or in the company of John the Baptist. As we shall see in the sections devoted to them, it is not always easy to insert these representations into an overall scheme respecting our normal canons of logic. Our own logic in fact does not seem to be the ideal means to reach an understanding of Mandaean traditions.

THE LITERATURE

Instruments

The Mandaean texts are usually books, as we understand them, or scrolls, usually called *diuan*. Paper is mostly used, although Lady Drower saw a treatise engraved on sheets of lead, so that they could be purified through immersion during the ceremonies. Leather is not used, even as a binding, since the skin of impure animals (cattle) is considered to be contaminating. The ink is produced by hand, by priests who are also scribes, with substances drawn from plants.

At the end of the various texts we usually find extensive colophons, where the scribe writes his own name (with those of his forebears), the name of the person for whom he has copied the text, the name of the owner of the book he has copied from, and sometimes extremely valuable information concerning the political situation at the time. In the luckiest cases the various scribes have copied again the old colophons written down by previous scribes, so that it is possible to reconstruct a history of the manuscript tradition of a given text. Unfortunately, the language and handwriting of the colophons are frequently not very carefully done, nor is it easy to uncover eventual gaps. Accurate scholarship is lacking for this too, and there is still no complete prosopographical study that would allow us, say, to single out and place in chronological order the various scribes and priests to whom we owe the salvation of Mandaean literature.[59]

The classical Mandaean language is a type of Oriental Aramaic, with features similar to those of the language of the Babylonian Talmud and with numerous external influences, especially Persian, evident in the religious terminology. Spoken Mandaean, called *raṭna*, uses a simplified language system and betrays considerable Arabic influences. The number of people who speak it is small when compared to the total population, but it seems destined to increase since all the recent evidence points to a renewed interest among Mandaeans in their own traditions and language. In Ira-

---

59. On this subject see now Jorunn J. Buckley, "The Colophons in the Canonical Prayerbook of the Mandaeans," *Journal of Near Eastern Studies* 51/1 (1992): 33-50; and idem, "The Colophons in H. Petermann's Sidra Rabba," *Journal of the Royal Asiatic Society* (Ser. III) 5/1 (1995): 21-38. In both articles, Buckley shows the importance of women as owners and/or scribes of manuscripts.

nian territory a school for Mandaean children where Mandaean is the language used has been established for some time.

The alphabet is made up of twenty-four signs, of which twenty-two represent the normal letters, the twenty-third is a double letter, and the last one is the repetition of the first ("a"). In this way a multiple of six is obtained (the number that symbolically indicates Mandaean things), as well as the correspondence to the number of hours in a day. Unlike what happens with other Semitic languages, the vowels in Mandaean do not appear as little dots or secondary graphical signs compared to consonants but are always written in their full form, being thought of as letters like the rest.

List of the Principal Published Mandaean Texts, Together with Information on Some Unpublished Ones

Works of a Mainly Exoteric Character

Liturgies

Text and English translation: E. S. Drower, *The Canonical Prayerbook of the Mandaeans* (Leiden: Brill, 1959). Text and translation (incomplete) in German: M. Lidzbarski, *Mandäische Liturgien* (Berlin: Weidmannsche Buchhandlung, 1920).

This is a set of collections of liturgical texts. The main collection is called *Qulasta* (originally "Hymns of Praise," then "Collection of Writings") and includes over 400 texts. Originally, the individual parts had an independent existence, written out and copied on to separate scrolls, and only later were they gathered together into a single book. The oldest extant manuscript dates from 1529. In addition to the *Qulasta*, other important parts are: *Sidra d-Nišmata* ("The Book of Souls"), containing liturgies for the *maṣbuta*, and then hymns and prayers for the *masiqta* — among the prayers, we should recall *Asut Malkia* ("The Greeting of/to the Kings"), a prayer for everyday purification; *Rahmia* (everyday prayers); *Abahatan Qadmaiia* ("Our First Fathers"), and then prayers for weddings, for ordaining priests, for *drapša, zidqa brika, klila,* and so forth.

Sidra Rba ("Great Book") or *Ginza* ("Treasure") *iamina* (of the right) and *smala* (of the left).

Edition: H. Petermann, *Thesaurus sive Liber Magnus, vulgo "Liber*

Adami" appellatus, opus Mandæorum summi ponderis, 2 vols. (Berlin-Leipzig [calcography], 1867) (abbreviation: Pet.).

Complete translation in German: M. Lidzbarski, *Ginza: Der Schatz oder das Grosse Buch der Mandäer* (Göttingen: Vandenhoeck & Ruprecht; Leipzig: Hinrichs, 1925) (abbreviation: Lid.). Work has been proceeding for some years on a new edition with translation.

The *Right Ginza* (abbreviation: GR) consists of 18 treatises on various subjects. The more ancient parts are to be found in the *Left Ginza* (GL), where there are legends on the death of Adam (actually these are not especially old), songs for the *masiqta,* texts on the fate of souls after death, with the description of the seven or eight celestial *maṭarata.* The collection of the various passages was carried out in the Islamic era.

Drašia d-Iahia ("The Book/Words of John") or *Drašia d-Malkia* ("The Book/Words of the Kings") (abbreviation: JB).

M. Lidzbarski, *Das Johannesbuch der Mandäer,* 2 vols. (Giessen, 1905 [the text]; Giessen, 1915 [translation into German]) (abbreviation: Lid.).

The book is made up of seventy-six passages of varying interest and on various subjects. Chapters 18-33 are one of the two original nuclei of the book, the one devoted to John, whereas another group of chapters makes up the "Speeches of the Kings." In the Islamic era other material was added (some of it ancient), which together goes to make up the present volume. Chapters 34 and 35 contain the most important texts for the "Legend of Miriai."

Haran Gauaita ("Inner Harran").

Text and English translation: E. S. Drower, *The Haran Gawaita and the Baptism of Hibil Ziwa,* Studi e testi 176 (Città del Vaticano: Biblioteca Apostolica Vaticana, 1953).

This is a kind of "History of the Mandaeans," from their flight under King Artaban to the coming of Islam, to the end of the world. The text, which is mutilated at the beginning and full of gaps, contains valuable information on the religious schism of Qiqil and the first years of Arab occupation. The colophon refers to a manuscript copied in 1088 E. (A.D. 1678).

TEXTS OF A DECIDEDLY ESOTERIC TYPE

Texts defined as *šarh*, "explanation, commentary." They contain rituals, instructions for their recitation, and explanations of the secret symbolism of the gestures and words.

Šarh d-Qabin d-Šišlam Rba ("Explanation of the Marriage of Šišlam the Great").

Text and English translation: E. S. Drower, *Sharh dQabin dShishlam Rba: Explanatory Commentary on the Marriage of the Great Šišlam*, Biblica et Orientalia 12 (Rome: Biblical Institute Press, 1950).

This contains the marriage ritual. Šišlam Rba (Šišlam the Great) is a quite recent figure in the Mandaean pantheon and is the celestial model of the Mandaean priest. Some of the prayers here are said aloud at the marriage of the priests. There is also a calendar with the propitious and unpropitious times for the wedding indicated.

Šarh d-Traṣa d-Taga d-Šišlam Rba ("Explanation of the Coronation of Šišlam the Great").

Text and English translation: E. S. Drower, *The Coronation of the Great Šišlam: Being a Description of the Rite of the Coronation of a Mandaean Priest* (Leiden: Brill, 1962).

This contains primarily the ritual for the ordination of a *ganzibra* and its (esoteric) explanation.

Among the unpublished texts should be noted *Šarh d-Paruanaiia* ("The Explanation of the Five Extra Days"), which has a description of the feasts for the five extra days of the calendar and an explanation of their meaning; *Šarh d-Ptaha d-Bimanda* ("Explanation of the Inauguration of the Bimanda"); and *Šarh d-Miša Dakia* ("Explanation of the Pure Oil"; on the oil ritual).

Alp Trisar Šuialia ("A Thousand and Twelve Questions") (abbreviation: ATŠ).

Text and English translation: E. S. Drower, *The Thousand and Twelve Questions (Alf Trisar Šuialia)* (Berlin: Akademie-Verlag, 1960).

The manuscript contains a treatise of the same title where in the form of question and answer among celestial beings the cult and the rituals are esoterically interpreted. This is followed by *Tapsir Pagra* ("Explanation of the Body"), a fragmentary text containing speculations on the correspondence between the microcosm (the human body) and the macrocosm (the universe). Then there is "Blow and Cure," a short treatise on purification (the "cure") for ritual impurities (the "blows").

Alma Rišaia Rba ("The First Great World"; or "Macrocosm") and *Alma Rišaia Zuṭa* ("First Small World"; or "Microcosm") (abbreviation: ARR and ARZ).

Text and English translation: E. S. Drower, *A Pair of Nasoraean Commentaries: Two Priestly Documents* (Leiden: Brill, 1963).

These are speculations on the relation between macrocosm and microcosm. ARR provides the esoteric explanation of the *masiqta,* while in ARZ Hibil Ziua explains the *dukrana.* The manuscript contains interesting colophons.

Diuan d-Maṣbuta d-Hibil Ziua ("The Book of the Baptism of Hibil Ziua").

Text and English translation in Drower, *Haran Gauaita.*

The text explains how a contaminated priest can purify himself (analogous to what Hibil Ziua had to perform having descended into the darkness in prehistoric times). The manuscript contains interesting colophons.

Diuan Abatur ("The Book of Abatur").

Text and English translation: E. S. Drower, *Diwan or Progress through the Purgatories: Text with Translation, Notes and Appendices,* Studi e testi 151 (Città del Vaticano: Biblioteca Apostolica Vaticana, 1950).

The scroll, with a wealth of illustrations, describes the journey of the soul across the *maṭarata,* the celestial purgatorial houses. The Abatur referred to in the title is the "Abatur of the balances," the judge of the otherworld. The text is relatively recent but is perhaps the oldest known in Europe since a copy was sent to Rome by Ignatius of Jesus around 1650 (and is now preserved in the Vatican Library).

Diuan d-Nahrauata ("The Book of the Rivers").

Text and German translation: K. Rudolph, *Der mandäische "Diwan der Flüsse,"* Abhandlungen der Sächsischen Akademie der Wissenschaften zu Leipzig, Philologisch-historische Klasse 70/1 (Berlin: Akademie-Verlag, 1982).

The text is a kind of geographical atlas with the religious and symbolic geography of the celestial world (and of Lower Mesopotamia, of which the celestial world is in some ways a projection). There are illustrations of canals, rivers, springs, trees, and hills. There is also Jerusalem and the temple, represented, respectively, by a rectangle and a circle (the scribe is thinking of the "dome of the temple") and both placed on the Euphrates-Splendor (Praš Ziua).

Diuan Malkuta 'Laita ("The Book of Exalted Kingship").
English translation: J. J. Buckley, *The Scroll of Exalted Kingship: Diwan Malkuta 'Laita*, American Oriental Society Translation Series 3 (New Haven, Conn.: American Oriental Society, 1993).
This text contains a detailed description of a part of the initiation ritual for the Mandaean priest, the *tarmida*.

Spar Maluašia ("The Book of the Zodiacal Signs")
Text and English translation: E. S. Drower, *The Book of the Zodiac (Sfar Malwasia)* (London: Royal Asiatic Society, 1949).
The text is extremely mixed in content. The various passages, of a composite nature, were written and rewritten between the sixth and sixteenth centuries.

In Mandaic a large number of magic texts have been redacted (usually with many illustrations). There are three kinds, depending on the material on which they are preserved and on the era of redaction.
1. On small tablets or scrolls of lead. These are talismans (to wear), and all the examples that have been discovered are very old. Their exact date is controversial, but they are probably prior to the fifth century.
2. On vases. Redacted between the fifth and seventh centuries, they precede Islam or are from very early on in Islam's age. They have been found in great quantities, within cups or bowls, that were then buried upside down so as to imprison forever the demon against whom the exorcisms or spells were addressed. Texts, translations, commentaries:
   H. Pognon, *Inscriptions, mandaïtes des coupes de Khouabir . . .,* vol. 2 (Paris: F. Vieweg, 1898-99).
   E. M. Yamauchi, *Mandaic Incantation Texts,* American Oriental Series 49 (New Haven, Conn.: American Oriental Society, 1967).

3. On little strips of paper that, rolled up, are placed inside little bags sewn with cloth. They are still being made today and can be sold to people who are not Mandaean. They are talismans, amulets, charms, and various formulas, mostly to wear. The priests are obliged to re-copy them, upon payment, for anyone who asks.

Bibliographical Suggestions[60]

Grammars and Dictionaries

Drower, E. S., and R. Macuch. *A Mandaic Dictionary.* Oxford: Clarendon, 1963.

Macuch, R. *Handbook of Classical and Modern Mandaic.* Berlin: Walter de Gruyter, 1965.

————. *Neumandäische Chrestomathie mit grammatischer Skizze, Kommentierter Übersetzung und Glossar.* Porta Linguarum Orientalium, n.s. 18. Wiesbaden: Harrassowitz, 1989.

Nöldeke, T. *Mandäische Grammatik.* Halle: Buchhandlung des Waisenhauses, 1875.

Studies

Drower, E. S. *The Mandaeans of Iraq and Iran: Their Cults, Customs, Magic, Legends, and Folklore.* Oxford: Clarendon, 1937. Reprint Leiden: Brill, 1962 (abbreviated: MII).

————. *The Secret Adam: A Study of Nasoraean Gnosis.* Oxford: Clarendon, 1960 (to be used with caution).

Gündüz, S. *The Knowledge of Life: The Origins and Early History of the Mandaeans. . . .* Journal of Semitic Studies Supplement 3. Oxford: Oxford University Press, 1994.

Lupieri, E. "Giovanni dei Mandei." In *Giovanni Battista fra storia e leggenda,* part 2, pp. 193-429. Biblioteca di cultura religiosa 53. Brescia: Paideia Editrice, 1988 (with further bibliography).

Pallis, S. A. *Mandaean Bibliography 1560-1930.* Copenhagen: V. Pio, 1933. Reprint Amsterdam: Philo, 1974.

60. Far from being exhaustive, these suggestions (almost all in English) will provide interested readers with the minimum data necessary to begin on their own a study of the Mandaeans and their language.

Petermann, H. *Reisen im Orient.* vol. 2, ch. xvii, pp. 83-137 n. 46 and pp. 445-65. Leipzig: Von Veit, 1965².

Rudolph, K. *Die Mandäer.* 2 vols. Forschungen zur Religion und Literatur des Alten und Neuen Testaments 74, 75. Göttingen: Vandenhoeck & Ruprecht, 1960-61.

————. "Mandaean Sources." In *Gnosis: A Selection of Gnostic Texts,* vol. 2, part 2, pp. 121-319. Ed. W. Foerster. Trans. R. McL. Wilson. Oxford: Clarendon, 1974.

————. *Theogonie, Kosmogonie und Anthropogonie in den mandäischen Schriften.* Forschungen zur Religion und Literatur des Alten und Neuen Testaments 88. Göttingen: Vandenhoeck & Ruprecht, 1965.

Segelberg, E. *Gnostica — Mandaica — liturgica: opera eius ipsius selecta et collecta, septuagenario Erico Segelbergo oblata.* Acta Universitatis Uppsaliensis, Historia religionum 11. Stockholm: Almqvist & Wiksell, 1990.

————. *Maṣbūtā: Studies in the Ritual of the Mandaean Baptism.* Uppsala: Almqvist & Wiksell, 1958.

Siouffi, N. *Études sur la religion des Soubbas our Sabéens. Leurs dogmes, leurs moeurs.* Paris: Imprimerie Nationale, 1880.

Sundberg, W. *Kushṭa: A Monograph on a Principal Word in Mandaean Texts.* Lund: Lund University Press, 1953, 1994.

Yamauchi, E. M. *Gnostic Ethics and Mandaean Origins.* Harvard Theological Studies 24. Cambridge, Mass.: Harvard University Press, 1970.

On Catholic Missions among the Mandaeans

Alonso, C., O.S.A. *Los Mandeos y las Misiones Católicas en la primera mitad del s. XVII.* Orientalia Christiana Analecta 179. Rome: Pontificium Institutum Orientalium Studiorum, 1967 (excellent).

Anonymous. *A Chronicle of the Carmelites in Persia and the Papal Mission of the XVIIth and XVIIIth Centuries.* 2 vols. London: Eyre and Spottiswoode, 1939 (many texts in English translation, but also many gaps and mistakes).

Gollancz, H., ed. *Chronicle of Events between the Years 1623 and 1733 Relating to the Settlement of the Order of the Carmelites in Mesopotamia.* London: Oxford University Press, 1927 (Latin text and English translation of a manuscript from Basra, with the history of the mission written by the Carmelites during those years).

2. The Mandaeans and the West: A History of Interaction

INITIAL CONTACT

It is said that the spiritual qualities that had inspired the first crusades were on the wane in the thirteenth century. The Christian lords of Europe seemed more willing to wear the cross for reasons of economic gain, or for a question of personal prestige, than for the salvation of their souls or to free Jerusalem. Thus, the Christian world saw Latin crusaders wreak destruction on the Eastern Roman Empire, sack Constantinople, strip both houses and churches, and carry off an infinite number of treasures. The gold and silver, drapes, trappings, and relics of Byzantium went to adorn and enrich the palaces and churches of the West, while Western sovereigns divided Greece and its islands into a series of feudal dependencies. The Fourth Crusade, indeed, was sidetracked from its original goal, and Jerusalem was to remain in Arab hands. It was an excommunicate emperor, Frederick II, who obtained the city of Jerusalem in 1229, but by means of diplomacy, without a fight. The excommunication was not lifted, however, and the Pope even went so far as to place Jerusalem under an interdict, an unprecedented move.[1] In any case, Western control over Jerusalem was not to last more than fifteen years.

1. Religious ceremonies thus lost their validity for the pious Catholic pilgrim in Jerusalem; at a stroke the pilgrim was deprived of confession and unable to take communion. The provision (legally above reproach, given that the head of state, the German emperor, was an excommunicate) aimed to dry up the flow of pilgrims and therefore drastically reduce the scale of economic activity in imperial territory.

This was a century of change for the Islamic world as well and, in particular, of decadence for Iraq. The Mongols arrived from the east. The first invasion, in 1231, did not bring about lasting changes, but in 1258 Hūlāgū (Hülägü) Khan, the grandson of Jenghiz Khan, advanced inexorably across Persia and Mesopotamia. With the title of Īl Khan, second only to the Great Khan who lived in the Far East,[2] he set up a domain extending from the Indus to the Mediterranean. The last of the caliphs of Baghdad, al-Musta'ṣim, who boasted of his direct descent from the earliest Abbasids, surrendered unconditionally on February 10, the first of ten days of ruthless sacking that cost the lives of hundreds of thousands of people in the capital alone. As was the custom among Mongol chiefs, Hūlāgū was careful to avoiding personally shedding the blood of the ruler he was about to succeed. He contented himself with having the unfortunate caliph and his son bundled into big sacks and trampled into pulp by his cavalry, so that it was the horses that actually did the killing. Īlkhan domination over Mesopotamia was to last roughly a century.

To the west of Mesopotamia a new power was emerging, for in Egypt the palace slaves had taken over. It was, in fact, the generals of the caste of Mamelukes who stopped the Fifth Crusade in 1217 and captured Louis IX in 1248. In 1260 they were able to defeat the Mongol army in Palestine, and on that occasion their leader, Baybars, proclaimed himself Sultan of Egypt. The Christians tried several times to make an alliance with the Mongols, encouraged by the fact that Hūlāgū had a Christian wife (Doquz Ḫātūn) and preferred non-Moslems in his state administration.[3] After Hūlāgū's death, though, the Mamelukes began to eliminate the Latin possessions in the east one by one. In 1268 they conquered Antioch and Jaffa, and in 1270 Louis IX's ill-fated African expedition ended with the king's death at Tunis. In 1280 it was hoped that a great Franco-Mongol alliance would block the expansionistic ambitions of Qalawun, the new Mameluke sultan, but in 1281 it was the Mongols and Christians who were defeated. Qalawun went on to take Tripoli in 1289, and his son, al-Ašraf, took Acre, Tyre, Sidon, and Beirut in 1291. While Cyprus remained in Christian hands, the mainland

---

2. Who at that time was his brother Kublai, who was going to play the host to Marco Polo.

3. After the conquest of Baghdad he even donated the caliph's palace on the Tigris to the Christian patriarch of Syria (a Nestorian or, in the terminology of the Westerners of the time, a Chaldaean).

feudal possessions of the Crusaders were swept away for good. In the meantime the Īlkhans converted to Islam.

Those were the years in which a learned Dominican from Tuscany, Ricoldo da Montecroce, or Ricoldo Pennini, was in Mesopotamia, perhaps trusting in the Mongol lords' goodwill toward Christians. As far as we know, he was the first Westerner to come into contact with the Mandaeans, around 1290. Born sometime before 1250, after finishing his studies in the liberal arts he became a monk. Having taught in Pisa, Prato, and Florence, between 1288 and the beginning of the fourteenth century, he traveled at length *in partes infidelium* on the orders of Nicholas IV. He went to Palestine,[4] Armenia, Turkey, Persia, and Mesopotamia. As he himself narrates in his voluminous "Confutation of the Koran,"[5] after "crossing many seas

---

4. Some believe that he chose to be called "da Montecroce," that is, "from Calvary," after visiting the holy places, although Montecroce is probably the name of the Italian village where he was born.

5. This composition was famous in the West for at least three centuries after Ricoldo's death. The work was translated into Greek around 1360 by Demetrius Cidon (or Cidonius). Cidon was a Greek imperial dignitary and friend of the emperor John VI Cantacuzene. When Cantacuzene was defeated by John V Palaeologus and subsequently chose the cloistered life, along with his imperial consort, Cidonius and other court intellectuals followed suit. The former emperor and his entourage continued their anti-Islamic struggle at a religious level, and Cidonius, who had studied Latin and Western theology in Milan, translated Ricoldo's treatise, which was also quoted and used by Cantacuzene in his works against Muhammed. The deposed emperor's historical-theological vision (like that of Ricoldo) revolved around the idea that when Heraclius finally destroyed the Persian army of Chosroes II in 628, humiliating the pagan world to such an extent that even the true cross, which had been carried off by the Persians, was given back (the cross was carried back triumphantly into Jerusalem, once again under Byzantine control, on September 14, 629), the devil decided to get revenge by having Muhammed appear at precisely that time: "During the time of Heraclius, Emperor of the Romans, a pernicious and mad man appeared. . . ." Muhammed was born poor and became rich with a widow's money, a gang leader who, unable to be accepted as king due to his humble birth, presented himself as a prophet, disguising his epilepsy with fantastic stories of angelic apparitions. This was the normal tone of religious and political polemics of the day. The Greek translation of Ricoldo's treatise, at any rate, became so famous that memory of its original Latin version was lost, and during the early sixteenth century it was retranslated into Latin by Bartolomeo Piceno. This version was dedicated to Ferdinand of Aragon, exhorting him, after having reconquered the "Provincia Betica," what remained of Moslem Spain in 1492, to move on to the conquest of North Africa and to drive toward Jerusalem. Throughout the sixteenth century the book was a bestseller, printed both in Latin (especially in Spain) and in vernacular languages. The German edition was edited by none other than Martin Luther (Wittenberg, 1542), only a

and deserts" he finally arrived in Baghdad, to begin studying Arabic and
the Koran and debating with Islamic scholars. He even began work on a
Latin translation of the Koran (which we do not know if he ever finished),
but, then, "full of bitterness" for the lies he found there, he set himself to
writing epistles and pamphlets against Islam, in particular his "Confutation." He was one of the few Westerners of his day to know both the Arabic
language and the Koran well. Indeed, when captured in 1291 (during the
confusion following the Mameluke victory) by two Moslem Mongols who
wanted to circumcise him, he was able to escape disguised as an Arab
camel driver.

Long after those difficult years in the quiet of the convent of Santa
Maria Novella in Florence, where he died in 1320, Ricoldo started work
once more on what must have been his travel diary. Written in Latin, his
"Itinerarium" or "Book of Peregrinations in Eastern Parts" had quite considerable manuscript success (it was even translated into French and Italian as early as the fourteenth century), but it was not printed until the
nineteenth century. The last chapter[6] is a sort of appendix entitled *De
monstris*. These *monstra* were the sort of bizarre things that any traveler to
faraway lands was expected to delight his readers with, and Ricoldo was
certainly not one to disappoint them. He tells of the strangest things that
he saw while in Mesopotamia, the last country he visited.

> In Baghdad, then, I saw many strange things worthy of wonder. There I
> saw pygmies, men a cubit tall. From the waist up they are in every way
> like men, handsome enough though very small; but their legs look like
> those of a chicken, or some other bird. They are brought from the is-
> lands of India and from the farthest deserts. It is of them that Aristotle
> says they procreate in their third year and die at the age of seven.[7]

---

couple of years before his death, within the context of his own activities against Turkish military and religious expansionism, not so long after the defeat of Ferdinand of Austria at Bu-
dapest (1541) and the destruction of the imperial fleet at Algiers.

6. Unfortunately only a couple of manuscripts preserved this chapter, and they were
not used by contemporary publishers. The printed editions of the book, therefore, do not
include it.

7. Ricoldo is not saying that the pygmies are in fact only one cubit tall, but is translating the term "pygmy" from the Greek *pygmē*, "cubit." Regarding their geographical origin he
is quite precise; the "islands of India" could indicate the pygmies of Asia, or "Negritos" (the
Andaman Islands, Malacca, and the Philippines), or pygmoid groups (Ceylon, New Guinea,

This description of the pygmies with chicken or ostrich legs, dressed up with a learned reference to Aristotle, corresponds to the then traditional view of pygmies. After describing human "monstrosity," Ricoldo moves on to the animal kingdom:

> In Baghdad I also saw a very strange *(monstruosus)* snake, that had four legs like a dog, but behind it a long horrible *(orribilem)* snake's tail. It was quite docile with its master, but was terribly *(orribiliter)* threatening with everyone else, in its movements and in sticking out its tongue. And an even stranger *(magis monstruosus)* snake appeared, with the face and hair of a woman, but with all the rest of its body like a terrible snake *(orribilis)*.

The first beast could be a monitor (the detail concerning the tongue would seem to exclude a crocodile), but regarding the second, which corresponds to certain iconographical representations of lasciviousness or the serpent (of Eden) trampled upon by the Virgin of the Immaculate Conception, it would not be prudent to advance hypotheses. I would like to point out, however, Ricoldo's care over his style, for in his repetition of the key words he provokes just the right degree of disconcerted surprise in the reader. It is at this point, as the last bizarre thing that he had observed, spiritual rather than physical this time, that Ricoldo describes the Mandaeans:

> A very strange *(monstruosa)* and singular people, in terms of their rituals, lives in the desert near Baghdad; they are called Sabaeans. Many of them came to me *(ad nos)* and begged me insistently to go and visit them. They are a very simple people and they claim to possess a secret law of God, which they preserve in beautiful books. Their writing is a sort of middle way between Syriac and Arabic. They detest Abraham because of circumcision and they venerate John the Baptist above all. They live only near a few rivers in the desert. They wash day and night so as not to be condemned by God, even to the point that a woman prepares the flour to make bread with one hand, holding the other in running water so that if she were to die, she wouldn't be condemned by God for

and Malacca), while the "farthest deserts" (where "desert" means "wild and uninhabited place") seem to be more generic definitions and perhaps allude to Africa and those pygmies that are known as "Negrillos."

having a hand covered with flour. They not only baptize their children, but also their animals, and when a cow gives birth they baptize both cow and calf. They say a kind of mass and sacrifice bread and raisins, and when they worship, they wear seven vestments. They have no contact with any of the other peoples of this land of any kind except to buy and sell; and they do not eat bread touched by a person of another religion. When they come to Baghdad or another city each of them buys flour at the market and then takes water from the river, making and then baking his own bread to eat. They pray very much and have a great respect for marriage. Muhammed praises them highly in his Koran.

Though only a summary, the earliest Western information concerning the Mandaeans is an accurate firsthand account, rich in detail. It is the Mandaeans who take the first step. They seek out the Western priest, take him to their village, and show him their manuscripts, which Ricoldo deems "beautiful." He may have seen an illustrated *diuan.* The information he provides on their religion is exact, though very superficial; there is a secret law, they hate Abraham, and they revere John the Baptist.[8] Other details are correct as well: their living near a river, the daily and nightly immersions, the baptism of children, the sacred use of bread and raisins, *rasta* composed of seven parts, contamination from contact with non-Mandaeans and consequent food taboos, much prayer, and the prohibition of adultery. Regarding the baptism of animals, while it is true that those destined for sacrifice (birds and rams) are regularly purified by immersion, the practice of baptizing cows and calves after birth is not confirmed by contemporary evidence today. Neither is there any confirmation of the practice of not using both hands in the preparation of bread, although the faithful, men and women, do have to wash one hand carefully in the *iardna* before receiving the sacred bread, holding the other hand out of the water. Could this be the basis for the "strangeness" Ricoldo noticed?

The final observation, that Muhammed praised them, refers to those passages in the Koran where the mysterious *ṣābi'ūn* or *ṣābi'ah* are granted the right to be considered a "people of the book," therefore enjoying the rights related to that status. The Sabaeans of the Koran are probably an Arabian people that we know little or nothing about. It is now commonly

8. It never in the least occurs to Ricoldo, however, that the Mandaeans might be Christians.

believed, however, that they must be a different people from the Yemenite Sabaeans.[9] It is practically certain that Muhammed was unaware of the existence of our Mandaeans, nor do we know if they were already called *ṣubba* by their Arab neighbors (who had not yet converted to Islam). Since the time of the Islamic conquest of Mesopotamia the Mandaeans have always played up the similarity in sound between *ṣubba* and *ṣābi'ah* in order to obtain a much-desired recognition from the local lords, not always with satisfactory results.

THE REDISCOVERY

Unfortunately, the information provided by Ricoldo lay buried in only a couple of manuscripts and was not published until the 1940s. In the course of almost seven centuries perhaps a few curious monks read Ricoldo's treatise, but this certainly did not lead to widespread European awareness of the existence of Mandaeanism. Mandaeanism was officially discovered by Catholic missionaries toward the middle of the sixteenth century. Having landed in India in 1498, the Portuguese attacked the Islamic world from behind, from their bases in Goa, Diu, and along the Malabar coast, at precisely the same time that Mameluke power in Egypt was crumbling and the Ottoman Empire was on the rise in Turkey. The Portuguese fleets were active even in the Red Sea and aimed at conquering Suez in the hope of gaining more complete control over the spice trade. In so doing they also hoped to come to the aid of the Christian Abyssinian Negus, who had always been more or less at war with his Islamic or Islamicized neighbors.[10] It was the Ottomans, however, under the sultan Selim, who were to sweep away what was left of the Mameluke sultanate and occupy Syria and Egypt (1517), definitively barring the path to Portuguese advance. Rather than occupying extensive heavily populated regions, the Portuguese, on the one hand, tended to create small, well-fortified

9. Those of Saba (Sheba), a well-known place in ancient times, thanks to its famous queen. Ancient scholars held that the name of the city and its inhabitants was derived from the name of a prince, one Saba, the supposed founder of the city and its first sovereign.

10. The idea of an anti-Islamic alliance with the Negus was an ancient dream of the Portuguese. Prince Henry, the adventurous son of King John, had succeeded in conquering Ceuta in 1415 and fondly imagined an occupation of the whole of North Africa as far as the borders of Ethiopia, from there advancing on Jerusalem together with the Christians of Africa.

strongholds with easy access to the sea, which they depended on for their survival. The Turkish Empire, on the other hand, after the conquest of Persia in 1514 and under the iron leadership of Suleyman the Magnificent,[11] had become a supranational organization whose power was equal to its geographic extent. Suleyman the Great's armies were able to penetrate Europe at will, while the Mediterranean risked becoming a Turkish lake, traversed by the ships of the famous corsair, Barbarossa.

In the east, the Ottomans were advancing toward the Indian Ocean. Having consolidated their power in Egypt, they built a fleet at Suez and got as far as besieging Diu. The captain general of the Egyptian fleet, the *qaptān,* was the legendary Pīrī Ra'īs (Pīrī Muhyī d-Dīn Ra'īs), world-famous navigator, corsair, and cartographer. There was direct conflict also in the Persian Gulf, where the Portuguese controlled Masqat, in present-day Oman, and above all Hormuz (and therefore the Straits). The various Arab lords in southern Mesopotamia and on the Arab side of the gulf[12] were forced to play off their independence in a difficult balancing act between Turks, Persians, and Europeans. Thus, when Suleyman decided to take direct control of the area, occupying it with his troops in 1549, the Arab Emir of Basra, who had been the sultan's vassal, appealed for Portuguese aid, as did the lords of Qatīf and Bahrain, who were already vassals of the Portuguese. With Qatīf and Bahrain firmly under control, the Portuguese set sail for Basra, without ever reaching it. A second Portuguese fleet sailed toward the Red Sea, occupied Aden, and reached Suez, though they withdrew from the latter almost immediately. The elderly Pīrī Ra'īs left Suez with thirty ships in 1551, regained control of the Red Sea, and occupied Aden. He then circumnavigated the Arabian Peninsula and took Masqat. He was unable, however, to capture Hormuz, and withdrew to Basra with heavy losses.[13] It was to be another legendary captain, the poet,

11. He rose to power in 1520.

12. Arabs, and therefore neither Turks nor Persians. Islamicized, the Arabs were often Shiites like the Persians and not Sunnites like the Turks. Islam, in fact, underwent an early split into two main branches. The Shiites, on the one hand, hold that religious and political leadership, illuminated through inspiration, passed to members of the prophet's family after his death, the Imams, the first of whom was 'Alī, Muhammed's son-in-law. The Sunnites, on the other hand, recognize the authority of the Caliphs, essentially political leaders of "lay" origin, since they were not related to Muhammed's family.

13. Under suspicion of having been corrupted by the besieged Portuguese. When it was rumored that the Portuguese fleet was approaching Basra, with just three ships he liter-

explorer, and oceanographer Sīdī Ra'īs (Sīdī 'Alī ibn Ḥusayn), who in 1554 forced the Straits of Hormuz with what was left of the fleet (fifteen ships). Due to the presence of the Portuguese fleet, however, and of adverse winds, he landed in the Indian Islamic sultanate of Gujarat, where he left his six remaining ships.[14] The hostilities continued with neither side gaining the upper hand; in 1556 bad weather and Turkish resistance combined to drive the Portuguese back from the gates of Basra, and in 1557 the Turks occupied Massaua and founded a province on the African coast of Somaliland, nearly cutting off communication between the Negus and the Portuguese possessions in East Africa.[15] In 1559 the Ottomans attacked Baḥrain, but, caught in a crossfire due to the arrival of the Portuguese fleet, they were forced to retreat and to pay compensation. A period of calm was to follow, lasting until 1581.

In 1555, right in the midst of these events, we find reference to the existence at Hormuz of some "Saint John Christians," or Mandaeans, in the papers of some Portuguese Jesuits. What Ricoldo hadn't even imagined now seemed a certainty in the eyes of the European missionaries. In India the "Saint Thomas Christians," held to be descendants of converts made by Saint Thomas, the apostle who is said to have been responsible for the conversion of India, had only recently been discovered. What was so strange, then, about finding "Christians of Saint John, Apostle and Evangelist"?[16] There was a considerable degree of cultural confusion at work (the missionaries did not realize that the John praised by the Mandaeans was not John the Evangelist but John the Baptist), but there was also a great deal of interest. The Mandaeans appeared to be a persecuted Christian community within the Turkish Empire; their existence alone would justify armed

---

ally fled to Suez, scuttling one of the ships in Baḥrain and abandoning the rest of the fleet in Iraq. Upon his arrival in Egypt a death warrant, signed by Suleyman, was awaiting him.

14. Here he finished his encyclopedic treatise on navigation in the Indian Ocean and then returned overland, taking two years to do so. On his return he received a pardon from the sultan.

15. A few years before the Negus had even claimed that he was ready to recognize papal authority and had asked, through the king of Portugal, that a Catholic patriarch be sent. This had given cause for great rejoicing to many, first and foremost Ignatius of Loyola, but in the end it all came to nothing.

16. At the time it was even possible to give a scholarly explanation of the discovery. It was commonly believed that the "First Epistle of John" — a sort of encyclical letter addressed to the Christian communities of Asia Minor — had been addressed to the Christian communities of Persia, and therefore the Evangelist had been aware of those lands.

Portuguese intervention in southern Mesopotamia. Just as the Mandaeans were enthusiastic about the Europeans' interest in them, so the Jesuits were equally interested in the information gathered by their missionaries. Shortly before becoming provincial, Antonio de Quadros[17] sent a long letter from Goa, capital of the Portuguese viceroyalty, to the provincial in Portugal, at the end of which he mentions the mission among "the Christians who call themselves Saint John Christians, who would like very much to see our priests there (in the Persian Gulf)." He sees this as one of the most promising missions and for this reason asks that many new missionaries be sent to India.

In another letter sent in the same month (December 1555), another Portuguese Jesuit wrote to the brethren of his order in his mother country telling of how a boy from Hormuz, originally from Basra, was being educated at the college in Goa. He describes the boy's people:

> They all observe Christianity, but it is not known how exactly; [we know] only that they have baptism and ecclesiastical priests and many other ceremonies. They say that the blessed apostle Saint John the Evangelist came to those lands and converted those people, though those who govern them are all Moors (Moslems), that is, for some of them the king of Basra (the Arabian lord, formally Pasha, and therefore vassal of the Turkish sultan), for the others the Shah [of Persia].

The Jesuit missionary seems quite prudent; he repeats that they have no precise information and that the boy was unable to inform them more accurately. Since they did not know what kind of baptism he had received, they had not yet given him Christian baptism for fear of baptizing a Christian twice over. Perhaps a few days after this letter was sent, however, a Mandaean from Basra arrived in Goa. His story, told to a Spanish Jesuit who then wrote to his brethren in Spain, is quite impressive. The following passage is taken from a copy made for the archives in Rome:

> During the past days a Christian of those called Saint John Christians came to this city in order to see a boy, a relative of his who was staying

17. Born in Santarem in 1527, Antonio de Quadros was provincial of the Indies from 1556 until his death in Goa in 1572. He is considered one of the main figures in the continuation, in India, of the missionary work of Saint Francis Xavier.

here with the others, and by way of an interpreter told us that they live in obedience to the holy Roman Church and that they keep all its sacraments and ceremonies. The Patriarch of Armenia sends them a bishop. They are the subjects of a Moorish king. The land where they live is called Basra. The Moorish king allows them to have churches and to say mass, but the Turks go there often and ruin their churches, forcing them into the mountains to say mass in places where the Turks do not go. He also said to us that there are up to forty thousand Christians, married with families, in that country.

The Mandaeans, therefore, are Christians ready and willing to obey the holy Roman Church and its temporal representatives (in other words, the Portuguese). They already know and use all seven Catholic sacraments and the related ceremonies in their lives. They regularly receive their bishops from the patriarch of the Church of Syria[18] and, therefore, must be considered members of the Catholic (Chaldaean) Church. They represented a true Christian stronghold (with no Lutheran doubts about the number or nature of the sacraments) in the heart of the Ottoman Empire, right in the area of Basra.

The story does contain some elements of truth, such as the Arab ("Moorish") ruler's toleration, Turkish persecution (a consequence of Turkish occupation in 1549), and the consequent flight to the mountains, that is, into Iranian territory. The last detail, though, the forty thousand

18. "The Patriarch of Armenia" was the usual way, in the sixteenth century, of referring to the patriarch of the Syrians or Chaldaeans. The relative confusion stems from the fact that after taking Byzantium, Muhammed II set up (1461) an Armenian patriarchate in Constantinople. The patriarch was recognized as religious and civil leader of all the "Armenian" Christians in the Ottoman Empire, including Nestorians, Chaldaeans, and Copts (the Christians of Egypt). At the time the term "Armenia" referred to an extensive region stretching from the Caucasus to the Mediterranean, including the northern territories of Mesopotamia (Harran, Edessa, Nisibi, and Mossul); therefore Syriac Christians (by language and by race) were also to be found in Armenia. The Armenians of western Armenia were Catholic, while the eastern ones often showed Monophysite tendencies, though there was a strong movement in favor of union with Rome, and a real schism did not occur until the early eighteenth century. In the end there were five Armenian churches, two led by a patriarch and three by a *katholikos* (literally "universal"), which were in constant disagreement with one another over questions of theology and observance. A few years ago a Western scholar developed a theory, based on the passage quoted above, that a bishop was sent from Armenia among the Mandaeans. I too believed this (*Giovanni e Gesù* [Milano: A. Mondadori, 1991], p. 153) prior to reading the original text.

families, is a pearl of a tall story prepared just for the Portuguese; 40,000 families would put the total Mandaean population near the unlikely figure of more or less 160,000 people. Although we certainly cannot say that the Portuguese decided to attack Basra in 1556 *because* our anonymous Mandaean only a few months before had gone from Basra to Goa to tell his version of the facts, the coincidence is definitely significant. However, the small number of Mandaeans must have been of little help to the Portuguese in the swamplands around Basra.

It is also significant that after what seemed to be such promising beginnings the Jesuits of Goa, as far as we know, do not mention the Mandaeans again for exactly forty years. The next reference to them, in fact, is by an Italian Jesuit, Alessandro Valignano,[19] who in September 1595 wrote a manual in Portuguese for the guidance of the missionary, the "Father of the Christians" as he was called in the East. This is what, with extreme caution, he recommends:

[The missionary] will take particular care over the foreign Christians that circulate in these areas, such as Armenians, Georgians, Chaldaeans,[20] Ab-

19. Born in Chieti in 1539, he was visitor and provincial; he died in Macao in 1606.

20. At the time, "Chaldaean" was still synonymous with Syrian, indicating all the Christians whose first language was Syriac. Today the term means only the Syriac-speaking Christians, originally Nestorians, converted to Catholicism since the sixteenth century. The Nestorian Church, composed of Syrian Christians who accepted the theological positions of Nestorius, was widespread in Persia, with missions as far away as China. Nestorius, a bishop in Constantinople during the fifth century, held that there was no true union between the human nature and the divine in Jesus Christ, so that, for example, Mary should not be called "Mother of God" but only "Mother of Christ" or "of Jesus (the man)." He therefore speaks of the Word's "indwelling" in Jesus, arriving at a certain dualism within his person, unacceptable to Catholics. Within Syriac Christianity the Monophysites (literally "those of a single nature") opposed the Nestorian Church. They believed that far from being a union of natures in Jesus Christ, there was only one predominant nature, the divine, his human nature being negligible. The Syrian Monophysites are also called Jacobites, after their great organizer Jacob Baradaeus. In the fifth century, against the will of Justinian but with the support of the empress Theodora, Baradaeus became bishop and organized a church in Antioch and the first Monophysite hierarchy. The church spread quickly, especially in areas where Syriac was spoken, and in the struggles that lacerated the area for centuries it always assumed an anti-Byzantine position. In Valignano's day a movement in favor of the union with Rome was beginning to grow also among the Jacobites, thanks to the presence of Catholic missionaries, leading in 1662 after various ups and downs to the creation of a Catholic patriarchate for the Syrians who had left the Jacobite Church.

yssinians, Greeks,[21] and Sabi, whom we commonly call Saint John Christians, and those of Saint Thomas,[22] to re-educate them and bring them back to the faith and the customs of the Roman Church, since many errors and customs contrary to it (the Catholic Church) are to be found among them, especially among the Sabi, of whom it is said that they are not baptized or that they do not perform a true baptism.

Gerolamo Vecchietti,[23] an Italian traveling in 1604 along the way between Baghdad and Basra, stopped in a small village where he found a group of Sabians or Saint John Christians. One of these had fled from Hoveyzeh, in Kuzistan, "because of bad treatment" by the local sovereign, a certain Mombarac.[24] The Mandaean spoke Portuguese and provided information to Vecchietti about his people (in all, he says, there were "around sixty thousand" of them) and about the language, which Vecchietti identifies as Syriac.[25] His account does not provide us with much information concerning their faith, but it does seem genuine. In Vecchietti's words:

> Of Christ they knew nothing but the name, and they did not know who he was. Of the Holy Trinity they had no knowledge, and they claimed

21. This term refers to two distinct realities. It can refer either to the Greek "Orthodox" (non-Catholic) Christians or to the Melkites. The latter term, coined by the Syriac-speaking Christians (from the root *mlk,* "king"), indicates those Greek-speaking Christians practicing the Byzantine rite who supported the "king," the emperor in Constantinople, while living in the territories where Semitic languages were spoken (Palestine, Egypt, Syria, and Mesopotamia). In Valignano's day, as in our own, there were two Melkite churches, the Catholics (in communion with Rome) and the "Orthodox." The text here is referring to the latter.

22. The Christians of India not only received the attentions of Catholic missionaries, but of Nestorian and Jacobite missionaries as well. This was partly why the Jesuits thought their Christianity was tainted by heresy.

23. Of a Tuscan family, he traveled through the East several times, often in the company of his brother, Giovan Battista. He was often entrusted with delicate missions by the Pope or some other European sovereign, and he was always on the lookout for information and fascinating novelties, especially manuscripts in Oriental languages.

24. Sayid Mubārak or, according to Portuguese sources, Çaide Mombareca. We shall be returning to him and his expansionist policies.

25. "I wanted to write a reminder of some of the words and, since the man was courteous, I sent for writing materials from the boat. Once I had written down many words I realized that the language was Chaldaean."

that there is only one God who is creator of all things. They had no information about Mary, nor of any of the ancient saints, much less the modern ones. I will say nothing of the sacraments, except that they continue washing themselves in the same river where they bring the child a few days after birth, but they understand nothing else. They could say nothing about the Gospels or any other book of the Scriptures and said only that they had a book of their Pigamber, which means prophet in the Persian language, more ancient than all the other prophets who had ever been on earth, [that is] Seth, son of the first father Adam, and they follow the rules [of this book].[26]

After arriving in Basra, among the gold and silversmiths of the bazaar Vecchietti ferreted out an elderly Mandaean who had been in Goa for a very long time, had converted to Catholicism, and spoke Portuguese quite well. Having gathered what he could from him in terms of news and information, Vecchietti deduced that the Mandaeans were "a generation of the ancient Chaldaean Christians," reduced to ignorance by Islamic persecution (which had been going on for a millennium), whose "bishops and priests" had died out and whose "books and scriptures" had been destroyed. Concerning their sacred text, it "was written in their native language and then in later times either for ignorance or cunning or both [it had been attributed] to Seth, in order to give it greater authority." In any case, Vecchietti was convinced that it would be easy to bring them back to the "true" faith, that is, Catholicism, especially since that is what had happened to those of them who had gone to live in Hormuz or in Portuguese territories.[27]

Everyone, then, considers the Mandaeans to be some kind of Chris-

26. The attribution of *Ginza* to Seth is present in the seventeenth-century European sources.

27. Gerolamo Vecchietti is at times the finest of narrators. Here is his description of some of the food available at the Basra bazaar during the spring and summer of 1604: "They eat a great quantity of salted fish and small fresh shrimp that are caught in infinite quantities in pools created in ditches when the river swells. They boil them, and stuff their throats and fill their bellies with them. I saw two things, new to my eyes, to eat in this city, on sale in the bazaar in booths. One of them was white truffles, dried and split in two; I ate these more than once cooked in rice with meat and butter and they were very good. The other was crickets, which made my stomach turn just seeing them, and I was careful to avoid that experience."

tians, though a few (especially the missionaries) were beginning to have their doubts, not about their orthodoxy, explicitly denied, but about their really being Christians at all, since their baptism was not valid. As for the John whose name they had taken, in a work published in Lisbon as late as 1600 a Jesuit historian, Joam de Lucena, could write that John the Evangelist had preached in the area around Basra.[28] Not long afterward, however, Sebastiam Gonçalves, another historian of the Company of Jesus, corrected him. When writing the first volume of his work in Goa between 1604 and 1608, Gonçalves still believed in the Evangelist's activity in Mesopotamia, but by the time he had finished the tenth volume in 1614 he was able to correctly identify John the Baptist as the Mandaeans' eponym.

According to Gonçalves, the Mandaeans were a group of Syrian (Chaldaean) Christians who had not accepted Catholic orthodoxy. "Very few [of them]," he says, "accept the baptism of Christ, or rather they receive [it] together with that of John [the Baptist], just as the Abyssinians [accept] the [baptism] of Christ and circumcision." There were said to be more than forty thousand of them scattered throughout the East, from Persia to Egypt, subject to Moslem lords who harass them considerably. Their priests were not ordained and their sacraments were not valid. Furthermore, they knew only of baptism and marriage, knowing nothing of extreme unction, ordination, and confirmation. Alongside Jesus and Mary they also worshipped John the Baptist and his mother Elizabeth. Some features of the account of the Mandaean who had arrived in Goa fifty years earlier reappeared here: "It seems that they were all subject to the patriarch of Babylon, whose ancient see had been in Antioch."[29] While other Chaldaeans, however, had entered in communion with Rome, these re-

28. In the Italian edition of his book, edited by another Jesuit, Lodovico Mansoni, in 1613, he writes: "And even today in Basra, at the mouth of the Tigris and Euphrates at the end of the Gulf of Hormuz, those barbarous peoples hold to a tradition that the Disciple beloved by Christ preached there and made many converts." It should be noted that even in this case the idea is presented as belonging to "those barbarous peoples," i.e., the Mandaeans themselves.

29. He is alluding to the Nestorian (or Syrian, or Chaldaean) patriarch. All the Christian churches of Syria claim Antioch ancestry. It was a city famous for its many Episcopal sees and the bitter conflicts between them, though the right to the original title, more or less well-founded historically, did not always coincide with where the see was actually located. For example, the two Melkite patriarchs "of Antioch," the Greek Catholic and the Greek Orthodox, reside in Damascus. The Chaldaean (Catholic) patriarch of Babylon resides in Mossul.

mained in error. Last of all, during the pontificate of Paul V (1605-21), they had decided to accept obedience to Rome since "These Saint John Christians did have one good thing, and that is that they recognized themselves to be ignorant in things pertinent to the Catholic faith and as such they wished to be enlightened by ministers of holy life and doctrine."

Gonçalves, in fact, witnessed the first official attempt of a group of Mandaeans to gain recognition as Catholics in order to escape being ruled by Islamic lords. In 1608 an embassy from Mubārak, then a vassal of the Shah of Persia,[30] reached Goa, asking for European help for the reconquest of Basra, governed by the Turkish Pashah. Mubārak ("Mombareca" in the text) says that he has had to move the capital of his kingdom to Hoveyzeh ("Oeza" in the text) in Iranian Kuzistan, but he claims to have dynastic rights to Basra, which he looks upon as the ancient and true capital. This was not the first time that Mubārak had come knocking at the Portuguese's door; he had already asked for the help of their fleet in 1603 and 1605. If the Portuguese were able to gain control of the Šaṭṭ al-ʿArab, he would attack Basra with cavalry and infantry, and, having taken the city, in return for their services he would give the Portuguese half of all the port's customs duties as well as the right to build a fort wherever they wanted in his kingdom. At the same time he allowed an exchange of letters between the Mandaean religious authorities present in his kingdom,[31] the (Augustinian) archbishop of Goa, and the Jesuit provincial. The 1608 embassy, however, marks a qualitative shift. One of the ambassadors, in fact, was Gonçalo d'Abreu, a "St. John Chaldaean Christian" who had been baptized as a Catholic and who had at one time been in the service (as a soldier) of the Portuguese commander at Hormuz.[32] He was also the nephew of the "patriarch of the St. John Christians," who is said to have been called Frey Symâo, "Brother Simeon," and who, Gonçalves noted, was married. Mubārak asked for ships while Frey Symâo asked for missionaries. According to the Augustinian sources, Simeon asked for Augustinian missionaries

---

30. This was Shah ʿAbbās I, called "the Great" for his expansionistic policies at the expense of the Turks and, later, against the Portuguese. One of Mubārak's sons lived at his court as a guest and hostage.

31. The Portuguese sources mention a "patriarch" and "bishops."

32. This was Geronimo Mascarenhas, who died in 1593 and was buried in Goa in the church of the Good Jesus. Besides being a valiant soldier, he is remembered by the Jesuits as a particularly pious person, having at his death left many of his possessions to the Company of Jesus. Gonçalo d'Abreu's baptism seems to have been due to Mascarenhas's religious zeal.

(knowing the virtues of the Augustinians of Isfahan). According to the Jesuits, he had asked for Jesuit missionaries. Gonçalo probably had letters for everyone, written by Symâo in support of Mubārak's military initiative. An Augustinian who was a witness to the events, Antonio de Gouvea,[33] tells us that from those letters it was possible to grasp the true reason why the Mandaeans were so actively involved. They were trying to enter into the good graces of their sovereign to put an end to his harassment of them. Their sovereign, in fact, treated them like slaves, subjecting them to forced (and unpaid) labor in the construction of his fortresses and obliging them to pay exorbitant sums even for the liturgical use of river water. The archbishop of Goa, who at that time was also the governor,[34] could not send military aid without the king's authorization, and the king's letters were late in coming. The ambassadors were kept in Goa for several months in vain expectation, and, finally, with the spring monsoons of 1609, the archbishop allowed the ambassadors to return home. He sent two of his Augustinian brothers with them "in order to carry out the primary duty of their profession (the mission) and also to exhort the Arab king to make war against the Turk."[35]

The two missionaries, Francis of the Presentation[36] and Matthias of the Holy Spirit,[37] reached Hoveyzeh together with the other ambassadors September 1, 1609, and had to explain to Mubārak that aid had not yet arrived. They also refused to let him have the galleon on which they had voyaged, which Mubārak would have liked to put to immediate use.[38] The atmosphere rapidly grew colder, and Mubārak suddenly abandoned the Company and headed for Basra with his army. The missionaries then turned to the Mandaeans, who gave them a warm welcome. We learn from a letter of one of the Spanish ambassadors of the group that there were

33. He deals at length with these facts in a book published in Lisbon in 1611.

34. As was often the case in the Spanish Empire. His name was Alejo de Meneses, and he took the place of the viceroy, Martín Alfonso de Castro, when the latter died in Malacca in 1607, before the arrival of the new viceroy from Europe (the changeover was to take place in 1609). De Meneses died in Madrid in 1617.

35. These are the words of Gonçalves.

36. Born in India prior to 1573, he died in Goa in 1629.

37. An Englishman about whom we know only that he arrived in the East in 1607 and died shortly after this mission.

38. Mubārak was ready to pay in horses (he did not have enough ready money) and to give his son to the Portuguese as a hostage, as a guarantee of eventual payment.

nineteen or twenty thousand Mandaeans ready to recognize the authority of the Pope, and that in the first two weeks more than one hundred had been baptized. Symâo himself wrote a letter to the archbishop of Goa, signed also by his bishops and priests, apologizing for not having sent a formal document of obedience to the Pope immediately. He said he wanted to call a synod to deal with the question. Everything seemed to be moving ahead splendidly, and even the king of Spain was informed of the progress being made. From a letter in the imperial chancery we find that the Portuguese were hoping to obtain from Mubārak the island of Kharg ("extensive, fertile and uninhabited"), where they would build a fortress, church, and convent, and to which the Mandaeans would have been able to move. Had the Arab sovereign created any problems they could have been transported to another island nearer to Hormuz. This must be the oldest document where the idea of transferring the Mandaeans away from their native lands appears, an idea we find in another letter written shortly afterward by the captain of the ship that had carried the ambassadors and missionaries to Hoveyzeh. According to him, it had actually been one of Mubārak's dignitaries who had suggested that the "Sabaeans" wished to move to Kharg.

In the same letter we also find details about the conclusion of the missionary activities:

> The said Fathers . . . were about to leave because they had nothing [more] to do . . . in their dealings with the Saint John Christians, since none of them were baptized, if not for the gifts that were given to them. Since they had nothing [more] to give, no one was baptized, and those who had been (that is, who had accepted baptism) then went through it again in their own way.

Like all other Europeans of the time the captain is rather violently prejudiced against all Arabs,[39] but his testimony is undoubtedly quite convincing because it anticipates what was to become a recurrent motif in all later missionary activity.

No matter what the outcome, this first contact lasted roughly one month and greatly enriched the Portuguese's knowledge of the Mandaeans.

39. The captain says of Mubārak: "Betrayal is the only law of conquest, his or of his neighbors."

Antonio de Gouvea devoted a chapter of his book to them, with some features that can also be found in Gonçalves and that reappear in later reports as well. The Mandaeans present themselves to the Portuguese as Christians and are believed to be such by the Portuguese, even though they are seen as a bit heretical and schismatic. According to the information gathered at that time, they believed in the Trinity and had a quite highly developed Christology (denying only the ascension). Mary was held to be virgin and mother and was said to have conceived Jesus by drinking spring water, as commanded by God. She had not died, though no one knew where she was. They believed in hell, purgatory, and paradise, and after Jesus and Mary their principal saints were John and Elizabeth. They celebrated mass with fermented flour, wine, oil, and olives. With these ingredients they made a sort of little loaf of bread taken by the priests and then distributed as in Catholic communion. They practiced baptism and marriage, but not confirmation and extreme unction. They had performed the other ceremonies in the past, but after the Moslems had destroyed their churches and images, they had let them fall into disuse. They even used a cross in their ceremonies, though a folding one, again for fear of the Moslems.[40] They were therefore persecuted Christians whose knowledge of religious things had fallen so low that, as the missionaries were to find later, much to their surprise, they did not even know how to make the sign of the cross. De Gouvea also observed that Symâo was not even a real bishop or priest since the Mandaeans had not had any regular ordinations for a long time. Roughly 150 years earlier, at a time of schism within the Nestorian church of Syria, they had broken communion with the patriarch of Babylon, on whom they had previously been dependent. This last detail is very interesting because it shows the Mandaeans' ability to reconstruct their own history. Whereas the Mandaean who had arrived in Goa in 1555 had been able to say that his co-religionists were then in communion with the Syrian patriarch, now, only sixty years later, it was no longer possible to try selling the same story to the missionaries present in their villages. The religious condition of the villages, which was right under the noses of the Augustinians, had to be presented as a de-Christianization due to an ancient schism and continuous Moslem persecution. Their "ignorance," however, could be remedied by an abun-

---

40. The discrepancy between what the Mandaeans tell the friars and the information gathered by Gerolamo Vecchietti five years earlier should be noted. Vecchietti was not a friar; it seems that Mandaeanism was able to change its skin according to who studied it.

dance of goodwill; we have seen that the missionaries baptized hundreds of people (and celebrated scores of weddings) before leaving. In actual fact they left empty-handed, as the ship's captain coolly pointed out.

The Barefooted Carmelites at Isfahan were also informed of the first missionary contact and wrote about it to Rome. At Goa, in the meantime, the Jesuits were champing at the bit. The provincial, Gaspar Fernández, did not at all approve of the Augustinian archbishop's cautious attitude, and most of all he did not like the idea that Augustinian missionaries were going to be first sent to the Mandaeans to open up the mission. Already at the end of 1608 he was writing to the provincial of Portugal and the general (Claudio Acquaviva), proposing that an ambassadorial trip to Rome and Madrid be organized for a Mandaean "bishop," first to visit the pontiff and then Philip III, who would concede the aid that the archbishop of Goa had not yet decided upon. At the same time, for such a promising mission the heads of the Company would have to dedicate themselves to obtaining exclusive rights from the Pope.[41]

Nothing was done. In February 1611 Gonçalo d'Abreu returned to Goa with a letter in Persian from the "patriarch Frey Symâo," addressed to the Jesuit provincial of Goa, who was now Francisco Vieira. The letter is a little masterpiece of deliberate religious and political equivocation. After a fairly sugary list of epithets in praise of the father provincial, ending with fulsome praise for his *own* zeal for "Christian things," Symâo proceeds, between things not said and high-flown sentences, in such a way that we realize he wishes to direct his people's "conversion" (forty thousand souls!) to Catholicism personally. Given his focus on the celebration of baptisms and marriages, nothing emerges from the text that is not the task of a Mandaean *ganzibra*. Now, however, his faithful have asked him to have them become Christians, and Symâo requests the provincial's permission to convert them. In actual fact he does not want any more missionaries to be sent; the provincial should authorize him, "with great certainty and tranquillity," and the reason is both political and religious: "both so that the Moors do not rise up against us, and because the people are still new to their faith and are spread out in several villages, and these people are not like the Portuguese, who have a great spirit, since they were born in the cli-

---

41. It would have been a good idea — we might add — for direct papal control over the mission to be maintained through the Jesuits, thus removing it from the jurisdiction of the archbishop of Goa, who was linked to Portuguese temporal power.

mate of India." We see that Symâo was using the Europeans' racial prejudices to his own advantage (the "Indians," both in Asia and America, were eternal children, weak and immature). At this point the Mandaean set out his political proposal clearly, a proposal that was to dominate relations between the Mandaeans and Europeans throughout the seventeenth century: "Most of the converts would like to pass over into your lands and live among Christians." The reason for this appears straight after these last words, though at first sight it may not seem to be so closely connected: ". . . and the Fathers who came here were very well received by king Çayde Mombareca, out of respect for Your Fatherhood, and therefore Your Fatherhood must thank him very much and the Lord Viceroy [must thank him as well], since [Mubārak] did as he was asked to do, and thus, without the help of the king, we would all suffer very great tribulation."

It is therefore harsh reality that has driven Symâo to write, and this should help us make allowances for his obsequious style. He had no alternative. The "thanks" that Symâo hoped for was the military support that Mubārak desired; the king was tolerant of the Mandaeans only to the extent that the Europeans, with whom he hoped to form an alliance, were interested in them. Any change in the political situation would bring an end to the temporary idyll. We can also see why Mubārak used a Mandaean to send his ambassadorial message to Goa; in the most pragmatic manner, he wanted to exploit the Christians' missionary zeal. He seems to have been willing to trade in a small minority of his subjects in exchange for military aid. For the Mandaeans too, however, the occasion was not one to be passed up. Neither Symâo nor his faithful followers were willing to truly convert, but being or becoming Christians, given the circumstances, could free them from the yoke of Islam without having to undertake an inevitably disastrous rebellion. It is clear from one of Symâo's final sentences, which in reality is not exactly obsequious, that the situation was felt to be extremely serious: "I remind Your Fatherhood, now that you have taken this question under your care, do not abandon it, so that we shall have nothing to accuse Your Fatherhood of on the day of judgment."

His Fatherhood either did not want to or could not meet Symâo's requests. In a courteous though firm and succinct reply,[42] it is clear that the provincial perfectly understood the religious risk contained in the Mandaean's letter.

42. He liquidates the preliminaries with a simple "Most Reverend Sir."

I was greatly pleased in Our Lord when I received the letter that Your Lordship[43] wrote to me, to the extent that (!) I found in it the zeal that you possess for the spiritual well being of your flock, which, for lack of preachers to teach them the path of salvation, have strayed so far from it. The Fathers of this minimal Company of Jesus would truly like to come and serve the Lord Our God and Your Lordship in this undertaking, in which such useful things could be done through divine grace, for the Lord who created us and redeemed us with his precious blood. And since Your Lordship suggests that I not send Fathers of the Company in your bishopric, and I cannot send them at present out of a necessary respect, I would at least like to fulfill in part the obligation that Your Lordship places on me, stating briefly the principal way by which your flock can be saved.

The provincial's letter was every bit as clear as Symâo's had been ambiguous. There follows a very brief, concentrated summary of the Catholic catechism (the way to salvation), aimed mainly at clarifying the relationship between the baptism of John and that of Christ. With fifteen centuries of theological reflection to back him up he is able to fire off a series of statements in quick succession, each with the support of ecclesiastical tradition. John's baptism "did not give grace, did not forgive sins, did not open heaven to sinners." Even when it had had a sacramental function, with the coming of Christ it had lost this, as in the case of circumcision, whose usefulness had ended. Just as one passes through a door to enter into a royal palace, to obtain forgiveness Christian baptism was necessary, "administered by an appropriate minister" (i.e., a properly ordained priest of the Catholic Church) with the Trinitarian formula (which the provincial writes out in its entirety, to avoid any possible misunderstandings). Just as when a new principality is created and the coins from the previous regime remain in circulation, these lose their value when they are replaced by new ones. In the same way John's baptism had fulfilled its historical role and then lost its value.[44] Having repeated the need for obedience to the Pope and adhesion to the apostolic and conciliar canons, the provincial

43. Note that the Christian priest refuses to exchange the title of "fatherhood."

44. The metaphor of old coins as a means of indicating something that is no longer valid is quite ancient. Probably of literary origin, it can be found in treatises of classical rhetoric (Quintilian 1.6.3), where it is used to demonstrate the uselessness of the words that fall from use in a given language.

concludes by exhorting Symâo to invite his faithful to abandon the baptism of John and adopt Christ's. He then draws everything to a close with a prayer that God might "inspire" the Mandaean and preserve his "reverend person . . . in order to do Him [God] many services."

The Jesuits did not open a mission among the Mandaeans of Hoveyzeh, whereas the Augustinians and Carmelites were going to succeed in doing so at Basra at nearly the same time (and not without antagonism) in 1623. As for the aid requested by Mubārak, he received only words of encouragement. Three years after this exchange of letters war broke out between the Persians, led by the governor of Šīrāz, and the Portuguese, who lost Gambrun (from that time onward known as Bandar ʿAbbās), a fortress on the mainland opposite Hormuz. Mubārak was to die in 1616 without ever having taken Basra. He even lost Hoveyzeh, militarily occupied by ʿAbbās I. Forty years later this same Mubārak (I believe) was described to Ignatius as having persecuted the Mandaeans terribly, destroying their churches and burning their books, to the point of having nearly swept them off the face of the earth or, at any rate, of having brought about their diaspora among the neighboring countries.

THE MISSION

By the beginning of the seventeenth century the political situation had changed greatly since the mid-sixteenth. The heart of the great Suleyman had ceased to beat some decades earlier and was now at rest in a faraway Hungarian village near Szigetvár, where the elderly sultan had gone to put down a revolt led by a Christian nobleman. As for Portugal, since 1580 the Portuguese crown had rested on the head of the Habsburg monarchs of Spain. Its colonies had become part of the Spanish world. If the enormous Lusitanian-Spanish power structure had suffered disastrous military defeats in Europe, mainly at the hands of the European allies of the Ottoman Empire (i.e., the French and English), in the Persian Gulf it was still the only European power capable of causing problems for the Turks and the Persians (having actually defeated the Ottomans in Africa near the end of the sixteenth century, at the siege of Mombassa in 1588).[45] A constant feature

45. In India and further to the east, the French, Danish, English, and Dutch were creating their own commercial and military bases. In a dizzy round of alliances and wars, usu-

was the instability of the Arabian tribes of both Arabia and southern Mesopotamia, sometimes pledging obedience to the pasha of Basra, sometimes
(especially the Shiite tribes along the coast) aiding Persian penetration. This
last was a new threat to Spanish interests since the Ottoman Empire's expansionist policies had been halted[46] and replaced by policies apparently
just aiming at survival. It was in fact a vassal of the Persian Empire who succeeded where the Turks had failed, and occupied Hormuz (April 22, 1622),
with the decisive help of the English East India Company, with whom the
booty was shared, and the Dutch. At any rate, perhaps as a remnant of the
anti-Turkish alliance, Catholic missionaries — Capuchins, Dominicans,
Augustinians, and, most importantly for us, the Barefooted Carmelites —
were allowed to live and travel within Persia, sometimes acting as ambassadors for the Western powers. Many of these friars were of Italian origin.

European knowledge of the Mandaeans grew. It was now clear to everyone that the John the Mandaeans spoke of was John the Baptist,[47] and
that their Christianity was at the very least heretical, bordering on the pagan. Throughout the seventeenth century (and indeed, even later) they
were confused with the semi-pagan "Sabaeans" of Harran, the "Carrhae" of
the ancient world so painfully familiar to the Romans, at this time little
more than a dusty village in southern Turkey (Urfa), a few kilometers from
the Syrian border. In antiquity the city had been splendid, with seven su-
perb temples built on seven heights, dedicated to the seven planetary divinities worshipped throughout Mesopotamia. Located near the center of the
fertile crescent, Harran had been a very important center along the ancient
caravan routes and had proudly resisted the Christianization of the
Byzantine world. The inhabitants had continued to practice their traditional ancient rituals, though with a fairly low profile. Around 830 Caliph
al-Ma'mūn found them still pagan, and Arab historians narrate that the Ca-

---

ally against the Spanish and Portuguese, they were laying the foundations of European domination over the rest of the world. Toward the end of the century the Dutch succeeded in
taking all of Ceylon away from the Catholic sovereigns.

46. The unsuccessful siege of Malta took place in 1565, and the defeat at Lepanto in
1571.

47. In actual fact, in a text published in Lisbon in 1665, the Jesuit Manoel Godinho,
speaking of his 1663 voyage from India to Portugal, still claimed that the Mandaeans were
the "descendants of those converted by the glorious Saint John the Evangelist, who is said to
have come with the illuminating rays of his doctrine to many lands of the East." He is the last
known witness to the misunderstanding.

liph, duly horrified, ordered them to convert. To avoid this (as well as circumcision), many of them declared themselves to be Christians, only to fall back into their "execrable superstitions" once the danger had passed. Many wrote about these "Sabaeans," some of whom became famous as philosophers and dignitaries at the Caliph's court, and some of the writings were somewhat over-imaginative; the situation was made all the more confusing by the fact that Islamic historians referred to all pagans as "Sabaeans," whether Romans, Greeks, Egyptians, or Babylonians. Some even placed the Harranians in relation to Egypt,[48] the pagan land par excellence, thus explaining both the paganism and the much boasted-of astrological knowledge of the Harranian Sabaeans. The picture is completed by our Mandaeans, whose astrological aspirations seemed to be the fruit of the ancient Sabaeans' divinatory arts. It was not until 1856 that the tangle was unraveled and the Ṣubba distinguished from the Harranian Sabaeans, thanks to a study published in German in St. Petersburg by a Lithuanian scholar.

There is a letter from Šīrāz of June 1622, two months after the fall of Hormuz, written by Pietro della Valle,[49] which is a good indication of the culture of the day. Della Valle traveled very widely in Islamic lands, using his money and friendships to weave a network of Christian solidarity in "enemy" territory. In the letter, Pietro tells of "a poor Chaldaean Christian . . . who was named Robeh by his own people, but the Portuguese called him John, since he had been to Hormuz several times and had spent a long

48. According to legend, the Sabaeans of Harran owed their name to their founder, whose name was Sabi and who was buried in the third of the three pyramids of Egypt (Seth and Adris — the father of Sabi — were supposedly buried in the other two).

49. Pietro della Valle was born in Rome in 1586 of a very noble and very rich family. An intelligent youth, energetic and imaginative, he loved literature and music (he designed and built two new musical instruments) and spent a few years in Naples, as was then the custom. From there he set sail to fight against the pirates of the Mediterranean. He is well known for the letters he wrote while traveling on a grand scale through the East with an enormous train of servants and baggage. He met Sitti Maani, of a powerful Christian family in Syria, also well known for her beauty and culture (she is said to have known twelve languages). Postponing marriage until a more suitable time, he took her with him with the intention of taking her to Rome, but just before sailing from Hormuz the young woman, who was pregnant, caught a fever and died. Pietro took her body to Rome where he organized a solemn funeral for her in 1627, four years after her death. At the family tomb in Ara Coeli, in a church overflowing with both nobles and commoners, he pronounced a eulogy that became famous and that drew to a close amid many tears, both his and of those present. Some time later he married a young Georgian woman that Sitti Maani had taken in as an orphan and had educated as a lady. He had fourteen children by her. Della Valle died in 1652.

time among the Portuguese there, had been well instructed by them in the Catholic faith, and regenerated with true baptism." Robeh-John's vicissitudes also mirror the times:

> He was also with the Portuguese during the siege of Hormuz, fighting and suffering alongside them. And when the fortress was taken, through the Arabic language, which he knew as well as the Chaldaean that came naturally to him, the little Persian that he knew, and the clothes customary in the country, and through mingling with the Moslems and perhaps pretending to be one of them,[50] he was able to avoid either being killed or enslaved. When the Persian army returned to Persia, since he still was not known to them, by mixing with the Persians he crossed the sea and arrived on the mainland. And with various groups of people, traveling on foot and following first one and then the other, and almost reduced to begging on the road, he arrived finally in Sciraz, and here was looking for refuge to survive.

It was Pietro himself who put an end to his wanderings: "Having clothed him, I took him willingly into my house and keep him as a servant."

Pietro did not know much about the Mandaeans. He was aware that they lived in a few villages, "some under Turkish dominion and others under Persian," in particular in Iraq, around Basra. He had also learned something about their language: "It is the Chaldaean language, which they speak in the vernacular, writing it with an alphabet of ancient characters that they alone use, very different from the common forms, ancient and modern, that all the other Chaldaeans and Syrians use in Asia." The information he provides regarding the various names of the Mandaeans is particularly interesting for us. The first is the one that they themselves use: "They call themselves Menadì,[51] I do not know why, nor do I know what it means." As for

---

50. The delicacy of this "perhaps" should be noted. It leaves open the possibility of less compromising behavior, to strengthen the coherence of the faith. In actual fact Robeh-John was a Moslem among Moslems, just as he was a Christian among Christians.

51. This version of the name has surprised contemporary scholars, since it does not appear in other texts. It is due to an error in the letter's transcription (published posthumously); "Menadì" stands for "Mendaì." "Mendai" (rarely "Menday") was a perfectly usual name, especially during the seventeenth and eighteenth centuries, for the Mandaeans. In our case the "ì" is the equivalent of an "ï"; in other words, the accent is not tonic but simply indicates that the vowel does not form a diphthong with the "a."

the name that had become famous, it corresponds to the ideas of the Portuguese: "But the Portuguese, who in these lands had had close contact with them, call them Saint John Christians. . . . The Portuguese maintain, and perhaps not without reason, that these Menadì Christians derived their ancient origin [from John's disciples]." The Portuguese, therefore, believed that the Mandaeans were Christians and that they were descendants of John's disciples. It should be noted that according to Pietro it was a Portuguese idea that they were descended from John, not a Mandaean one. Concerning their faith, he considers them Christians, but he observes, "some of our men call them Sabaeans, from an ancient and heretical Sabba, and there is an opinion that he thus infected them with some heresy." This phantom Sabba would seem to be the result of the fusion of an idea typical of ancient heresiologists, who held that if there was a heresy there had to be a heresiarch, together with the idea in seventeenth-century erudite circles that the Sabaeans (of Harran) got their name from one Sabi. At any rate, Pietro tends to share the Portuguese belief that there was some link between the Mandaeans and John the Baptist "since in their rituals, together with the name and appearance of Christianity, there have mixed together many superstitious ceremonies that have a Jewish air about them."

The continuous state of belligerence between Persians and Portuguese after the fall of Hormuz led the latter to avoid Persian ports and shift the focus of their marine activities toward Basra. This city, a door to southern Mesopotamia, was the seat of the Pasha Afrāsiyāb. Formally a vassal of the Turks, in practice the Pasha had been independent since 1612 and was the first of a dynasty that would hold on to Basra until 1658. While the English and the Dutch were continuing to penetrate Persia, the alliance between the Portuguese and Afrāsiyāb became virtually a necessity, especially when the Shah succeeded in occupying Baghdad, wresting it from another pasha who was formally a Turkish vassal. At this point the Augustinians and Barefooted Carmelites who had lost their respective convents in Hormuz turned to Basra, and Afrāsiyāb welcomed them with open arms, as he did all the Portuguese.

The first to arrive was a Portuguese Carmelite,[52] Basil of Saint Fran-

---

52. Augustinian sources assure us that right from 1622 the Augustinians had been invited by Afrāsiyāb and that in Isfahan they had been preparing for the departure of their missionaries for Basra. When the Barefooted Carmelite superior of Isfahan became aware of this, he would have hurriedly sent a friar so that his order could be the first to found the mission.

cis, who founded the local mission, which still exists, in Basra.[53] He dedicated himself body and soul to the salvation and conversion of the Mandaeans,[54] steadily gathering information about them, as we can see from the reports he sent to Rome to the "Sacra Congregazione di Propaganda Fide."[55] Basil knew of three names for the Mandaeans: Saint John Christians among Christians, "Sabba" among the Moslems, and "Mendaia" among themselves. Their language was as different from Syriac as Italian is from Spanish or the various romance dialects from one another. Basil had taken some Syrians with him so that they could speak to the Mandaeans, but "they understood each other very little." "The characters are also quite similar to the Chaldaean (Syriac) ones, though they are different, and the names of the letters are very different." They had a very ancient book that they called *Sidra* and that was said to be by Adam (the *Ginza*), or that may have been written by John the Baptist.[56] They hated Negroes and the circumcised, and their priests never shaved either their beards or their hair. A list of their villages in Iraq and in Persia[57] was sent to Rome together with an estimate of the number of their families. According to one of the three *ganzeure* (ganzivri) that Basil knew, there were approximately twelve hundred Mandaean households. This seems finally to be a realistic estimate,[58] though Basil adds that he "doubts there are so many."

53. Father Basil was born in Santarem in 1595 and died at Mount Carmel in 1644. The official date for the mission's foundation is April 30, 1623. We will primarily be following the history of the Barefooted Carmelite mission given the abundance and availability of the documents, preserved in archives in Rome, but also because almost all of the friars were Italian and because the vicissitudes of Basra can really be considered an example of what was then happening in Catholic missions in the East.

54. The first Augustinian missionary, Nicola Peretti or Perete, perhaps Italian (but he was also known as Nicolás Veiga), arrived in Basra on July 3, 1623. He worked without falling into conflict with Basil, but he died in December of that same year. So, we cannot know just how much he may have worked with the Mandaeans.

55. This had recently been organized by Gregory XV (Alessandro Ludovisi, pope from 1621 to 1623) as a new papal instrument for the organization and management of Catholic missions on a worldwide scale.

56. Basil claims he possessed a copy and hopes to have it translated into Arabic in order to understand its contents.

57. The missionaries prepare a geographical map of the region, with the location of the villages. It was to be printed a couple of times during the seventeenth century.

58. Perhaps on the low side. A contemporary source puts the number at twelve thousand families, and thus there may have been an error in the transcription of Basil's letter.

The missionary had no doubts, however, about their not being true Christians:

> [For] a long time . . . I have been resolutely convinced that they have no baptism and as a consequence no sacrament at all; and I have had plenty of evidence of this, [having] spoken with their Fathers (their priests) and very carefully extracted from them the words they use when they perform that ceremony, which is none other than an ablution, a very common thing in this region. . . .[59] And in Goa they baptize those [Mandaeans] that go there, since everyone in general is suspicious of their Christianity. . . . At present they do not seem to me to be Christians . . . [however] I say that they seem to be descended from Christian forebears . . . since they call themselves Christians, observe Sunday, worship the cross,[60] and perform this ceremony (baptism).

In spite of his clear view of things and his full awareness of the "inconstancy of these people and the little credit that can be given to their words,"[61] Father Basil did not remain idle. His pragmatic spirit led him to

59. Here Basil was being openly polemical with the Augustinian Antonio de Gouvea, whose culture and Episcopal rank are remembered. Basil interrogates the two Mandaean priests *in situ,* asking them to repeat the formula they said out loud at the moment of baptism. One of them actually gives him the Trinitarian formula of Christian baptism. Some time later, however, Basil learned that the Mandaean had just been to an Augustinian missionary in order to learn the formula.

60. This story about the worship of the cross comes up regularly in the Christian missionaries' reports. Usually it is a misunderstanding of the rituals with the *drapša,* white banners hung from two pieces of wood in the form of a cross. As well as these wooden crosses that can be taken apart (the supports for the *drapša*), Ignatius of Jesus, however, also mentions little crosses embroidered onto the priests' robes (going so far as to call them "the marks of priesthood"), even though they were hidden from sight for fear of the Moslems. These could be simple ornamental additions in the form of a cross, passed off as Christian crosses by the Mandaeans to convince the missionaries of their sincere Christian faith. Ignatius also tells of Mandaean priests whom he had seen kissing such crosses "to show me the devotion and respect they have for it." At the present time, little necklaces with a "wrapped cross" are often worn, in much the same way as Christians wear crosses. In these modern forms, which must be little models of *drapša,* the two poles holding up the Mandaean standard are replaced by two boards, as in the traditional depictions of the Christian cross. This makes it difficult to distinguish such images from Christian images (especially from certain Calvary crosses, wrapped in drapery, and either with or without the instruments of the passion).

61. The text continues: "With much reason I fear that after Your Illustrious Lordships

believe in the feasibility of a project that today would be called deculturization.

> Once they are among us and established under our dominion, to me this appears very easy (their conversion), even though at present they are still overly attached to many superstitions and much too little to the faith. . . . They tell me that if they were among us they would do as we command, and if we are not fully satisfied with those of the present generation, in any case, since their children would live under our doctrine and in our countries, they will soon forget their ceremonies, especially since their Fathers (the Mandaean priests) will soon have all died out, because they are few, and will not be replaced.

The plan corresponds to the project we have already seen in the Jesuit correspondence and in the Spanish chancery's correspondence, attested to at Mubārak's court, and finally expressed unambiguously in the letter of Frey Symâo: an exodus of the entire Mandaean population to Christian lands. It would seem that the first ones to have tried to put this plan into action were the Augustinians. Their missionaries from Goa arrived in Basra as early as 1624 (unaware of the efforts of their brothers from Isfahan and of the presence of Basil).[62] They established themselves near the area inhabited by the Mandaeans and as soon as possible set up a school for Mandaean children where Arabic was taught (so the children could inscribe correctly written phrases on jewels for Moslem clients), as well as Portuguese (for contacts with the Christians) and some Latin for serving mass. In 1625, while Pietro della Valle was passing through Basra with his caravan, twenty-five Mandaean leaders and priests meeting to-

---

(the cardinals of Propaganda Fide) have much labored on this and obtained this, as They desire, then [the Mandaeans] do not want to put it into practice."

62. The origin of this mission places the Augustinians under the authority of the archbishop of Goa, whose parish priests they considered themselves to be — and hence the only ones authorized to administer the sacraments to the Christians of Basra. The juridical problem consists in deciding whether or not Basra may be part of the diocese of Goa and in clarifying the relationship with the Barefooted Carmelites. The latter group, who could claim to have arrived first and be directly responsible to the Pope, by way of the Congregazione di Propaganda Fide, defended their independence from Goa, whose jurisdiction they did not intend to recognize. Luckily, the conflict took place only at the highest levels of the two orders in Rome and in Goa, while the missionaries present in Basra usually collaborated with each other.

gether in the Augustinian chapel signed an official document of obedience to the Roman pontiff.[63] The Augustinians also succeeded in obtaining a document from the pasha, ʿAlī,[64] authorizing the Mandaeans to frequent their convent and obey their orders. With these successes behind them, the Augustinians of Goa and Basra tried to put into action their plan to move the Mandaeans elsewhere. They had some of the latter reach Goa, and, according to Augustinian sources, they received the pasha's authorization allowing the Mandaeans to leave his territories.[65] It was Ruy Freyre de Andrade, captain general of the Straits, who had taken the whole affair very much to heart, who put Father Basil in charge, having been angered, apparently, by the contents of a sermon preached by an Augustinian. We thus arrive at the year 1630.

Basil tells us that in that year the Mandaeans would willingly have settled in Bahrain, had that region not just been occupied by the Persians. They then decided on Duba, in Oman, which was then under Portuguese control and was not far from Masqat, the last Portuguese stronghold in the area. Here the Mandaeans could really have made themselves useful. Since they already served as mercenaries for the Arab Moslem lords, when the "Moors . . . make war against Moors," they could be even more useful serving in Christian armies. The Mandaeans seemed to be happy about the move as well. By way of Basil they even sent the Pope a letter expressing their thanks.

63. The original, redacted in Arabic, is preserved in Rome, brought there by Father Rodrigo of Saint Michael (Rodrigo Aganduru Móriz). A monk of the reformed branch of the Catholic Augustinians, he was a true adventurer of the missions. He introduced himself to the cardinals of the Congregazione di Propaganda Fide and to the Pope himself as the one person truly responsible for the Mandaeans' conversion. He asked for and obtained privilege after privilege for "his" mission at Hoveyzeh and Basra. Pietro della Valle, who had by that time settled in Rome, wrote about this to Father Basil (with whom he had become a close friend) on behalf of the Congregation of Propaganda Fide. Regarding Father Rodrigo and his document of submission to the Pope, Basil replied: "Your Illustrious Lordship knows well that it is a very ordinary thing for people who live in or pass through these lands to make an elephant of an ant." At any rate Father Rodrigo never again went back to the East; he traveled to Spain to obtain the political protection of the Catholic king, and he died there in 1626.

64. ʿAlī succeeded Afrāsiyāb in 1624. The latter had died during a Persian attack on Basra. The attack had been repulsed thanks in part to five Portuguese men-of-war that the pasha had hired for Basra's defense. Relations with the Portuguese, therefore, were very good, and it is easy to understand why the pasha was interested in keeping them like that. In 1624 he even donated a house to the Barefooted Carmelite missionaries.

65. According to Carmelite sources, however, they were the ones who had obtained that authorization.

The dream seemed to come true in October 1632 when Basil sent "seven hundred souls" of both sexes and every social extraction under the Mandaean leader Roboán. The trip was free, indeed paid for, as the viceroy of the Indies even gave them 1,200 piasters as reimbursement for their expenses. Unfortunately, however, relations between the pasha and the Portuguese broke down just before departure.[66] The Portuguese and Mandaeans therefore made a punitive raid on Basra while the Moslems of the area attacked the missions. In the confusion an Augustinian missionary died of a heart attack. In the meantime the Arabs of Oman rose up and drove the Portuguese from most of the region. Even De Andrade, who had been charged with organizing and settling in the exiles, died shortly after their arrival. The seven hundred Mandaeans were split up and shifted from pillar to post in the various Portuguese possessions of the region.[67] When the spring monsoons arrived (1633) Roboán went to Goa with about ninety adults, where he was received with great honors. With the new name of Luis de Sousa, he received from Don Miguel de Noronha, the viceroy, the title of captain, membership in a Portuguese knightly order, and the *encomienda* for Duba and its neighboring territories.[68] Upon arrival in Goa some of the Mandaeans were immediately enlisted[69] in the army and sent to various parts of India and Ceylon, while the others waited for the autumn monsoons in order to return to Oman.[70] Once there, however, they found that the situation had worsened further. With a rather precarious peace agree-

66. The pasha demanded that the Portuguese hand over to him two Persian ships that they had captured in waters that he apparently considered to be his.

67. Philip of the Holy Trinity, an Italian Barefooted Carmelite who visited those lands some years afterward, saw in this chain of disasters a clear sign of the intervention of the devil, jealous at the Carmelites' increasing success.

68. The *encomienda* was a sort of nonhereditary feudal possession much used by the Spanish and Portuguese sovereigns to entrust the lands that had been (or were going to be) conquered to the *conquistadores*.

69. One year later a Barefooted Carmelite was to write: "Among the seven hundred souls [of the emigrant Mandaeans] there are three hundred musketeers already engaged in the armies and fortresses of this State to the great satisfaction of all." Their fame as soldiers was such that nearly all adult male Mandaeans were enrolled in the army.

70. In the meantime, the Augustinians and Carmelites found ways of quarreling over which of them was to be responsible for the mission in Duba. The Augustinians claimed that it should be theirs, since theirs was the parish of Masqat, while the Carmelites claim identical rights because they were responsible for the exodus from Basra. The viceroy was to support the Carmelites' claim.

ment the Portuguese had recognized the Arabs' de facto independence,[71] and the local sultan had not the slightest desire to hand over any of his recently conquered lands to the Mandaeans. Some of the Mandaeans settled in Goa, others on Ceylon, though most of them refused the viceroy's offer to settle in India. Some returned to Basra. Within a year and in spite of the considerable efforts made especially by the Carmelites (including those of Isfahan in Persia, and of Goa) to find a satisfactory new settlement for the Mandaeans, no one was satisfied. In the meantime a letter from the imperial chancery in Madrid arrived and expressed total disapproval of the viceroy's actions, because the king considered it dangerous to arm thousands of soldiers from a single, non-Christian ethnic group and to include them in the small European army in India. The Mandaeans were not to be trusted. With his pride injured the viceroy replied firmly, though we can understand why he would be unwilling to insist on the project later. Even Basil in Basra, where he had been able to come to an understanding with the pasha, was now isolated and powerless; due to the political situation no Portuguese ships arrived there from India for more than a year, and Basil, therefore, was unable to receive any letters. In one of his last surviving letters mentioning the Mandaeans, he asks his superiors to "negotiate with the Sacra Congregazione [di Propaganda Fide] so [that], before all [the Mandaeans] become extinct, some order be sent by the King of Spain recommending these people." Basil was to be called back to Rome in 1636, and his successor[72] did not take a very great interest in the Mandaeans — or at least that is the impression we get from the letters that have been preserved. He was more involved in getting himself sent on a much more challenging and riskier mission, to Japan.

Basil returned briefly to Basra to continue his work,[73] but it was an-

71. An angry Carmelite chronicler wrote that this peace had somehow been organized by the Augustinians of Masqat (who must therefore have played the role of mediators) who were no longer interested in looking after the rights of the Portuguese and the Mandaeans since they would anyway not have been charged with taking care of the souls of those who settled at Duba.

72. This was the young and brilliant missionary Stephan of Jesus, born Decio Minerva. Born in Naples in 1609, he died in Goa in 1673.

73. The Congregazione di Propaganda Fide had sent him to the East on a very delicate mission, to make contact with Elias IX, the Nestorian patriarch of Babylonia (who resided in Mossul), in order to bring him nearer to Catholicism and eventually to union with Rome. Evidence of the high regard Rome had for Basil is also provided in a 1627 letter of Monsignor Ingoli, first secretary of the Propaganda Fide, addressed to Pietro della Valle: "I

other Carmelite, Ignatius of Jesus,[74] vicar from 1641 to 1652, who was to truly follow in his footsteps. On a cultural level, Ignatius is of a certain importance, for as a missionary he was concerned with providing his Carmelite brethren with the cultural instruments necessary for carrying out their work.[75] Of particular importance for us is his manual for missionaries involved in the conversion of the Mandaeans, with the lengthy title, *Narration of the Origin, Rituals and Errors of the Saint John Christians. Followed by a Discourse in the Form of a Dialogue in Which 34 Errors of These People are Confuted.* He dedicated his work to the cardinals of the Sacra Congregazione di Propaganda Fide, and in fact the book was published in Rome (in Latin) by the Congregazione in 1652. The manuscript dates from 1647, and from one of Ignatius's letters of that year we learn that he had already redacted the complete work in Latin and in Persian and was in the process of writing an Arabic version as well. It is a real treatise, composed according to the scholarly canons of the day.[76] The first part is a carefully ordered description of the Mandaeans and their customs, paying particular attention to the religious aspects of their culture. An analytical

---

have seen [the] letter from Father Basil, Barefooted Carmelite, and from it and from others written to his Superiors I understand that he is a very prudent Father inspired by a zeal out of the ordinary, and that the Sacra Congregazione must take him in great consideration, and I will not miss any occasion to let him be known as such to the Cardinals."

74. His name was Carlo Leonelli, and he was born in Sorbolongo (Pesaro) in 1596. With a degree in civil and canon law, he became a Carmelite at the age of thirty (1626). He was immediately sent as a missionary to Persia, to Isfahan in 1629 and Šīrāz in 1634. From 1641 he was the superior of the convent in Basra, where he worked for fourteen years. In 1656 he was transferred to Palestine, and he was finally recalled to Rome in 1664, where he died in 1667.

75. Many of the missionaries active in the area were experts in Eastern languages and have left us numerous grammar books and dictionaries, especially on Arabic, Persian, and Turkish. Ignatius, writing in Latin, composed various grammars and dictionaries of Turkish and Persian and translated Bellarmine's *Doctrina Christiana* into Persian. This text, an expression of the Catholic "Counter-reformation" and its ideals, had already been translated into Persian at least as early as 1629 (translated and edited by Father John Thaddaeus of Saint Elisha). It circulated in Arabic and was customarily used by missionaries as an instrument of religious penetration in Islamic countries. Ignatius's work, however, which provides the Italian text, the Persian text with the transliteration of the Persian between the lines, and a literal Latin translation of the Persian, was a book to be used by future missionaries in order to learn Persian.

76. It has been noted in recent years that some passages in Ignatius's text correspond closely to the text of De Gouvea, which he must have used as his source.

list of the sect's principal errors then follows, the errors being presented in the same order as the features previously described. The book's layout was obviously very carefully planned; he first describes the phenomenon and then lists the "errors" according to Catholic orthodoxy. In keeping with the then prevalent style in missionary literature, Ignatius inserted at this point a lengthy Dialogue, a discussion in which he himself confutes a Mandaean priest, one Scech Baram,[77] following the same order as before, one "error" after another. In the end Scech Baram, the ideal Mandaean from the missionaries' point of view, is converted.

Like the other missionaries before him, Ignatius was convinced that either originally or at some time in the past the Mandaeans had been Christians, so their conversion was in reality a return to their lost faith. It therefore made sense to speak of "errors." He claimed that in Baghdad they would have been considered Christians, and for that reason called Chaldaeans or *Suriani,* that is, Syrians. He believed that they had broken away from communion with the patriarch around 170 years earlier.[78] Perhaps without fully realizing the contradiction with respect to what he had just claimed (that the Mandaeans were Christians), Ignatius was also convinced that they were the descendants of those baptized by John the Baptist. As the Jesuits had done before him, he compared them to the Saint Thomas Christians. Since the John that gave them their name was not the Evangelist but John the Baptist, it was not possible to suppose a mission to the east by the Baptist. Ignatius therefore fully developed the historiographical theory of a Mandaean exodus from the west, with a gradual and parallel distancing from Catholic orthodoxy. Islamic persecutions since the times of the first caliphs, with the consequent periodical destruction of churches and books, provided a good explanation for the limitations of their orthodoxy.

As far as names went, for the Arabs and Persians they were *Sabbi,* but they called themselves *Mendai* or, "for as long as they can remember," *Mendai Iaia,* meaning "disciples or followers of John the Baptist." This last claim is another red herring fed to the missionaries by the Mandaeans. In

---

77. I.e., Šayḫ Bahram; Bahram or Bihram is quite a common name among the Mandaeans.

78. De Gouvea, who wrote nearly forty years before Ignatius, claimed that 150 years had passed since the schism. Should we think that the various Mandaean informers of the missionaries rounded off the figures as they saw fit? Or was it Ignatius who updated Gouvea's chronology?

Mandaean John (the Baptist) is called Iahia Iuhana, where Iuhana is Mandaean for Yuḥanan-John and Iahia is formed from the Arabic Yaḥya, again, John. Thus the use of the Mandaean name Iahia should not be dated before the Islamic conquest of Mesopotamia in A.D. 639, while the expression *mendai iaia* or, rather, *mandaiia [d-]iahia,* is not to be found in any known Mandaean texts.

We can see from some parts of the treatise that by this time there was cultural interaction of the profoundest kind between the Mandaeans and the Catholic missionaries, thanks to which ideas that were Christian or Western in origin had been appropriated by the Mandaeans. They had then been reprocessed and presented to the missionaries as though they were Mandaean. A considerable proportion of this phenomenon can be attributed to the Mandaeans' desire to appear to the missionaries in the best possible light, in other words, as near as possible to Christianity. We have already seen the embroidered cross being kissed; Ignatius even has Scech Baram tell of a Mandaean belief that John the Baptist ordered his disciples to crucify him after his death, in order to be like Christ in every respect. Such an idea is completely extraneous to all known written Mandaean traditions, where we see a rather violent conflict between Iahia Iuhana and Išu Mšiha.[79] It would therefore make no sense at all that John should desire to be crucified, even after his death, and, even less so, to be similar to Jesus.[80] What we have here is an exaltation of the cross as a means of winning over the goodwill of the missionaries.

Not all of them, however, were willing to go quite so far in order to present themselves as Christians. Some told Ignatius that in the past the Mandaeans had also used the sacrament of confession, now fallen into disuse, both in its particular form (with a priest) and in its community form. "Others, however, claim that this is a lie and that [the Mandaeans] have never used confession." Some bizarre notions, however, seem to have been dictated by a desire to distinguish themselves from the Christians, and to create a tradition or reputation capable of rivaling or counterbalancing them. Thus Ignatius relates the legend that in Persia, near the city of Šuštar,

79. Jesus Christ, where Mšiha is the equivalent of Messiah.
80. The Christian legend preserved in the "Acts of Peter" narrates that Peter asked his executioners to crucify him, to imitate Christ, but upside down as a sign of humility. I believe that the idea of "being crucified to imitate Christ" probably reached the Mandaeans who told it to Ignatius by way of the preaching of the missionaries, perhaps during the festivities of Saints Peter and Paul when it was commonplace to emphasize their martyrdom.

the center of an important Mandaean community, "in a certain field . . [there is said to be] a house, where they claim the tomb of Saint John the Baptist is and that his body lies there. They say that a river flows from the house and claim the river is the Jordan." John had died (a natural death) in Šuštar, and his body supposedly lay "in a glass sarcophagus *(in sepulcro crystallino)* miraculously constructed." Everyone knew that one of the most famous and venerated heads of John the Baptist — and some said his entire body — was in the mosque and ex-basilica of Damascus, where it is still the object of intense veneration by both Christians and Moslems. All of Christendom, Latin, Greek, and Syriac, was full of heads, jawbones, teeth, fingers, hands, arms, legs, and ashes of Saint John. Relic worship in general was known to the Mandaeans and had been severely criticized in one of their texts. Through it, however, the Christians could point to all the concrete proofs of which the faith of ordinary people had need. What was so strange, then, about the Mandaeans creating a noble relic of their own, if even only in words? The expedient, however, did not work as its authors had hoped; even Ignatius's reaction must have been quite firm and severe, as can be seen from his written confutation. The story stopped being told, and when asked about it repeatedly by Western scholars in the nineteenth century, the Mandaeans rejected it as preposterous.

The interaction between Mandaeans and missionaries also emerges in a passage in Ignatius's book where his Mandaean interlocutor is made to set out a theory regarding their origin that corresponded to Ignatius's beliefs, and not those of the Mandaeans themselves. To justify worship of John the Baptist at Šuštar, Scech Baram says:

> As can be deduced from clues and conjecture, it seems to me that our people emigrated from the lands of Judaea to these of Persia and Arabia. Since, however, our people worshipped Saint John the Baptist, his tomb, the River Jordan and the other things regarding this saint with the greatest of loves, and since these things could not be brought away, when they arrived here, driven by devotion they imposed the names of those things on the realities of this region. And thus they believe that they still live in the places where our forebears lived in ancient times.

This is a clear and coherent expression of a theory that has turned up periodically in Western studies on Mandaeanism since the late eighteenth century. The entire nation of the Mandaeans supposedly moved from its original home in Palestine to Mesopotamia. The absolutely European way of presenting the theory should be noted; it is a deduction based on clues and conjecture. This scientifically precise Western language has no equivalent in Mandaean literature. It should also be noted that the fictional speaker is an educated Mandaean, aware of Christian culture and ready to convert, while the final sentence proves that the "normal" Mandaeans of the time believed that they lived in the same lands as their ancient ancestors. All the same, Ignatius did not see anything strange in presenting his own theory of a flight from the west as Mandaean, though it seems hardly logical that following persecution by the Moslems the Mandaeans fled from Islamic Palestine to the equally Islamic region of Mesopotamia. Since the Mandaeans found it useful to present themselves to the Christians as "followers of John the Baptist," and since missionaries like Ignatius were convinced that there was a historical link between the Baptist and the Mandaeans, unable to have John go to Mesopotamia (as he was not the Evangelist!) they had the Mandaeans come from Palestine. The Mandaeans must have understood immediately that this is what the Europeans wanted to discover, and, as with the veneration of various "crosses," they found it quite easy to play along. Thus in the contemporary Mandaean oral tradition the idea of a Palestinian origin is widely held, whereas despite the many efforts made to find it, no evidence to this effect exists in their written texts. It would seem that Ignatius's passage, not by chance to be found in the words of "Scech Baram," bears witness to an already advanced phase of cultural exchange that explains many aspects of modern Mandaeanism.[81]

81. It would be worth comparing Ignatius's passage to a similar one of Basil where, however, the missionary distinguished between the Mandaean oral tradition contemporary to him and his own reflections: "These Saint John Christians hold as tradition that their country is near Syria and Jerusalem and they give it the title of Gebel el Agdar, which means Green Mountain, and even today in the present they say that their Mandaia live there. And to me this does not seem beyond probability, because if we consider these men to be Chaldaeans, both as a consequence of their very ancient Christianity, and also because [they are] so strongly bound to the glorious precursor of Christ, it is not improbable that they are those that the said saint converted in ancient times in those parts with his preaching. [And from this] I gather that this Green Mountain must be Mount Lebanon . . .; it also seems reasonable that these people together with those who live on Mount Lebanon today, who are Maronites, in ancient times were the same nation." Some contemporary Mandaeans hold that Ǧabal al-aḫḍar is in Jordan and that it constituted a step (before Harran) on the ancient Mandaeans' flight from Palestine.

Ignatius, however, was not only a man of letters. He was vigorously committed to continuing Basil's work. The Mandaeans were now convinced that, if they wanted to emigrate, they needed to go to India, and thus at yearly intervals (i.e., when the European fleets returned to the East with the annual monsoons) groups of them sailed for Goa and for Ceylon. Ignatius worked together with the captain general of the Strait of Hormuz, Juliano de Noronha, and with Rome's support. He even received a papal brief from Innocent X, probably during the first year of his pontificate (1644), addressed to "all the Saint John Christians." The papal text does not go beyond general terms, but it does exhort the "dearest children" to keep the faith now that they have sought refuge "in the sacrosanct bosom of the Roman Church, as in a safe and well-defended haven," and to observe obedience to the missionaries, "from whom you must drink up the word of God, as though it came from Our mouth." Ignatius refers to the fact that many Mandaeans were ready to leave, to the point of selling "houses, fields, and other real estate and furniture." Two hundred families even abandoned a village in Persia and set up a camp near Basra, ready to move. The pasha of Basra, however, went back on his word (he was perhaps no longer interested in friendship with the Portuguese) and sought to block the departures, which from that point on took place only on a much smaller scale. In some years Ignatius was able to send no more than four or five, fifty being the maximum, apparently in 1646.

Ignatius sent a few Mandaeans to Rome along with some manuscripts.[82] We know the Christian name of the first Mandaean sent, Manuel

82. It is usually believed that he sent only one manuscript, a richly illustrated and annotated (in Latin, in his own hand) copy of the *Diuan Abatur* that is currently in the Vatican Library. In a letter dated December 1646, however, he writes, "The Sacra Congregazione had me ask for these Christians' books. I found some, which I am now interpreting with the help of some [who are] knowledgeable in their language, and will then send them to the Sacra Congregazione, which I hope will be greatly pleased to see them." Roughly one year later he repeated, "Concerning the ritual books of the said Nation, I have already found a few, that are written in a special language not understood by the people, but only by a few, whom they call Scech, and who are like priests. And these are tough and reluctant to declare their things. . . . If it is impossible to have the entire explanation of the said books, I will at least find the substance." In reality, Ignatius's explanations for the drawings in the Roman *Diuan Abatur,* which in general do not correspond at all to the previous Mandaean captions, show to what extent the missionary (or his helpers) could deceive himself. His plan to send off other manuscripts to Rome could explain the presence (quite certain in the past) of other less famous Mandaean manuscripts in Italy.

Carvalho. With a couple of brothers he went as a pilgrim to Rome and Santiago de Compostela, and then on to Portugal to deal with some business of his own. These must have been the first Mandaeans to set foot in the eternal city. Two more, the brothers Abdelsaid ('Abd as-Sa'īd) and Abdelahed ('Abd al-Aḥad), were baptized solemnly in San Giovanni in Laterano (in 1653, it seems) and received the names of Isidoro Pamphili (from Pope Innocent X's family name) and Giovanni Battista Orsini (from the family name of Cardinal Orsini, who was particularly interested in their case). We also have a letter from a Carmelite missionary proposing to the Propaganda Fide that Isidoro be named Catholic bishop of Hoveyzeh. One of his uncles was "governor" there, their family being one of the leading Mandaean families.[83] The two brothers remained in Rome from late 1652 until the beginning of 1654, asking for all sorts of favors and financial help. First they sought the status of a bishopric, and then, not having obtained this, they asked at least to be named knights. In the end they settled for requesting their appointment as official missionaries of the Propaganda Fide. They were entrusted to Abraham Ecchellensis, a most erudite Roman Maronite we shall be meeting again, who was to act as a kind of preceptor in questions of faith. When Abraham became aware of the decidedly schismatic aspects of their Christianity, he was able to block their passports for Portugal (where they had hoped to obtain imperial favors). In the end, with many Christian books in Arabic and very many letters of introduction, they set sail for the East. Along the way they were captured by pirates, and an Armenian Christian from Cyprus paid their ransom. They found themselves in Aleppo as guests of the French consul and again received financial help from the Propaganda Fide. Before returning to Basra they tried once again (in vain) to be ordained bishop and priest, respectively, by the Maronite patriarch of Lebanon.

Compared to the successes in Rome of Ignatius's missionary policy,

---

83. The letter, by Barnabas of Saint Charles (whom we shall be talking about below), is interesting for several reasons. On the one hand, it denotes an interest on the part of the Carmelites and the Propaganda Fide in creating a new bishopric, independent of Goa, in order to resolve the questions of jurisdiction once and for all. On the other hand, it shows that some Mandaeans were also involved in the administration of the lands where they lived (at that time Hoveyzeh was under direct Persian control). That they were relatively well-off (apart from the quotation from the Gospel) is confirmed by a letter of introduction written by Ignatius, according to which the two had abandoned their house, wives, children, and also much material wealth in order to turn their attention to the wealth of the spirit.

in Mesopotamia it did not bear much fruit.[84] The various plans for transferring the Mandaeans to Christian lands did not work out. Arming the Mandaeans was even considered at one point, to send them off to conquer the Maldive Islands under the leadership of a deposed king, but this was another project that never got off the ground. The Mandaeans who took refuge in Goa or in other Portuguese territories most certainly became Catholics, but in Basra no baptisms were performed. Besides Ignatius's eloquent silence, we also have the disconsolate and bitter testimony of Matthew of Saint Joseph, who spent a number of years in Basra from 1649.[85] In a letter of that year he mentions having written a treatise in Arabic entitled "The Road to Perdition and the Road to Salvation," dedicated and addressed to the Mandaeans to show them "the deceptions of their Sheiks and leaders." He considered them to be "apes" (and also a "race of vipers"), since they aped everyone — Turks, Persians, Indians, Jews,[86] and even Christians — in their customs, while their writings were clearly derived from the Koran. This initiative did not bring about the desired results either, but at least it is an example of Christian cultural propaganda in the language of the people to be evangelized.

> Thirty years [have gone by] with great diligence on the part of the Augustinian fathers and our own; not even now [however] has a real Christian been made among this Nation. . . . Besides they make fools of everyone, of us in particular, and say they would sooner become Turks . . .

84. Ignatius seems to have a quite vague idea even regarding the number of Mandaeans. In a 1646 letter he says that there are fifteen to twenty thousand families, and in his book he claims that there are as many as twenty to twenty-five thousand.

85. Born Matteo Foglia in Marcianise (Caserta) in 1612, he died in Cochin, just south of Goa, in 1691. He was an Arabist, a doctor and botanist as well as a fine draughtsman. In India he composed a text on botany *(Viridarium Orientale),* with splendid drawings, published in Holland as an integral part of a botanical encyclopedia in twelve volumes (Amsterdam, 1678-1703). In Basra in 1649 he compiled the oldest Mandaean dictionary with a grammar known to us (which is still in manuscript form): "Elements of the Mandaean or Sabaean language, with Rules, Syntax and Prosody" ("Elementi della lingua dei Mandei o Sabbei, con Regole di Sintassi e Prosodia"). There is an anonymous manuscript of a Mandaic-Arabic-Latin-Persian-Turkish dictionary now preserved in Holland that the previously mentioned Rudolph Macuch has referred to several times, without, however, being able to discover who wrote it. It must, at any rate, be a product of the mission in Basra.

86. According to Father Matthew, "from the Jews they have borrowed the custom of checking whether their brides are virgins or not."

than Roman Christians. And sometimes they may say they want to go with the Portuguese; but they say this to free themselves of the tyranny of the Turks, not to abandon their superstitions and laws. And anyone who writes the contrary to the Sacra Congregazione is living a lie and seeks flattery. This is the pure truth.

The attack on Ignatius's policy could not be more explicit. Matthew was discouraged personally and asked to be transferred to a different mission. In short, "there is not the slightest reason to hope for anything from the Saint John Christians."

The new vicar, Barnabas of Saint Charles,[87] was of the same opinion, at least during the first phase of his stay in Basra:

> Neither I nor Father Matthew nor Father Ignatius himself, who has been vicar here for nine years, have found one [Mandaean] willing to be baptized; besides, every day some go into Portuguese lands, and many return, and of those that return I have not seen one who became Christian, [except] one poor soldier who spent 16 years in Masquat. . . . I believe that we must arrange their departure to Christian lands, so that slowly either the fathers or [the] sons will become Christians.

The differences between the missionaries seemed irreparable. Matthew left and even Barnabas went to Isfahan, returning to Basra only after Ignatius had been called back to Rome.[88]

There is also an external source that provides a glimpse of the missionaries' difficulties. During the spring and summer of 1649 Monsieur François de La Boullaye-le-Gouz, "un gentil-homme Angevin," arrived in Basra from India after an adventurous crossing of the Persian Gulf. He knew the Italian Carmelite mission and emphasized the "complete freedom to discuss religious matters, as in Persia and the West Indies." Like all the Europeans passing through the area he was guest of the Barefooted

---

87. Born Francesco Bertarello in Melegnano (Milan) in 1610, he died in Šīrāz, in Persia around 1665, after having tried in vain to found a mission in Madagascar. He was in Basra between 1649 and 1661. Among other things, he composed a multi-lingual dictionary (Turkish-Persian-Arabic-German-Latin-Italian-French), a grammar, and a Turkish and Persian version of the *Doctrina Christiana*.

88. His removal could have been a consequence of the written protests of his brethren, who could no longer stand the way he managed the mission.

Carmelites and most certainly met Ignatius and perhaps also Barnabas and Matthew, gathering his information on the Mandaeans from them.[89] His account corresponds to the content of Ignatius's book, both in general and in some specific details as well (in a letter Ignatius mentions he had shown him his book), and it also contains the first drawings of Mandaeans to arrive in the West. A priest with a turban, beard, and mustache can be seen baptizing children, sacrificing a hen, officiating with "bread, wine, and oil," and sacrificing a ram. What is most interesting, though, is his very critical judgment of the situation. In his opinion, and he does not hide his own Catholicism,[90] the most recent persecution of the Mandaeans was the attempt to deport them to lands controlled by the Portuguese, under the leadership of missionaries and with the pasha's consent. Now things were going badly for the Portuguese: "the same rigorous behavior towards the Sabaeans can no longer be seen, and they have all returned to their old religion, or have converted to Islam, and there are not even four Christians left." In contrast to Ignatius's optimism, here we can see Matthew and Barnabas's disillusionment coming through, but from the perspective of a politicized "layman," one of the first witnesses to be not personally involved in an attempt to save the souls of the Mandaeans.

In Basra, in the meantime, Barnabas of Saint Charles was giving a demonstration of his determined character. He stated outright in a letter that he was hoping for the forced conversion of all the Moslems living in Christian territories, whether freemen or slaves, in order to counterbalance the religious policy of the Turks. He received in his house and helped some Dutch, even representatives of the Dutch East India Company, and in return received substantial offerings, which allowed him to survive the weakening of bonds between Portugal and Rome.[91] He also wrote to Rome

89. The French traveler claims that the Mandaeans drew their knowledge of John the Baptist and Jesus from the Koran. This, however, was not Ignatius's idea, but rather that of Matthew of Saint Joseph.

90. His book, published for the first time in Paris in 1653, one year after that of Ignatius, was dedicated to Cardinal Capponi. Capponi, born in Florence in 1585, archbishop of Ravenna, was then prefect of the Vatican Library, a position that he held until his death in 1659.

91. In 1649 Masqat fell to the Arabs, and the Augustinian mission in Basra, too closely linked to Goa, did not survive the collapse of Portuguese power in the region. In his letters to his Carmelite superiors, Barnabas makes no mystery of the economic difficulties caused by the mission passing under the direct control of the Congregazione di Propaganda

asking for advice on how to behave toward the Dutch since it could be assumed that they would be acting against Catholic interests in the region.
With many gifts (he had some clocks sent from Rome for the purpose) he
won over the Islamic authorities of the area, to the point of being able to
claim the personal friendship of the pasha. In 1657 he even went as far as
to say that the missionaries were more honored in Basra than in Rome itself. He was removed in 1661, after a quarrel with the pasha.

Before that date, however, he had had occasion to change his opinion
of the Mandaeans. Around 1655, in fact, dozens of baptisms of Mandaeans
were performed, with the two brothers baptized in Rome taking an active
part in the missionaries' efforts.[92] The Carmelites were now trying to convert the Mandaean women, though they considered them particularly "obstinate." Father Barnabas in particular hoped that, since Father Matthew
was also a doctor, he would be able to win their confidence.[93] The times,
however, were not propitious; in 1657 all the Jews and Mandaeans of Persia were forced to convert to Islam, and the missionaries feared that the pasha of Basra, enjoying de facto independence from the Sultan of Turkey,
would want to follow the Persian example. With hindsight, we can see how
the increase in the number of baptisms around that date was the outcome
of a calculated move; faced with the Islamic threat, the position of the
Christians was less weak than that of the Jews or the Mandaeans, who
could not count on any foreign powers for protection.[94] At any rate, it was

---

Fide. This had made the mission independent of Portuguese interference (they had wanted
to drive out any friars who were not Portuguese nationals), but it had also created some
problems: "I think it is certain that if that income is placed in the hands of the priests, then
we will die of hunger and it will be necessary to leave the mission. . . . All of this business is
due [to the interference] of the Devil . . . but in the end God is in heaven, above the priests!"

92. They even convinced their own parents, who were baptized in 1655. Barnabas
hoped for a more decisive intervention from them within the family, composed of around
forty people. On the one hand, he had them write to their godfathers in Rome, and, on the
other, he invited his Carmelite superiors to "persuade the Lordships of the Sacra Congregazione di Propaganda, that it would be good to send some gifts to *Signor Giovanni Battista*
and to *Signor Isidoro*, so that they will be the more edified and the more compelled to show
the truth to their Nation."

93. "I hope that, if God in His grace lets Father Matthew come, he will obtain the favor of these Sabaean women through medicine, which is highly regarded here, especially
when it is *muoffz*, as they say here, that is, free of charge."

94. In that same year Barnabas wrote, "Everyone is afraid, and in particular the
Sabaeans, that is those who have not received the faith of Christ, [more] than the ones I have

only a passing flare-up of enthusiasm, since only a few years later (1660) a French Carmelite, Anselm of the Annunciation,[95] was writing this in his "Brief and True Report on the Current State of the Mission in Basra":

> [The Mandaean race][96] being one of the falsest and most dissimulating among all the nations, as well as one of the most wretched and miserable that exist on earth. . . . I call the Sabaeans foxes, because of their falseness and dissimulation. . . . In general, I say that if one of them converts to Christianity it is only to receive a loan in order to increase his own commercial gain, or in the hope that during the monsoon season the rev. Father, Vicar of this house, will get them hired by the English or the Dutch or other merchants who pay them well. . . . It is true that if we had many sequins and escudos we could make a great number of Christians and maintain them. . . . When we make a Catholic of a Sabaean, if we want to keep him Christian we must send him to Goa where the Portuguese and the Holy Inquisition will see to keeping him in line, but sending these Christians to Goa or other places in the Indies is a charitable act that we can manage only with a few of them, since the Portuguese, who were willing to take them with their ships, no longer come to the market in Basra after losing the port of Masqat and the island of Ceylon.

THE FAILURE

The Mandaean exodus to Christian lands had thus virtually come to a halt, and the political climate was deteriorating. The pasha of Basra allied with Persia and in 1666 rebelled against the sultan, so that Turkish armies moved on the Persian Gulf. During the various phases of the long period

---

baptized" (the sentence is then corrected to "that have received our faith"). "I have hope in God's goodness that will defend them." Actual examples were not lacking, as recounted by a Carmelite visitor who tells of a converted Mandaean who had been mistreated by the Moslems, of Barnabas's resolute intervention, of the pasha's consequent order to leave "the Christians of the father" in peace, and the resulting wave of requests for baptism. Barnabas responded "with every prudence and circumspection."

95. Born in Paris in 1614, he died in Tripoli in 1681. He was visitor general of the Barefooted Carmelite missions in Syria and Palestine, which he visited several times and from where he sent his reports to Rome.

96. He considered them to number eight or nine thousand in all.

of war that followed, the mission was sacked twice and burned once, and even the doors and its other fixtures were stripped from it and carried off.

The situation in the mission was further complicated by new tensions among the missionaries themselves. We have a secret memorandum of 1666 in which a number of the Basra monks asked for some really valid missionaries to be sent out who had completed regular courses in theology, who had some knowledge of the religious problems of Eastern sects as well as northern heresies (given the passage of northern Europeans via the port of Basra), and who were ready and willing to study and learn the local languages. The report was delivered anonymously to a high-ranking prelate so that its main points could be discussed by the Congregazione di Propaganda Fide, without, however, having the report itself brought to light. The document concludes, "We beg that you relate that Father Athanasius and Father Matthew are profoundly disturbed, that Father Blaise and two others are worthy of removal, that Father Felix is worthy of great reprehension for the reasons that Your Most Illustrious Lordship knows and [that] were told to him in person." The mission was entrusted to French Carmelites, and their attitude toward the Mandaeans was at times quite harsh. Thus Angel of St. Joseph,[97] having received permission from the pasha to reexhume a Mandaean who had been baptized as a Christian but buried according to Mandaean rites, had the body buried in the Christian cemetery. The times seemed to call for energetic characters, and the last vicar that we shall deal with here, Agathangel of St. Theresa, certainly fits the bill.[98] Together with another French monk, Toussaint (All Saints) of Jesus,[99] he thumbed through the church registers and found that in

---

97. Joseph Labrosse, born in Toulouse in 1636, died in Perpignan in 1697. He was an Arabist and a pharmacologist of note. He also made a number of voyages of a certain political significance. He went, for example, to Constantinople in 1678 to obtain written permission from the Sublime Port guaranteeing the survival of the mission in Basra, which had just fallen into Turkish hands again. Among his works, apart from the usual dictionaries, an encyclopedic text on pharmacology translated from Persian is worth remembering, as are his translations into Persian of Thomas Aquinas's *Summa Theologica* and the "Aphorisms" of Hippocrates. His "History of the Mission in Persia," composed in London sometime after 1681, was destroyed by fire.

98. A Frenchman from Aquitaine, where he was born around 1642. He was in Basra between 1674 and 1686 and died in Bandar 'Abbās just after leaving Basra in 1686. During his stay among the Mandaeans, he was able to procure Mandaean manuscripts, the oldest today to be found in Great Britain, for Robert Huntington.

99. Born Antoine Boucher in Paris in 1640, he died there in 1696.

spite of the numerous baptisms, not one Mandaean had been buried in the Christian cemetery, with the sole exception of the one mentioned above. Similarly there had been only one Christian wedding, and the many Mandaeans baptized even in relatively recent times did not even bother to come to mass on Sundays.

> The two above-mentioned fathers,[100] new missionaries, deploring so much neglect, immediately set themselves to bringing them to their devotions — in fact they had not yet understood the hypocrisy and dissimulation of this sect — and taking the names of those who were registered as baptized, they invited them all to attend church services and to preach to the others so that they would abandon their irreligious behavior and embrace the true faith. In a few days our church was full of Christians — if they can be called such — and catechumens, and there was not even one Sabaean that did not say he wanted to be baptized. Once warned, however, that it was first necessary to leave the *terminus a quo* in order to arrive at the *terminus ad quem,* there was not even one who wanted to leave the sect of the Sabaeans.

Agathangel had no further illusions at all:

> An erroneous opinion is dominant among them (the Mandaeans) that the three or four drops of the Christian baptism does not damage the full scale immersion of the Sabaeans, which takes place in a river and is repeated as often as one likes. On the other hand, marriage and burial are against their law and for this reason, since our Fathers came to Basra, while they have baptized many, they have not united anyone in matrimony, if not one who had repudiated his rather elderly Sabaean wife, in order to marry a young and beautiful Christian, as the rest of the story well illustrates. In fact, when this wife left for India with her daughter, the bride of an English captain, the Sabaean complained for some years and in the end, old and blind in body and mind, he abjured the Christian faith.

This was a particularly traumatic event, because the old man in question was none other than Abdelsaid Isidoro Pamphili, one of the two Sabaeans baptized in Rome twenty years earlier. Agathangel understood

---

100. Agathangel is writing in the third person.

Abdelsaid's problem and even offered to have his wife sent back from India. The Mandaean refused, however, encouraged by his children (according to Agathangel), who had promised to find him another wife, if he turned apostate. Thus on June 6, 1679, the second day of *paruanaiia*, he was baptized again, by a Mandaean priest who was not from Basra.[101] Agathangel found bitter consolation in seeing the wrath of God fall on Abdelsaid's children; the eldest ended up in prison immediately afterward, while the second died "miserably" that autumn, followed by his sister, and Abdelsaid's only daughter.[102]

God's punishment of the mission's enemies is a recurrent theme in Agathangel's narration. Thus an Armenian Christian who had pretended not to understand Agathangel's warnings was stabbed by an apostate (converted to Islam), while his brother, a Catholic convert, was healed in five days from a disease he had had for five months. Another anti-Catholic Christian was killed by dogs in keeping with a prophecy made unwittingly by Agathangel himself. He also tells the story of a Mandaean woman, the wife of a Mandaean who had been baptized Christian, who fell ill during the month of December 1678. The Virgin Mary appeared to her with the baby Jesus in her arms. The Madonna scolded her harshly for not following the path chosen by her husband. The latter then ran to tell Agathangel, who went and found her ready to be baptized. Knowing the dissimulation typical of the Mandaeans, this time it was Agathangel who delayed things, making her

101. The local priests had refused, since they held that anyone who had repudiated his Sabaean wife and married a Christian in a Christian ceremony could not be baptized. They even had the incautious priest suspended and sent for illumination from the "ganzebra," whose reply was that "what is done is done and if he wanted to return again to his sect he should be admitted."

102. Agathangel is not a fair judge of Isidoro-Abdelsaid. I have had the opportunity in Rome of checking the original registers of the church of Basra, and it appears that when Idisoro married the Christian Cathun (Hatun) in 1660, she was perhaps beautiful, but she certainly was not young for those days (having been baptized thirty years earlier) and, most of all, she had already been widowed twice, with children. In addition, since Cathun had married the first time in 1648 and the second time in 1659, one year before she married Idisoro, it cannot be believed that Abdelsaid, who had gone to Rome in 1652 (ambitious to become a bishop), had been baptized there in 1653, and had then been an active promoter of the Christian faith during the second half of the 1650s, converted to Christianity just to marry Cathun. Cathun's complex marital status, however, explains why she left her third husband in order to go off with her daughter from her first marriage (and therefore not Abdelsaid's daughter), who had married a Protestant.

promise to receive the proper instruction and then be baptized after she had recovered from her illness. In only a few days she was healthy again but was no longer interested in being baptized, in spite of Agathangel's warnings:

> And I warned her to fear God's punishment, as what then happened demonstrated. Indeed, towards the end of January of the following year of Our Lord 1679, one day she was quite well and went to bed in the evening in perfect health and the next morning she was found, strangled by an invisible force, and by God's righteous judgment.

The missionaries, with little real help from such divine acts of revenge, decided to call another meeting of the Mandaeans that same January 1679 in order to clarify the situation. Not only did the baptized Mandaeans claim to know Catholicism well, but all Mandaeans said that they were ready to convert, on only five conditions. The first of these was that the Pope send them an annual pension, so that they could pay the tribute due to the sultan; the second that they could continue to baptize and rebaptize as was their custom; the third that they could continue to perform weddings in keeping with their customs; the fourth that they could continue to bury their dead following their customs; and the fifth that they could continue to refuse to eat meat butchered by non-Mandaeans. The missionaries replied that the first point depended on the pontiff's generosity and that the fifth point did not constitute a problem. The other three conditions, however, were unacceptable. The Mandaeans protested heatedly:

> They answered that they had always believed that in order to be Catholics it was sufficient to be baptized in church, but that it was acceptable to be baptized and re-baptized, take a husband or a wife, and in short live according to their old customs. . . . Those baptized as adults answered that they had not understood these things at all, and that if they had understood them they would not have agreed at any price to being baptized by the Fathers. Those who had been baptized as infants said that they had not known what they were doing and that they wanted absolutely to live and die according to the Mandaean custom.

Pained and astonished at having allowed some of the Mandaeans present to confess and to take communion in the past, the Carmelites decided not to baptize any more Mandaeans unless they were on their death-beds, in hopes that at least in those circumstances the conversion would be sincere. Agathangel continues:

> Even though experience proved the contrary. Indeed, the only one of those baptized on their deathbeds who overcame his illness, afterwards reverted to his old habits. Two years later he became ill again and before dying declared that he was dying as a Sabaean and that he wanted to be buried by the Sabaeans and not by the Christians.

Agathangel also recounts the case of Sahed, a Mandaean educated in the Christian faith from childhood. He was baptized and given the name Gonzalve de Sousa and then sent to India, where he served in the Portuguese army for more than thirty years. Having returned to Basra as an old man in 1675, he continued to go to church, and the missionaries were convinced that he was a sincere Christian. He fell ill, though, and repeatedly postponed confession and extreme unction until, once he realized that he no longer needed the "material aid of the missionaries," he called for some witnesses and had a certain bag brought to him.

> [He] took out the crown [of the rosary] of the Blessed Virgin Mary and threw it at us, as an insult to our holy Religion, and the next day he died, obstinately clinging to his unbelief. And we have told this story here so that those responsible may see with how much caution they must deal with the conversion of these Mandaeans, who shamelessly usurp the name of Saint John Christians for the benefit of Europeans (but certainly not among themselves), in order to better deceive those who all too easily believe them.

This was in June of 1683. The Catholic mission among the Mandaeans had truly drawn to a close.

THE ERUDITE AND TRAVELERS

In Rome Ignatius's policy (which had also been Basil's) had been positively accepted by the Sacra Congregazione di Propaganda Fide, so much so that his work had been printed. In that same city, however, and at the highest levels of Catholic cultural circles, an extremely authoritative voice began to make itself heard in criticism of the historiographical basis of Ignatius's book. In fact, in 1660 Abraham Ecchellensis,[103] the learned Maronite[104] scholar, devoted a lengthy note in one of his books[105] to the Mandaeans, confusing them with the Harran Sabaeans, as often happened in those days. He claimed to know the Mandaeans well, having had occasion to discuss questions of faith with some of them.[106] He obviously distinguished between Mandaic and Syriac and was able to describe three of their books with a fair degree of accuracy: the *Ginza,* the "Book of John,"[107] and the "Book of the Zodiac," of which he possessed some manuscript passages in Mandaic. Having read their texts, Abraham Ecchellensis was probably the first person in Europe to realize that the Mandaeans were a sect of Gnostics betraying certain dualistic features. He explicitly criticized Ignatius on strictly historical grounds; those baptized by John the Baptist were circumcised, practicing Jews that did not convert to Christianity. How, then, could the Mandaeans be their descendants, if they abhorred both circumcision, Abraham, and all of Judaism?

The definitive critique of Ignatius's work in Catholic circles was to come at the beginning of the eighteenth century from yet another

103. Born in Hāqil (and therefore called *al-Hāqilī,* Ecchellensis) in Lebanon in 1605, he died in Rome in 1664. He was professor of Arabic and Syriac at the universities of Rome and Paris. He was engaged in the Latin translation of the works of the Eastern Fathers and historians. A historian himself, he worked on monumental projects such as a polyglot Bible and an Arabic Bible (later published by the Congregazione di Propaganda Fide). He was also involved in a polemic against the Protestant Orientalists, in defense of the Catholic orthodoxy of Eastern ecclesiastical writers.

104. The Maronites are another group of Syrian Christians, descendants of Aramaeans evangelized and converted by Saint Maro and his monks. Due to irreparable conflict with the Jacobites, in the second half of the seventh century they began a general exodus toward Lebanon. There are Maronite communities in a vast area extending from Mesopotamia to the Mediterranean, including its eastern islands. Their Catholic orthodoxy has never seriously been called into question, and the title of "Antiochian" has been recognized for their patriarch by the Roman pope since the times of the Crusades.

105. Published by the Congregazione di Propaganda Fide, like Ignatius's book.

106. This should be an allusion to the two brothers, whose story we narrated earlier.

107. Abraham seems to be familiar with a shorter text than the one we know, containing only the legends about John (the current chapters 18-33) and with some variants compared to the text we have. Perhaps these were the texts sent by Ignatius and brought to Rome by Isidoro and Giovanni Battista.

Maronite scholar active in Rome, Joseph Simon Assemani.[108] In a book of his of 1728[109] in which he showed himself to possess a considerable historical sense, having gone to the trouble to read Ignatius's letters preserved in the Congregation's archives, he noticed the contradiction we have pointed out above. He objected that if the Mandaeans were in some way descended from John's disciples, then they certainly could not have been part of the Syrian church, which boasts of an apostolic foundation and tradition, not based on John the Baptist. Furthermore, Ignatius provided no explanation of the schism that he claimed took place 170 years before his own time, or sometime around 1480. Finally, if the Mandaeans had ever really been "Chaldaeans" or "Syrians," as Ignatius claimed, they would have been Nestorians, but there is not even a trace of Nestorian doctrine in Mandaeanism.

While scholars in Rome were attacking the fragile historical reconstruction of Ignatius and the other early Catholic missionaries, in Mesopotamia the last missionaries had abandoned all attempts to convert the Mandaeans *en masse*. The Portuguese were less and less powerful in the region, and conversion thus became less useful to the Mandaeans. There were still to be some isolated cases, but nothing in comparison to the events of the seventeenth century. In contrast to the missionaries' diminishing interest, there were more and more Europeans traveling through the Orient and then writing travel accounts for a European reading public longing for the exotic. Some of these books were reprinted several times and became rather well known, reaching readers whose curiosity had been aroused during the late seventeenth and throughout the eighteenth centuries. Often these books were written for what we would call a "secular" audience, at any rate, distant from the world of missionaries and the archives of Catholic Rome. In European libraries the number of books and encyclopedias containing information on the Mandaeans grew greatly. This does not necessarily mean, however, that true progress was made in the knowledge of Mandaean matters. The case of Jean Baptiste Tavernier is

108. As-Sim'ānī is the name of an illustrious Lebanese Maronite family, four of whom were famous Orientalists. Joseph Simon was born in Tripoli (Lebanon) in 1687 and died in Rome in 1768. Prefect of the Vatican Library, he was named archbishop and was a personal envoy of the Pope. Charles IV of Naples named him the kingdom's historiographer and made him an honorary citizen. A few months after his death a fire destroyed his personal library, which contained very rare manuscripts and equally rare printed works.

109. Again, published by the Sacra Congregazione di Propaganda Fide.

emblematic, for in a book that was reprinted several times,[110] he merely proposes a sort of summary in French of Ignatius's work. He claims to have personally seen everything that he tells of and to have written it all down in his diary, yet passages seem to have been lifted whole from Ignatius, and Tavernier does not even bother to correct the dates (the 170 years of separation from the Syrian church, e.g., are not updated). Tavernier adds on his own initiative that the Mandaeans call raisins *zebibes* "in their language," when it is the normal and widely used Arabic word — by no means used exclusively by the Mandaeans. At any rate Tavernier's text enjoyed great success and influenced dozens of European scholars and writers.

Much imprecise information reached the West in the form of hearsay presented as eyewitness accounts. The search for strange tales to amaze the reader led practically to slander in some cases. The height of this type of literature was perhaps reached in this nineteenth-century travel account that narrates, among other things, the following:

> [For the Mandaeans] touching the dead is explicitly forbidden; they are neither washed nor buried. In order to reconcile respect for the law with necessity, they have arrived at this frightful solution. When they believe that someone dying is near his end, they strip him, wash him and after dressing him again in his best clothes they wrap him in his funeral shroud and lower him into a grave that his friends have prepared and there they let him die in peace while family and friends pray and wail all around, until he has breathed his last breath. They then close the grave and, after one last prayer, each one goes to his own home.

Up until the last century, though, apart from the works of missionaries, which were usually unknown with the exception of Ignatius's, travel accounts and rare manuscripts in the libraries of Europe were the only sources to be drawn upon for those who wished to set out to study Mandaeanism.

---

110. *Les six voyages de J.B.T. etc., en Turquie, en Perse, et aux Indes,* 1st ed., Paris, 1676. Tavernier passed through Basra several times, the first time being in 1639.

PROFESSORS AND DIPLOMATS

With the end of the eighteenth century, European university culture, in particular German university culture, made its vigorous appearance and occupied the center of the stage. Among the many scholars of theology, history, and Oriental languages to be interested in the Mandaeans, there is just one I would like to recall, the Swedish scholar and traveler Matthias Norberg, active for more than forty years toward the end of the eighteenth and beginning of the nineteenth centuries. Norberg transcribed a number of Mandaic texts in Syriac characters so they could be read by a certain number of specialists, but more importantly he translated several passages of Mandaic literature, including finally the entire *Ginza*, into Latin. Unfortunately, he allowed himself to be carried away by some very personal ideas, so that even the Syriac transliteration answers to criteria of a linguistic theory of his own that turned out to be unfounded. From a strictly scientific point of view, the text is completely useless. For his reconstruction of the history of the Mandaeans, he followed Ignatius's idea of their Palestinian origin,[111] and he also believed in the fantastic stories of one Germano Conti of Aleppo, vicar of the Maronite patriarch of Constantinople. Conti provided him with an inaccurate account of the Nusairs of Lebanon, based on legend, and Norberg saw in them a branch of the Mandaeans who had remained near Palestine at the time of the migration to Mesopotamia. The Nusairs, sometimes identified in the West with the "Assassins," so-called because of their supposed use of hashish before going into battle, are an 'alīdic Islamic sect,[112] rather close to the Druses.[113] As was definitively clarified in the course of the first fifty years of the twentieth century,[114] there are in fact some similarities in the rituals of the Mandaeans and those of the Nusairs: the use of myrtle, the repeated handshakes, and the use of a surrogate wine made from raisins and dried figs

111. Which he came to know through the work of Engelbert Kämpfer, 1712.

112. In which the superhuman and practically divine aspects of 'Alī (the first imam) are exalted, while Muhammed remained only a human prophet, the "Prophet of 'Alī."

113. "Imamists," like all Shiites, believe that the succession of imams after Muhammed was regular only through the seventh imam and then was interrupted. They are therefore referred to as "Seveners," while the Shiites of Iran claim that the last imam was the twelfth and are therefore called "Twelvers."

114. Thanks most of all to French scholars active in Lebanon (often with diplomatic coverage) during the period of the French mandate.

(rather than dates) macerated in water. There are no really substantial similarities, however,[115] and Conti's fables concerning the Nusairs' exaltation of John the Baptist are simply not true. In the Maronite prelate's account the "Nusairs" had always believed in legends such as one about how John killed a monster who lived in the Lake of Tiberias,[116] or had developed features in their rituals deriving directly from John — for example, a sort of Eucharistic communion with locusts and honey, or their priests' custom of wearing a camel-hair tiara.

Ferocious criticisms of Norberg's works were heard, and his theories were disproved in scholarly circles. It has to be allowed, however, that he did open up new horizons so that an increasingly broad public was able to access Mandaic texts. His attempt to compare the contents of certain passages of the Gospel of John to their texts bore some fruit in the long run, though today the analogies are not usually explained in terms of a direct relationship but by the derivation of Mandaeanism from Gnostic traditions linked to the Fourth Gospel. At any rate, his having discovered the analogies opened up new directions in New Testament studies.[117] Among Norberg's critics, we should remember the German Orientalist, Heinrich Petermann. To grasp the importance of his work, we should bear in mind that his Mandaic edition of the *Ginza* (1867) is still the standard edition referred to in studies on Mandaeanism, and, apart from his studies, he is also important for us because of the account he wrote of his three-month stay in southern Iraq in 1854 while gathering information directly from the Mandaean priest Iahia.[118] The text is written in the typical travel-literature style of the day, and there are some unforgettable passages, like those on wildlife with four (or more) legs with whom he has to share his home, and his efforts to keep at least the biggest of them out of his bed.

115. The precise meaning of the term "Nusairs" remains to be clarified. Its similarity to *naṣuraiia* is quite astonishing, though it should not be overestimated.

116. A similar legend does exist, but as far as I know it is preserved in Iran and the lake is different.

117. We have proof that prior to Norberg, and besides Abraham Ecchellensis, Richard Simon had read some Mandaean texts (as he himself claims in his work of 1685); he too recognized in Mandaeanism a Gnostic sect. Richard Simon was a French Catholic priest and one of the fathers of the critical study of the Scripture. He suffered a great deal of persecution for this by the ecclesiastical authorities, who feared that his inquiries would undermine the faith.

118. On Petermann's and Iahia's adventures, see now Jorunn J. Buckley, "Glimpses of a Life: Yahia Bihram, Mandaean Priest," *History of Religions* 39 (August 1999): 32-49.

Alongside these Petermann also provides what is probably the first scientifically modern, balanced description of the world of the Mandaeans' ideas. He understood their Gnostic aspects perfectly, distinguishing the Mandaeans from the Nusairs, as well as the syncretic features of their doctrines. He recognized the parallel nature of the figures of Manda d-Hiia and Jesus Christ, considering the former a derivation of the latter. With considerable acumen he saw the ideal root of this phenomenon in Gnostic Christological dichotomy.[119] He learned many things from Iahia, including the contents of the *Haran Gauaita,* a text that would become known in the West only during the twentieth century, and both ancient traditions and more recent theories — for example, the theory of "the four false prophets" (Abraham, Moses, Jesus, Muhammed), in opposition to the only true one, John. The risk in his approach is that, without realizing it, he adds material of his own to the material provided by Iahia, as when he mentions that the priest spoke to him of Pontius Pilate. The surviving Mandaean texts never mention that Pilate was called Pontius; it is not clear whether Iahia had learned from the Christians what his ancestors had not known or whether Petermann has made explicit for the reader what the Mandaean himself did not say.

Iahia, though, was not an ordinary Mandaean. The plague of 1831 had decimated the population and almost completely wiped out the priestly class, leaving only Iahia and his cousin and brother-in-law, then both young *šgandia.*[120] With no clergy left, the two "deacons" joined up with a group of keen cultured laymen *(ialupia)* and, under the guidance of other older *ialupia,* full of virtue and knowledge, they prepared themselves for the priesthood, studying the sacred texts, prayers, and rituals. Finally, with the permission of the local Arab sheik they built a *manda* and ordained each other priests, in what was clearly an unorthodox manner. In equally irregular fashion they then chose a *ganzibra* from among themselves and went on to ordain him, so that marriages could be celebrated. Chance, or that strange set of coincidences that we call destiny, just so has it that at least one of the manuscripts that Lady Drower purchased was copied by this same Iahia, who added a long autobiographical colophon to

119. See above, p. 37.

120. In other words, both already had the equivalent of the Catholic minor orders but were not necessarily destined to become priests. Regarding the epidemic, Petermann distinguishes clearly between the plague of 1831 and cholera, which was endemic. Also in 1854 two Mandaeans died of cholera (which was at any rate a lower number than in other years).

the text. At times Petermann's account and Iahia's colophon correspond even in the smallest details, as in the case of the harassment perpetrated by the sheik of the Arab Muntafiq tribe (a sort of feudal lord of the area), which led to the flight of the Mandaeans, including Iahia, and Petermann's forced return to Baghdad.[121] Iahia's text is permeated with regrets and bitterness: wars, flight, persecution, the theft of his personal possessions, and the futility of appealing to the Moslem courts, even the death of a daughter, far from home and without even a sufficient number of Mandaeans in a state of purity to celebrate the funeral in accordance with the prescribed norms. In certain moments desperation led the Mandaeans to break ancient taboos. About a hundred of their brethren, "men and women, boys and girls" who had been forcibly circumcised on the orders of a sheik, rather than being considered impure and untouchable, were welcomed "in baptism and marriage."[122] Iahia's memories turn to happier days, when he was an adolescent before the plague and witnessed the successes of his father, a *ganzibra* of profoundly revered memory. It would seem from Iahia's account that his father had not only once won a theological debate with an English missionary[123] at the house of the English consul general, but he had even convinced the Englishman, *mistar tilar*, a Mr. Taylor, in his heart of hearts to convert. The "queen of London (*landun*)" had apparently been angered about this.[124] Iahia also recalls having learned the "language of the Franks," that is, English, as well as Armenian.[125] He had also seen some of the amazing things brought by the Europeans "whose kingdom is great in the East"; "they have carts of fire made entirely of iron, except the part un-

121. Iahia never presents himself as *šganda* in the colophon, but as *ialupa*. The two definitions do not necessarily contradict one another, and it is possible that Iahia wanted to emphasize the "near regularity" of his priesthood before the foreigner, while in the text for the use of the Mandaeans he preferred to place the emphasis on his cultural preparation.

122. This is how Lady Drower translates a text that is difficult to understand. The information conflicts, however, with everything we know about the behavior of the Mandaeans in this regard and provokes a skeptical reaction in modern Mandaeans as well.

123. He is a *padria,* that is, a "padre," with an English pronunciation, called *iuspia* (Joseph?) *uilip* (Philip?).

124. Another coincidence had it that the son of this Colonel Taylor, in his turn English vice-consul, while excavating what would later be identified as the site of Eridu, dropped in to see Petermann in the period when he was taking lessons from Iahia. He was the only European to pass by in three months.

125. Albert Socin, the German professor who tried in vain to extract other information from Iahia besides requests for money, confirms Iahia's knowledge of English.

117

derneath, which is wooden and goes in the water."[126] He also mentions a wheel with pistons and a propeller or spinning blades; these are steamships "that cover a month's distance in a day," capable of going "from Basra to Baghdad in three days."[127] He had seen these, a large number of them, though he had only seen a "picture hanging [in the house of] Christians who are lords" of "carts that go in the sky, and rise up to three parasangs high." This must have been a drawing or a print of some aircraft "with wings like the wings of birds, which are a system for turning, and it also has a wheel, a wheel that takes in air from above." Iahia's world was the world of the vanquished, who are witness to the power of others, Moslems (Turks or Persians or Arabs) and Christians (Franks, in other words, Europeans), and are unable to take part in it. He was able to repeat, though, with pride, that he had never given in to the temptation of apostasy.

Roughly twenty years later, however, a grandson of one of the two *šgandia* who had survived the plague did leave the faith. The young man, named Adam, probably Iahia's grandson, was accompanied by a missionary to a meeting with Nicolas Siouffi, the French vice-consul in Mossul, in 1875. Siouffi had arrived in Baghdad in 1873 and had tried in vain to gather first-hand information on Mandaeanism. He was delighted to be introduced not just to any Mandaean but the son of a *tarmida,* and one who had finished the curriculum necessary to enter the priesthood shortly before converting to Catholicism. It would seem, therefore, that the two main nineteenth-century sources of knowledge of Mandaeanism available in Europe originated in the same Mandaean family, perhaps even grandfather and grandson.[128] As with

126. Some of these words have a technical meaning and appear only here; the translation is fairly loose.

127. Against the current; François de La Boullaye-le-Gouz's boat took exactly thirty days to make the trip in 1649.

128. Adam tells us that his grandfather, Sheik Bulād, and the latter's brother-in-law, Sheik 'Abdallāh, were the only two *šgandia* who survived the great plague of 1831. In some points Adam's account coincides perfectly with Iahia's, but in others it does not, as with the proper nouns. We can suppose that Iahia had told Petermann his proper Mandaean name (which corresponds to the name on the colophon, whose author calls himself Iahia Bihram), while Adam told Siouffi the Arabic names of his grandfather and great-uncle. This is confirmed by the manuscript of the "Book of the Rivers," copied in 1843 by one 'Abdallāh, whose Mandaean name was Ram Zihrun and who claims to be one of the two survivors and to have consecrated eleven priests up until that day. According to Iahia's colophon narration, Ram Zihrun is his brother-in-law, the one who ordained him priest. In which case Iahia was Bulād, Adam's grandfather.

Petermann and Siouffi, neither of the two was aware of the other's actions.[129] Siouffi was an enthusiast, but he was not familiar either with the critical work of his own time or with Petermann's work. Communication between Siouffi and Adam was also hindered by the language barrier. Siouffi had no problems with Arabic,[130] but Adam understood it only with difficulty. Adam spoke only his own language *(ratna)* fluently and knew how to read and write only classical Mandaean. Siouffi candidly confesses that he often put the Arabic words that his interlocutor could not come up with into his mouth, going on to explain their meaning "in order to be sure that that was what he really meant to say." In the end Siouffi learned to read and write Mandaean, to be able to transcribe what his improvised teacher dictated, and to read or copy sentences from the manuscripts that Adam showed him.[131]

Despite its limitations, the book Siouffi published in Paris in 1880 was the most wide-ranging and detailed work on Mandaeanism ever written by a European witness. The mass of information covers all aspects of their lives, rituals, the calendar, taboos, religious traditions, and legends. Unfortunately, Siouffi did not have the tools to distinguish the more ancient aspects from what seem to us to be recent additions, nor was he interested in such a "philological" approach. His aim was to present the reader with an understandable, "logical" outline of Mandaeanism, with as few contradictions and as little confusion as possible. The various myths and legends were therefore linked to one another and organized in a nearly chronological manner, in contrast to all the sources known to us. Some aspects of his presentation of things were completely new. In the first place, the religious imagery used by Adam seems decidedly Christianized. He even provided some Trinitarian (or three-member) baptismal formulae, like that of the Christians. According to one of these, which was supposedly the oldest and even used by John the Baptist, baptism was performed "in the name of Alaha (Allah!), Mara d-Rabuta (the Lord of Greatness),

---

129. Iahia was still alive in 1870; see above, n. 125.

130. He also wrote a short manual of the pronunciation of the letters that were most difficult for Europeans to pronounce. Besides Arabic, he also knew Turkish.

131. At some point Siouffi most certainly had had the "Book of the Zodiac" and the "Book of John" before him. He quotes from them and transcribes some brief passages, whose text does not always correspond exactly to the texts now known. There are no exhaustive studies on this topic, but the Mandaic reproduced by Siouffi is probably more similar to spoken *ratna* than to the classical language.

and Manda d-Hiia," while another, which according to Adam was then in use, presents the insertion of Iahia, the Baptist, in the same way as the Christian presents Jesus, the Messiah. The stories of John and Jesus also paralleled one another very closely. As in the Islamic legends their mothers were sisters. Both became pregnant miraculously by drinking a special water prepared for that purpose by divine beings. There is a difference, however, in that the water that made Elizabeth pregnant was prepared by Manda d-Hiia, the true "father" of John, while that of Mary was prepared by Ruha d-Kšaia, the *male* and good version (no longer a devilish figure) of Ruha d-Qudša. In the Christian story, though, was it not the Holy Spirit that performed the typically male role of getting Mary pregnant while she, in a very widely known legend, was gathering water from a spring? The two babies conceived in such an extraordinary way[132] also remained in the womb longer than normal: nine months, nine days, nine hours and nine minutes. Both of them were then born from their mothers' mouths. There is a long Mandaean tradition behind this bizarre idea. The oldest document referring to it known to me is an anti-monastic text in the *Ginza*. There it was said that the Christian nuns refused normal sexual activity, which the Mandaeans considered both necessary and praiseworthy, and devoted themselves to practices that could not exactly be considered desirable for normal girls. Their punishment consisted, then, in a sort of auto-conception followed by oral childbirth. That type of childbirth, however, had already been attributed to Elizabeth in the "Book of John," without the text having anything at all critical to show about her behavior (the way John was conceived is not described, though we are led to understand that it lies outside the realm of the ordinary). The birth of John, Adam continues, following the story of the "Book," was the result of a trick by Lilith, a female demon who assists women in labor and who helped Elizabeth. The

132. In reality, from a Mandaean point of view, taking into account speculation on the water of life, it is not absurd to think that new life should come from water. In even more recent narrations a legend appears according to which Elizabeth and 366 Jewish women get pregnant by drinking from the river Jordan (which is imagined as flowing by Jerusalem). As early as the early seventeenth century, however, De Gouvea had been told that Mary had become pregnant by drinking water. The same thing had been told to Basil of Elizabeth (and reported in Eugenius of Saint Benedict's 1627 report). In another legend told to Ignatius, John had been conceived without real sexual relations, and every time he desired a son he asked the divinity, who granted him one miraculously from the waters of the Jordan (John, then, gave each one to his wife to be breast fed).

Jews, in fact, had learned through dreams of John's imminent birth, had decided to kill him, and had involved all the midwives in the plan. Lilith, however, was able to deceive them all, having the baby born in an unexpected way and entrusting him immediately to Anuš 'Utra, who took him off to a distant, blessed mountain where the boy could grow up in peace. An absolute novelty, though, was the idea that Jesus, too, was born from the mouth of Mary to preserve her virginity. This is the most unusual feature of all because, while it is normal for the Mandaeans to think that Jesus had been conceived by a virgin since he was a demonic entity, there was absolutely no reason for them to believe in a virgin birth. In the context of the story Adam shows considerable sympathy for his heroes, even the Christian ones, and it is not possible to tell if these sympathies come from Adam's personal attempt to reconcile his situation as an apostate, which still preserves a very close cultural link to his world of origin, or if they are a product of Mandaean circles, for centuries impregnated with forms of deliberate religious equivocation aimed at attracting the sympathies of the successive Western people they came into contact with.

We do not know why Adam converted to Catholicism. Siouffi tells us that he was going at times to mass, which he heard in Syriac (it was therefore the Chaldaean ritual), and proudly declared that he "understood almost everything." In another context, however, it is clear that he had never read the Bible, and, one morning, he came from mass and asked Siouffi the following question:

> How is it possible that the Christians claim that speaking of Iša (Jesus) John said that he was not worthy of untying the laces of his shoes? Aren't Iša and Iahia cousins, and therefore equal? Weren't they born of equal parents and aren't they equal in the World of Light, where they live together? I believe that the Christians attribute this great superiority to Iša over Iahia, because they say their lawgiver is a god and they call Mary "mother of God." But how is it possible to say such a thing? God cannot be born or generate! And you Franks believe such things!

The French Barefooted Carmelite, a missionary in Baghdad, who had taken Adam to Siouffi, claimed that Adam was a convert, that he had burned the bridges with his former world, and that his former brethren in religion considered him an enemy. They had excluded him from the community (in fact Adam now lived with the missionaries). Adam's words, however, reflect certain precise points of Islamic propaganda that the Mandaeans had perhaps adopted as their own and, at any rate, that demonstrate that Adam considered the Christian world as external to his own. It would seem, then, that the same ambiguous situations of the seventeenth century were still coming to the surface even at the end of the nineteenth.

THE "MANDAEAN QUESTION"

For about fifty years there were no books on the contemporary Mandaean world that surpassed Siouffi's in accuracy, and his work marks the end of an epoch in studies on Mandaeanism. While scholarly research remained firmly in the hands of university scholars, for the most part German, at a lower cultural level the old ideas of Norberg enjoyed an ambiguous notoriety among theosophist and spiritualist groups. What the "friends of Renan" or Blavatsky herself found fascinating was the possibility of arriving at an ancient tradition, the heir to John the Baptist's preachings, via Mandaeanism. A general revival of interest in Gnostic theses accompanied in particular by speculation about John the Baptist, placed in relation to the primordial androgyny, fascinated the curious and dreamy Europe of the Belle Époque. Even among academics, however, hand in hand with the growing availability of Mandaean texts a growing need was felt to reconsider what had seemed scientifically certain. Analogies were discovered and then studied in depth between Mandaeanism and the world of Iranian ideas, and attempts were made to find a historical link to Zoroastrianism and its direct Indian descendant, Parsism. Parsism and Mandaeanism were considered fossil religions, preserved through the centuries by two ethnic minorities that resisted the cultural siege of the outside world by closing in on themselves. After the end of the First World War the time was ripe, in official science, for a revolution in the evaluation of the antiquity, origin, and historical significance of Mandaeanism.

One of the most outstanding individuals involved in the debate was Richard Reitzenstein. A comparative historian of religions, famous scholar, and brilliant popularizer of his subject, he provided a basis from a perspective of the history of religions for the thesis that had formerly been that of Ignatius and Norberg, though for different reasons and within a different historical framework. In other words, the Mandaeans came originally from Palestine. According to Reitzenstein, the disciples of John the Baptist that did not convert to Christianity were persecuted by the Jews before the fall of Jerusalem in A.D. 70 and fled to the East. Having first settled in northern Mesopotamia, they were later persecuted by the Christians of the Byzantine Empire and finally took refuge in the south, where they still live. Such movements would explain the cultural influences of Judaism, Christianity, and Zoroastrianism on the Mandaean texts, which would therefore be based on very ancient foundations. With a certain philological optimism Reitzenstein believed he had discovered the remains of a presynoptic apocalyptic text, written by disciples of John the Baptist before A.D. 70, in two passages of the *Ginza*. He was convinced that for the Mandaeans John was a messianic figure, the true Christ, in contrast to Jesus the deceiver. The New Testament showed traces of dependence on Mandaeanism, and indeed the Fourth Gospel was the consequence of a polemic against primitive Palestinian Mandaeanism.

Mark Lidsbarski took up a position alongside Reitzenstein's. Lidsbarski was a Polish Jew who both materially and ideally abandoned the village ghetto atmosphere in which he grew up and became professor in a German university, deservedly winning fame as one of the greatest Semitists of his time. He was also lucky enough to die of natural causes in 1937, before the application of the racial laws against the Jews. Basing his work on study of the Mandaic language, he held that its peculiarity could be explained by supposing a Palestinian origin and prolonged contact with Persian. Such contact would have occurred while the Mandaeans were settled in northern Mesopotamia.

In the jealously protected garden of New Testament studies the theories of Reitzenstein and Lidsbarski had the effect of tremendous bombshells fired from a great distance. Everyone, both exegetes and theologians, began to study Mandaic, and no biblical commentary from those years feels it can avoid dealing in some way with the "Mandaean question." Some adhered enthusiastically to the new theories, the most famous of these supporters being Rudolf Bultmann, perhaps the best-known New Testament scholar between the two world wars. Criticisms, however, soon began to make themselves heard and within about twenty years had gained the upper hand. It was demonstrated not only that the Mandaean passages dealing with Christianity were more recent than the New Testament but that they were not even derived directly from it, being reelaborations of apocryphal legends written centuries afterward. Some tried to demonstrate that Mandaeanism was a sort of degenerate form of Syriac Christianity from the Islamic period or shortly before. Some even went so far as to say that had Mandaeanism disappeared without a trace, the history of religions would be none the poorer. The so-called Mandaean fever, then, passed quite quickly, at least in the field of New Testament studies, to the point that more recently it has even been asserted that the "Mandaean question" had been "killed" at the end of the thirties.

Those were precisely the years in which Lady Drower began publishing her work, however. With her wide-ranging labors carried out over several decades, the enthusiastic English scholar was to a very large extent responsible for the renewal of interest in Mandaeanism in Western scholarly circles. Untiring in her work of translating and editing Mandaean texts, she provided Western culture with manuscripts, photographs, accounts, and even recordings that are irreplaceable today. Unfortunately certain specific limitations are to be placed alongside the enthusiasm and dedication. Lady Drower clearly knew Mandaic and the world of the Mandaeans very well, but she had no philological or historical preparation. It is clear in her first works that she was not familiar with the scholarly literature on the topics she was dealing with, nor was she aware, for example, of the Gnostic meaning of the works she was analyzing. The works she edited and translated are often very complex and derive from a devastated textual tradition, and her lack of knowledge in the field of textual criticism is clearly felt.[133] All the same, her books and articles are invaluable instruments for anyone wishing to approach Mandaeanism seriously. Furthermore, concerning the origins of Mandaeanism, in the earlier years of her work Lady Drower did not think a Western origin possible, but she was later convinced of it, probably under the influence of her brilliant colleague Rudolf Macuch.

Macuch was a Slovakian Semitist philologist who taught for many years at the University of Tehran. He worked with great commitment on Mandaeanism for around forty years, involved among other things in the historical reevaluation of some of the information contained in the *Haran Gauaita* and in the analysis of the historical information to be drawn from

133. There is no scientific description of the codex or scroll. Obvious mechanical errors in the text are not eliminated, and discovering that words or entire lines have been lost (in some cases altering the meaning) is an easy task. Everything is translated in the same way, or, in other words, there are rarely any indications as to whether we are faced with additions between the lines or in the margins. Finally, noticeable oversights in the translation exist.

the colophons of the known manuscripts. He was deeply convinced of the Western origin of Mandaeanism, even though, on the basis of archeological and philological evidence, he held that they arrived in southern Mesopotamia in quite a short time. By the end of the second century A.D. they had probably already settled the area where they live today.

Perhaps the greatest living scholar of Mandaeanism and the Mandaeans is Kurt Rudolph. An East German, Rudolph took refuge in the West before the fall of the Berlin wall and now teaches at the University of Marburg. A scrupulous philologist and careful historian, his works are always of the highest scholarly level, despite the large extent of his literary output. He too is almost entirely convinced of the Western origin of Mandaeanism, though he is very cautious when dealing with this topic, and indeed has taken a different stance from Macuch on a number of occasions.

In conclusion, the combined if varied activity of Drower, Macuch, and Rudolph has relaunched a kind of second phase of the "Mandaean question." Now nearly everyone is convinced that the information regarding John the Baptist and Jesus are derived from the Christian apocrypha and not directly from the New Testament, which most certainly antedates them. The question of the historical and geographic genesis of Mandaeanism remains completely open, however. No matter which approach is taken to the question, new difficulties appear. Let us suppose that the Mandaeans really were a Jewish sect founded by John the Baptist along the banks of the Jordan and later, sometime between A.D. 30[134] and 70, the year Jerusalem was destroyed, took refuge somewhere in the East. The first problem is Josephus Flavius's silence. The Jewish historian was a contemporary of the events he relates and was even a personally and passionately involved witness to many of the events of those years. He clearly demonstrates that he was well informed about John the Baptist and his death, dedicating a couple of pages to the topic. Furthermore, in his reconstruction (however subjective, idealized, and "theologized") of what was for him recent history, he appears very attentive to symptoms of degeneration in the powerful in Palestine prior to the war, which he interpreted as divine punishment for the sins of the Jews. He would hardly have omitted from his narrative the persecution and flight of the Palestinian disciples of John the Baptist, a figure he presents in a positive light. The second really seri-

---

134. John the Baptist was executed shortly before Jesus, at least according to the Christian sources. According to the Mandaeans he preached for forty-two years.

ous difficulty is that if the Mandaeans are actually the direct descendants of John's disciples, why do they not have any traditions of their own concerning their founder but derive everything they have to say about him from Christian traditions, sometimes even dating from some centuries after the New Testament? However, if the Mandaeans have always been where they are now and are not related directly to John the Baptist, why did they go and "recycle" a saint (and only that one!) from a rival and hostile religion?

3. Legends and History

In antiquity, except in rare and exceptional cases, no one wrote the history of the defeated, and the Mandaeans, as a distinct ethno-religious entity, have not left a mark on history as winners. Their legends are often stories of harassment and oppression, of flight, and of defeat, maybe with an ending bringing salvation. It is some consolation that the survivors of what must have really been pogroms managed to reach Mšunia Kušṭa, the earthly paradise, or else a mysterious Mandaean kingdom to the north, beyond impassable mountains, unscathed. Yet these fables aiming to console, in which the highest happiness lies in an existence without persecution, tell us nothing of the actual facts, except that the reality was so tragic that it meant an obligatory happy ending to the stories, a tranquilizing fantasy in which to believe. What knowledge we have of Mandaean reflections on their story, past, present, and future, ranks them among the cultural productions of oppressed peoples, similar, for example, to those of the Indios of America. The bitterness they share, the background to any number of stories, is an awareness that the world by now belongs to a power "come from beyond," which for nearly five centuries in the Americas and for more than thirteen centuries in the Land between the Two Rivers has enjoyed total domination. In the stories of the defeated, this has to lead us to forgive those aspects of exaggerated, exalted self-esteem, of a somewhat arrogant vainglory, as well as the distortion of events, which we can learn about from different sources. They are defense mechanisms, necessary for the preservation of a cultural identity.

In Mesopotamia, in the eyes of a local population like the Mandaeans, the date that marks a watershed in their history, one for which it certainly makes sense to talk of a before and after, is the date of the Islamic invasion. In A.D. 639, year eighteen of the Hegira, the overflowing armies of the Prophet resolved the eternal conflict between the Byzantines (at that time recently victorious) and Persians, throwing both out of the Middle East and immediately striking a mortal blow at the Sassanid Empire. Of course, over many centuries government passed through many hands; Arabs, Persians, Mongols, and Turks, just to name the main ones, alternated in power. Nevertheless, the marks of a fundamental continuity were always present. In the first place, all the rulers adopted Islam as their official religion. Second, the local administration in southern Mesopotamia was almost always in the hands of Islamicized Arab lords, holding feudal allegiance to the empire of the day. Third, the Mandaeans were always excluded from whatever power system was ruling at whatever time.

The bitter memory of the Arab or Moslem conquest (for the vanquished Mandaeans the ethnic identity and the religion of the conquerors coincided) is still very much alive. But what about beforehand? What do the Mandaeans recount of their past before the invasion? To judge from the few written records that deal with the subject, and the numerous oral traditions, which only from the nineteenth century were collected together with an eye for accuracy, Mandaean history between the Flood and the Arab occupation provides us with certain basic motifs, and some apparently factual information, whose chronological relationship is not always clear. A first motif, an important feature above all of the oral traditions, which with the passing of time is becoming ever more important, is the existence of an independent Mandaean kingdom, situated somewhere to the north. Called *Ṭura d-Midai*, "The Mount of Media," or more frequently *Ṭura d-Madai*, in the more recent texts it has crystalized into *Ṭura d-Maddai* or *d-Mandai*, "The Mount of the Mandaeans." This is sometimes identified with Mšunia Kušṭa,[1] a kind of Mandaean earthly paradise, and sometimes with a land between the latter and Tibil. It is occasionally closely though unclearly associated geographically with Harran. Placed beyond impassable mountains, which only a handful of Mandaeans in the past managed to reach after long and perilous journeys, over the centuries it offered a place of refuge for the persecuted and provided a reserve supply of living Mandaeans, to which the divinity was able to turn to rebuild Mandaeanism whenever it was destroyed. A second motif, again increasingly important the nearer we get to the present day, is the knowledge that

1. See above, pp. 45-46.

the Mandaeanism of the epoch since the Flood, just like the whole of humanity of the ages before it, has passed through periodic extinction and has then been miraculously restored to life by divine intervention. These two motifs, variously combined or alternative to each other, make up a kind of plot or background on which several sets of events are projected. The first set deals with the Exodus of the Israelites from Egypt. According to the Mandaean stories, the Egyptians were the Mandaeans of that era, led by two sovereigns who were brothers, King Pharaoh and King Artabanus. The second set of events concerns a campaign of persecution against Mandaeans in Jerusalem, and the consequent destruction of the city as a divine punishment, at the time of a heroine called Miriai (Mary), or else after the death of John the Baptist, or when Anuš 'Utra appeared in Jerusalem. This last event is sometimes believed to be a reaction to the teaching of Jesus Christ, but sometimes it is believed to be quite independent of this, from an age whose collocation is uncertain. Finally, from oral evidence gathered in the twentieth century, there is the idea that the Mandaeans come from Ceylon. Connected in various ways to these legends is the memory of a foundation of Jerusalem, sometimes placed on the Euphrates. There is also the conviction that its destruction was unique and definitive. Finally, there is an awareness that things got worse in Mesopotamia for the Mandaeans when a dynasty of tolerant Persian kings was succeeded by another dynasty of persecutors. This may refer to the defeat of the Arsacids and the Sassanian takeover of power, around A.D. 226 (the Sassanians were fervent Zoroastrians).

BETWEEN EGYPT AND INDIA

To try to make a coherent whole of the data collected so far would lead to a historical monstrosity, making Mandaeanism into a Hydra that springs up and is repeatedly reborn along a curve starting from Egypt and passing through Jerusalem, Harran, Media (or at any rate the mountains to the north), Mesopotamia, and finally, leaving the Persian Gulf, reaching Ceylon. Looked at more closely, however, the direction this curve takes is by no means inexplicable; it follows the Fertile Crescent from Egypt to India. This is the same route caravans and fleets followed for thousands of years, trading and exchanging things, people and ideas. Apart from Ceylon, it is also the line along which biblical history after the Flood unfolds. Abraham

was born in "Ur of the Chaldees" in southern Mesopotamia and takes off
for Harran (Gen. 11:31), arriving first in Palestine and then Egypt (where
he sells his wife to the Pharaoh, Gen. 12:10-20). His Palestinian descendants preserve close links with Harran (where Jacob takes refuge when
persecuted by his brother, Gen. 27:43) and later go to Egypt. From there
they go back to Canaan, where David and Solomon rule and set up the
temple at Jerusalem in the heart of their new kingdom. Finally (but here
we begin to have historical data available, not just legend), some are exiled
in Babylonia and some of the descendants return to Palestine, with various, periodic flights into Egypt, as the events affecting Jeremiah (Jer. 43:5-
28) or Onias IV[2] teach us.

Recent historical criticism does not believe in the Israelites' comings
and goings *as a people* along the paths and trade routes of the ancient
world. It is now believed that behind every story of a movement *en masse*
we should be seeing a derivation or a relationship of cultural, economic,
and political dependence.[3] It is also true, of course, that ideas and things
shift with the people who carry them, but in order to explain a linguistic, a
religious, or, in a broad sense, a cultural derivation, it is not at all necessary
to imagine entire populations, like flocks of sheep, subjected to highly improbable periodical migrations, impressive as these may seem. Those who
think in this way continue to fabricate historical myths but cannot be writing real history. In the ancient world there was even greater mobility
among people than we might think existed, but in many cases of cultural
transformation the missionary activities of some preacher, or the station-
ing of troops, or the foundation of a colony is sufficient. The new arrivals
may often be absorbed gradually into the socio-cultural fabric of the place
in which they settled, but by the time that happens new ideas, new words,
and new customs will have gained currency. Behind every syncretism lies
contact between different realities, but not every syncretism has gone on a
pilgrimage via ports and cities to learn the individual features of which it
consists. Think of this example from Mandaean ritual. As we noticed
above,[4] the fruit, fresh or dried, serving as ingredients for certain sacred

2. The son of a high priest, he fled to Egypt after the murder of his father in 170 B.C.
and built a temple there devoted to the cult of Yahweh, as Flavius Josephus narrates in *The
Antiquities of the Jews,* XIII, 3, 62-73.

3. I refer the reader to a fine if polemical Italian work, Giovanni Garbini's *Storia e
ideologia nell'Israele antico* (Brescia: Paideia, 1986).

4. See above, p. 28.

meals, is partly of local origin, partly from Persia, and partly (e.g., the coconuts) from India. Yet this is no reason to believe that the Mandaeans or their ancestors had to wander off to India or Persia to find their nuts or other fruit, as if discovering their virtues by staying in Mesopotamia was almost impossible. The most suitable place for this ritual syncretism was precisely southern Mesopotamia, and indeed especially the region they lived in, known in the ancient world first as Mesene and then as Characene (from the name of the city of Charax, the capital), always a crossroads for the traffic connecting the Far East to the Middle East.

With this in mind, we shall now see why the Mandaeans consider the Egyptians to be their ancestors, and how Artabanus, a king of Persia, also became a Mandaean, as well as a brother of the Pharaoh of whom the book of Exodus speaks. It is a story a few centuries old, but it cannot be so very ancient. The only written Mandaean text, in fact, that contains the story of Exodus reproduces the Judaic legend without Artabanus and with no Mandaeans. The passage that interests us is of the eighteenth and last treatise of the *Right Ginza,* a kind of universal history from the creation to the end of time. Since the end of Arab power is forecast for seventy years after the invasion, the prophecy must be prior to this date, and hence the book may well have been composed in the second half of the seventh century.

> Then Abraham was made, the father of the Jews. He and the whole of his race journeyed (?) to the land of the Egyptians, whose king had the name of King Pharaoh (Pirun). The Jews had to suffer much under the Egyptians and King Pirun. Then Iurba, Ruha and the god they worshipped led them out of the land of the Egyptians. The Jews hurried, when their god led them, and in one day crossed the sea. He (the god) divided [it] for them, and the water of the sea rose up into two great walls, like two mountains, so that all the Jews could cross. They then wandered about in the solitude of the desert. Then they went to Jerusalem and settled there.
>
> Then King Pirun went after them, he and all his army, 70 myriads, 770,000 Egyptians accompanied King Pirun. He saw the sea without boat, raft or ford. Then King Pirun saw a way along the bottom of the sea, while the waters of the sea were drawn back like two mountains. Then the entire army of King Pirun followed in the wake of the Jews; and the sea closed over King Pirun's army. Only King Pirun and his friends and assistants in the mistakes escaped.

The first part of the story follows the Bible quite closely, at least in terms of the general train of events,[5] but the final part is an addition, probably connected to a Judaic legend of the haggadic kind.[6] This already told of the salvation of the Pharaoh from the waves and is to be found in medieval Judaic traditions. In our text Artabanus does not appear, nor is any particular sympathy expressed for the Egyptians, and not by any stretch of the imagination are they thought of as Mandaeans.

The name of Artabanus does appear, however, about a page away from the passage just quoted above. He is the last of a list of sovereigns, after a Chosroes and before the coming of a new dynasty of Persian kings. The text is unfortunately rather mangled, but the part that interests us goes as follows:

> . . . and Abas (?) Iasdis of Ṭib (?) who was called King Artabanus (Ardban), reigned 14 years. After him there were Persian kings. They reigned 382 years. [There follows a list of Sassanian kings].

In actual fact, in A.D. 224 Artabanus V, who had been unable to suppress a revolt of the satraps and had taken refuge in northern Mesopotamia, suffered a decisive defeat. With his death (in 226) the Arsacid dynasty ended and was succeeded by the Sassanians, who reigned for over four centuries, until the Arab invasion. So, there are traces of a historical memory in this passage, though the numbers are wholly unreliable. Though it is not expressly said that Artabanus is a Mandaean, it does seem that the redactor wishes to present him as coming from Ṭib, a city in southern Mesopotamia whose name occurs several times in Mandaean texts, and which is considered a city of Mandaeans. The text, not being intact, does not enable us to make statements with full authority, but we may deduce that the redactor believes he knows the true name of Artabanus (Abas [?] Iasdis) and his place of birth (in "Mandaean" territory). Does this mean that in the sec-

---

5. It is of no importance that Abraham is made to remain in Egypt or that the Israelites are led at once to Jerusalem, whose foundation had already been narrated before the history of the Exodus.

6. The additions to the sacred text, in Judaic traditions, are of either haggadic or halakic kinds. Halakah is the name given to those of a legalistic kind that introduce into the text greater detail concerning the observance of individual laws. Haggadah is an addition that serves to clarify moral aspects of the text. The latter usually introduces legendary narrative features, useful for ethical reflections and for preaching in the synagogue.

ond half of the seventh century Artabanus was already considered a Mandaean sovereign?

We now jump more than a thousand years of history and turn to the data collected by Lady Drower. In her volume on "The Mandaeans of Iraq and Iran," she published two versions of the story of the Exodus, one ("F") narrated by an Iranian Mandaean priest and the other ("G") of Hirmiz bar Anhar:

Story "F" (MII 261)

Six thousand years later [after the Flood], the planets, who are the children of Ruha and 'Ur, built the sacred House, that is 'Ur Shalam — Jerusalem.[7] . . . In Jerusalem Ruha gave a share of her kingdom to Musa (Moses) of the Beni Israiil. Musa was against the Mandai and had quarreled with them in Egypt. Ardwan (Ardban) Melka King of the Mandai had a vision and heard a voice coming out of the House of Life saying, "Rise, go out of this place because of your health and well-being." He rose and took the Mandai and they went out of Egypt and came to the sea which became shut off, leaving a road with mountains of sea on either side. Thus they went from Egypt.

But Firukh Melka (King Pharaoh), brother of Ardwan Melka, remained in Egypt and fought with the Jews there and was surrounded and discomfited by them and fled. Seeing the road through the sea still remaining, he went with his people upon it, but when they were in the midst of the sea, the mountains of water closed upon them and they were all drowned.

Ardwan Melka with his sixty thousand Mandai traveled and traveled till at last they came to the Tura d Maddai. The mountain opened to them, for it was high, big, and impassable, and they entered and went behind it. It closed again and Hiwal Ziwa said to Ardwan Melka, "Remain here with the Mandaeans, and the Twelve [signs of the Zodiac] and the Seven [planets] shall not rule over you." Musa pursued them, but when he reached the Tura d Maddai, he could go no further and so returned and went to 'Ur Shalam.

---

7. 'Uršalam is the Mandaean transliteration of the Arab name for Jerusalem, here identified with the temple.

Story "G" (MII 264ff.)

Para Melka (King Pharaoh) was obstinate, and was punished for his obstinacy. The people of Egypt were of our religion, and Musa (Moses), who was brought up with Para Melka, learnt something of our knowledge.[8] . . .

The people of Musa and the people of Para Melka quarreled, and Para Melka made it so difficult for the Jews that they wished to escape from the country and pass over the Sea of Suf. When they came to it, they went to the ferry which belonged to Para Melka, and said to the ferryman, "Ferry us over in your ship." The ferryman replied, "I have no orders to ferry you across," and, try as they might, they were unable to persuade him.

Now Musa had a staff, and knowledge of secret names. This staff had been given him by Ruha. . . . He struck the water and uttered names, and the water became solid like the ground, so that people could walk upon its surface. Then the Jews passed over the Sea, but Musa himself remained standing in the middle and did not remove from it, for, had he come out, the power of the names would have gone with him, and his people been drowned. When the last of them had passed over, he followed them.

Then Para Melka and his people came in pursuit of them. Para Melka asked the ferryman.[9] . . .

Then Para Melka (having the same knowledge) struck the water with his *marghna* (ritual staff) and it became land. . . . When Para Melka passed over, he did not stop in the middle, but crossed over before all his army. Then, as soon as he had reached the other side, the waters closed upon those who were following him, and they sank beneath the surface.

Oral traditions are slippery and treacherous for historical reconstruction, and there is the risk that we will follow in the unfortunate footsteps of the Pharaoh and come to the same end. We can, however, see that

---

8. Hirmiz bar Anhar always insists on the importance of the secret knowledge of the Mandaeans when he tells a story. The sentences that follow, which I do not quote here, on the necessity of nonviolence are also characteristic of Hirmiz's thinking.

9. The anecdote of the ferryman, who tells the Pharaoh what happened, seems to be an embroidering (by Hirmiz himself?) of the phrase in the *Ginza* according to which the Pharaoh "saw the sea without a boat, a raft or a ford."

something has happened to make the stories circulating today very different from those of long ago. Pharaoh, on his own (in G) or with his brother Artabanus (in F), has become the king of the Mandaeans. The fusion of the two kingly figures and their becoming Mandaean is certainly not a recent phenomenon, especially if one takes into consideration that there is a ritual meal and a special feast in memory of the Mandaean-Egyptians who perished in the Sea of Sup (or Suf, the "Sea of Reeds"). A custom of that kind is not invented in one day.

We shall now go back in time to see what can be discovered about the process that the text of the *Ginza* has undergone up to the time of the present-day legends. The first step takes us back to 1875, to Siouffi's account; then we shall find ourselves in 1854, examining Petermann's. Unlike Lady Drower's methodology, the two nineteenth-century witnesses do not set out various big extracts from the stories, having listened to various informants, but attempt a harmonized reconstruction of the ancient history of Mandaeanism on the basis of the evidence of just one person. The risk of presenting the ideas of just one Mandaean rather than Mandaeanism itself is all the greater. Yet in these reconstructions, especially Siouffi's, the periodical disappearance of Mandaeanism is much stressed, probably since both still feel the effects of 1831 and the related irregular reconstitution of the priesthood.[10] This is why the story Siouffi records underlines that with every catastrophe the priesthood was extinguished, and that in the aftermath of the last catastrophes it was reconstituted in an unorthodox or irregular way. It is easy to understand also that Petermann's informant, one of the two survivors of 1831, had no personal interest in pointing out this irregularity, whereas his nephew, by that time an apostate, could reveal to Siouffi those explanations he had heard from within his own family. In particular, concerning the irregularities of the reconstitution of the priesthood that had occurred in the cases prior to 1831, it is not the account of past events but a "normalization" of the present. It aims to demonstrate that in 1831 nothing new happened. The most recent priesthood, although irregularly constituted, was as permissible as the previous ones.

10. See above, p. 116.

HISTORY

Siouffi

The previous events. The Mandaeans are extinct. Mara d-Rabuta, through Manda d-Hiia and a miraculous water, gets Elisabeth pregnant. John will be the "supreme head" of all the Jews, who in effect convert en masse, except for their "head," Eleazar and his followers. John dies and leaves 366 "disciples, all *ganzibria* or *tarmidia*." Into their temple enters Mariia, a princess and daughter of Eleazar, and converts. A massacre follows. Only Mariia and around thirty others survive. Anuš 'Utra, appearing in the guise of a sparrow hawk, drowns the Jews. The few Mandaean survivors, Jerusalem being demolished, are taken to "another place" by Anuš 'Utra.

The history. "Before leaving the Ṣubba, Anuš 'Utra chose from among them two brothers, whom he invested with sovereign powers. . . . The elder was called king Pharaoh (Parak) and the younger king Artabanus (Ardauan). . . . It then fell out that after Anuš 'Utra went away, the Ṣubba and the Jews multiplied. . . . At that time Moses appeared, the Jews' prophet, who decided to take revenge for the Jews Anuš 'Utra had killed. Also king Pharaoh wished to take his revenge on the Jews for the Ṣubba that Eleazar had had murdered; but then Abatur sent him a letter ordering him not to make war on Moses and to leave the country with his people and settle elsewhere. The king of the Ṣubba took not the slightest notice of this celestial command and declared war on the Jews."

There follows a duel between Moses and Pharaoh. Moses, defeated, throws himself into the sea with all his people, and the sea opens up before him.

"[Moses] stopped in the middle of the sea, that had divided into two for him, to allow his whole army to pass in front of him and go out last. King Pharaoh had followed him with his army, at the head of which he was marching with his brother.[11] At the very instant Moses set foot on land, the waves closed over the army of king Pharaoh and everyone drowned, with the exception of Pharaoh himself, his brother and about thirty Ṣubba, men and women, who had set foot on dry land almost at the same instant as Moses."

Now Moses pursued the survivors, who took refuge in Šuštar, "where

---

11. Who reappears here, having previously been absent from the story of the war.

136

the two brother kings left their unfortunate companions in misadventure, to continue their journey as far as Mšunia Kušta." Here Pharaoh dies, and his soul, which Abatur upbraids, is sent for punishment to a *maṭarta.*

The later events. "The Ṣubba remaining at Šuštar were without priests and hence could not marry. To get round this drawback, they chose, among the most virtuous, certain ones who carried out among themselves the functions of the *tarmidia,* without being invested with the legitimate and regular priesthood, that they no longer possessed."[12] The Mandaeans multiply, but fall into great ignorance, so that Adam Abu l-Faraǧ is sent to them.

Petermann

The first false prophet, a servant of Adonai, the sun, was Abraham; the second, Moses. At the time of the latter, the Egyptians were in possession of the true religion and [also] Pharaoh, their king and high priest. . . . He persecuted Moses and the Jews, against the divine will and therefore his brother Artabanus with 60,000 Egyptians separated himself from him. All these, after their deaths, were taken to Mšunia Kušta. But not even Pharaoh died in the Red Sea, but managed to get out of it nude, with his followers. And they also were taken to Mšunia Kušta. With them all the Mandaeans had disappeared off the face of the earth. . . .

The third false prophet for them is the Messiah, that they call Enbu Meschicha. . . . 42 years before him appeared Jahja, or Jehana . . ., under the government of king Pontius Pilate. . . .

Despite the different general organization of their material, Petermann and Siouffi provide us with proof that the legend of Artabanus and that of the Pharaoh merged and were consolidated in Mandaean traditions, at least from the whole of the nineteenth century to our day. This enables us to take a further step backwards, to 1678, 1088 of the Hegira, the year of the final redaction, according to the colophons, of a scroll entitled *Haran Gauaita,* meaning "Inner Harran." The text, of which Lady Drower

12. The problem deeply felt in 1831 was that the new priests were laymen.

procured two copies, both nineteenth century, has come down to us with the beginning section missing and full of gaps and corruptions. Its present beginning speaks of Artabanus, and I believe it can quite easily be integrated with the data of the stories dealt with so far. These are the first lines of the *Haran Gauaita,* with its abrupt start:

> And Haran Gauaita welcomed him and that city in which there were Naṣurai, since there was no road for the king of the Jews. Over them was king Ardban. And 60,000 Naṣurai abandoned the sign of the Seven and entered into Ṭura d-Midai, the place where no tribe had power over us. And they built *bimandia* and stayed in the voice of the Life and in the power of the Most High king of light, until they reached their end.[13]

The *Haran Gauaita,* the true title of which should be "*Diuan*[14] of the Great Revelation," was rebaptized Haran Gauaita by the Mandaeans because the present text actually begins with these two words.[15] However, at least in those parts that now form the beginning, the expression *haran gauaita* is clearly quite important, since it wishes to represent the geographical location of Ṭura d-Madai. This can be seen from phrases like: "Anuš 'Utra went to Ṭura d-Madai, that is called Haran Gauaita." Yet where is this "Interior Harran," and why did a literary phenomenon of this kind occur?

The geographical connection with the city of Harran is clear and uncontroversial. Nevertheless, it has to be admitted that the term "Harran" indicates the region as well as the city, as happens for instance with "Babylonia." It thus makes sense to speak of an "inner" or "interior" part of the Harran region. The problems arise when a precise identification is

---

13. There follows the story of Jesus and then that of John, sent by the Life to earth to fight against the success of the Messiah of the Christians.

14. Literally "scroll"; hence "explanation."

15. Among other things, this shows that the Mandaeans themselves know the text only in its actual state, with an entirely random beginning. There are other manuscripts, unpublished, in the titles of which the word *haran* appears, positioned first, and which present themselves as original and "complete" versions of the *Haran Gauaita.* However, the very fact that the first word of their titles is *haran,* which is the first word of the commonly known text, shows that the supposedly "complete" versions are later reworkings and enlargements of a text which already began with the word *haran.* But this is the *Haran Gauaita* we know, with its mutilated beginning.

required, especially if one considers that since it is identical to Ṭura d-Madai, it should be mountainous. The Turkish village that corresponds to the Harran of antiquity is to be found in an area that is now desert, in a fairly flat or at the most what may be called rolling countryside. The river changed its course many centuries ago, leaving to a reddish dust the task of invading the streets, of finding its way into the chinks and crannies in the walls, and of covering the seven hills on which the seven temples once rose. The mountains are quite some way away. Even the mountains of the Media to which Ṭura d-Madai refers are some hundreds of kilometers away, toward the northeast. These are difficulties to us, however, only through the cultural parameters of our twenty-first-century Western humanity, or to Lady Drower, who would frequently ask where Ṭura d-Madai was to be found, and once received this for a reply: "It's to the north, towards Damascus and Jerusalem." It is hence only by ignoring the nature of the documents we are examining that we can persevere in the attempt to find exact correspondences, in either the history or the geography. We just have to accept what is told us, in this case that Ṭura d-Madai coincides with the territory of Harran.

We can then realize just what "that city where there were naṣurai" may mean. It is the same Harran, inhabited by those mysterious Sabaeans, with which our Mandaeans (Ṣubba) were identified, by Arab historians as well as by European scholars, for many centuries, precisely in those years in which we have assumed the *Haran Gauaita* was redacted.[16] This identification is what the book propagates. All the crucial moments of Mandaean history linked with Ṭura d-Madai are now connected with Harran. This, undoubtedly, was one of the reasons why the redactors brought out the book in the first place. Finally, the date this occurred would be a time when such a cultural operation was possible. From one perspective, it ought to have been quite close to a time in which the Harran Sabaeans were considered to be a politically significant reality; from another, this reality had to be by that time in the past, so that it was possible for the Mandaeans to appropriate it without fear of contradiction. If this is true,

---

16. The idea that the ancient Sabaeans of Harran were their biological ancestors is today accepted as historical fact among Mandaeans. Another idea I mention for its curiosity value — to be deduced from Lady Drower's reports and from contemporary narration — is that the Mandaeans are the heirs of the ancient Babylonians (as archaeological discoveries would apparently demonstrate), who fled to the marshes of the south after being thrown out by the Assyrians or the Persians.

the more likely era would seem to be the final phase of the Caliphate of the Abbasids, during whose golden age important people from Harran shone as philosophers, ministers, and dignitaries at the court in Baghdad. Since those Sabaeans were tolerated and indeed welcomed at court, it is reasonable to suppose that the Ṣubba, constantly seeking a status acceptable to the Islamic powers that be, and always playing on homophony, were persuaded that they had at least ancestors in common with those. I believe the actual appropriation took place afterward, when the Sabaeans, like Pharaoh and Artabanus, were also just a memory.

Artabanus, however, is placed here at the head of the Sabaeans-Mandaeans. While in the legends closest to us we have seen him lead the sixty thousand Mandaeans in flight from Moses, here he seems to take up those that, as the text says, "abandoned the sign of the Seven," that is, the power of the planets and hence the Judaic threat. If this interpretation is correct, only Pharaoh is missing from the roll call. I believe that when our text, after the initial mutilation, starts off with "And Haran Gauaita welcomed him," it is speaking of Pharaoh, whose name has gone missing in the gap at the beginning. Thus *Haran Gauaita* becomes a link in the chain of development of the legend of Pharaoh and Artabanus and loses a great deal of the air of mystery that has surrounded it. The text continues, indeed follows, a familiar pattern: a peaceful life of independence and the periodic extinction of Mandaeanism. We can say nothing about what went before. Since the present text leads the reader to the end of the world, it may be supposed that the "Explanation of the Great Revelation," as is the case with other texts of a "historical" character,[17] began with the creation, or else the Flood. The place where the scroll was torn apart would have been toward the end of the story of the Exodus.

Artabanus and Pharaoh do not yet appear to be brothers, but they are both leaders or heads of the Mandaeans, one of the Egyptian variety and the other of the Sabaeans-Mandaeans. The reasons why they were transformed into Mandaeans, as far as we can see, are not the same. Pharaoh is the king of the enemies of the Jews and so appears in the guise of a natural ally, a protagonist fated to be attractive to the Mandaeans. He humiliates the Jews, and this is inevitably deeply satisfying to the Mandaeans, whose vitriolic hatred of the Jews is evident at every level of their litera-

---

17. See, e.g., the Book XVIII of the *Right Ginza*, excerpts from which follow on pp. 200-201.

ture. It is not easy to tell whether this is inherited from Christian Gnosticism, is the consequence of the obstacles to coexistence that minorities often experience, or is a mixture of the two. In addition, Pharaoh, with the catastrophe of the Red Sea, becomes a victim of Judaism; and therefore in this too he is identified with the idea the Mandaeans have (or had) of themselves, as a minority persecuted by the Jews. A slight modification of the biblical tradition is therefore enough to create a way out for Pharaoh and allow him to become the king of the Mandaeans.[18] For Artabanus, a much closer and real figure than Pharaoh, the reasons are of a more historical nature. They lie in the different religious policies of the last of the Arsacids and the Sassanians. The latter, by adopting Zoroastrianism as the state religion, forced its observance on everyone and persecuted all dissidence. We have the stele of a certain Kirdir,[19] who at the end of the third century boasted of having persecuted Jews, Christians, Manichaeans, and Naṣurai, the latter perhaps being Mandaeans. It is natural to look back with longing on the past when times are bad, and see it through rose-tinted spectacles. Under the heel of the Sassanians, the memory of the Arsacids reemerged, especially the figure of the last sovereign, Artabanus V, defeated by the Sassanians, now enemies and persecutors of the Mandaeans. He had been a sovereign defeated and in flight, just like the Artabanus of the Mandaean legends (who unlike Moses did not even persecute the Jews), and like the Mandaeans themselves, at least in their own

18. In a story in neo-Mandaean, recently published by Macuch, "King Pharaoh" *(farruch malka)* is the name of the *'utra* who was in the guise of the white falcon and was sent by Hibil Ziua to destroy the persecuting Jews. Other legends, related to me orally, are of clear Arab origin and show the Pharaoh in evil guise: he wanted to marry the sister of John the Baptist and was responsible for the killing of the latter (usually denied). The Mandaean-Egyptians who were fleeing from the Pharaoh (who, however, was a Mandaean since he was praying on the banks of the Nile) and who drowned in the sea were the good ones. Other stories reduce the number of survivors. There were only seven of them, or maybe twelve. The ancient root of the positive figure of the Pharaoh and of the drowned Egyptians may be found in a Gnostic reading in the Old Testament that stands the story of salvation on its head. According to this vision, the biblical evil ones are in fact the spiritual ones who opposed the demiurge Jahvé (from Nimrod to the Sodomites to the victims of the Flood), offering through their physical death a testimony to the truth, in contrast to the arrogance of the demiurge. However, the Gnostic speculation at that stage is far away from the content of known Mandaean texts.

19. Or Kartir. He was a leader of the Zoroastrian priests and a high-level dignitary of the imperial court. In the last analysis, the persecution and death of Mani are due to him.

legends. Since the Arsacids were not remembered by the Mandaeans as sovereign persecutors, here too a mechanism of identification was triggered off, so that the Mandaeans appropriated to themselves the last sovereign under whom they remembered being able to live and let live. His identity is projected further into the past; his dynasty becomes Mandaean; and his name, considered that of an illustrious ancestor, appears in what is perhaps the best-known of Mandaean prayers, that is, "Our First Fathers." In a colophon of the "Book of the Rivers," he is even made into the founding father of a modern priestly family, whose most ancient hero is called "the son of the sons of king Artabanus." In the *Haran Gauaita*, however, there remains the memory of the crisis the Sassanians brought with them:

> and then the kingdom from Baghdad was taken away from the sons of the sons of king Artabanus. And the Hardbaiia[20] took over the kingdom. 170 *drapšia* and *bimandia* remained in Baghdad.[21] And then the king of the Hardbaiia reigned 360 years,[22] and then the son of the Arab butcher (or: the son of the butcher, the Arab) took power, and took a people for himself and practiced circumcision.

Finally, we should not be too astonished that Artabanus and Pharaoh became brothers. Apart from the realization of the actual kinship between sovereigns, common in the ancient world, the Mandaean mythopoeic imagination must have thought it natural that two "kings of Mandaeans," already brothers in the faith and, according to the tradition in *Haran Gauaita*, active at the same time, were also actually brothers. Beyond this, it is difficult to see.

Along the long curve we traced on the map at the start of this chapter, following the Mandaean legends, at the opposite end to Egypt we find

---

20. The term, whose various written forms are a little different, indicates the "Persians." It occurs again quite close to this passage, when the text says: "He (Muhammad) governed all this and dominated the lord of the mountain of the Persians, who are called Hardabaiia, and took away their kingdom."

21. Previously, the *Haran Gauaita* says that the Mandaeans had reached the number of four hundred places of worship in Baghdad. With the arrival of the Arabs, these were further reduced to 60. The numbers are symbolic, but they do give an idea of the Mandaeans' awareness of the deterioration that had come about.

22. The 382 years of RG 18 have become 360, a number even further away from reality but one with greater symbolic value (a year of years?).

Ceylon. Since it was a distant country, absent from their immediate experience and from Mandaean literature, Lady Drower found its unexpected mention in some of the replies to her questions astonishing, and she did not conceal her amazement. This is what she reports of the words of a *tarmida* of Iranian origin:

> The story of our nation is this. Two hundred and fifty years ago the Ṣubba, who are the true children of Adam Paghra and Hawa Kasia,[23] lived in Serandib (Ceylon). They were all cut off by plague except one pair, whose names were Ram and Rud. . . . But after 150,000 years, by the command of Hiwel (Hibil) Ziwa, the whole earth broke into flames and only two escaped.

The text, continuing with a version of the history of the four ages of the world, can only be understood when the reader realizes that it is widely recognized throughout the Eastern and Islamic world that Adam and Eve lived in Ceylon, the best of all possible worlds after being thrown out of Paradise. Since the Mandaeans were the only true descendants of Adam, it must appear natural to place themselves in the same land as their progenitors. What is really surprising, even among the sovereign incongruities of the data in the Mandaean texts, is the mention of those 250 years. In the context of a discourse on Adam and Eve, that number would seem to be rather small. In actual fact, the Iranian *tarmida* does not tell Lady Drower that Adam and Eve were still in Ceylon 250 years before; he says that the Mandaeans were there, and he justifies his claim with the explanation of the (ancient) story of Adam and Eve. What remains to be explained is the idea that 250 years previously the Mandaeans were in Ceylon. As with all the numbers in Mandaean chronography, this too should not be taken literally; here we are probably dealing with the memory of the exodus to Ceylon attempted by the Mandaeans in the seventeenth century, under Christian sponsorship. That Lady Drower's *tarmida* is around thirty years short in his calculation is rather insignificant. His words are perhaps the only evidence that something remained in Mandaean thinking of the attempt of the Mandaeans and Carmelites. I believe that we have here a remnant of what must have been the official theological justification of the

---

23. The narrator is referring to a legend according to which the Mandaeans descend from the earthly Adam and from the Eve of Mšunia Kušṭa.

Mandaean clergy regarding the abandonment of Mesopotamia and the exodus to Ceylon. Since the human soul is so profoundly conservative, there is no better way to introduce something new than to present it as a return to ancient custom and tradition. Thus, thanks to the Adam legend, Ceylon was presented to the Mandaean faithful as the lost ancient fatherland to which it was then possible to return. This particular detail also shows how the Mandaeans and the Catholic authorities of the seventeenth century were following very different ideals. Among the Mandaeans there is no trace of an idea of conversion to Christianity, or reference to a desire to live under Christian monarchs. The exodus to Ceylon is felt to be and understood to be a return to their own Mandaean roots. Thus, the pessimists among the Carmelites had been right, and from a historical perspective Ignatius's idealistic position was mistaken, and destined to fail.

JERUSALEM, JOHN THE BAPTIST, AND THE OTHERS

In Mandaean literary and oral traditions it is widely reported that a massacre of Mandaeans took place in Jerusalem, and that the city was consequently destroyed in punishment. According to numerous contemporary Mandaeans, the idea of a flight of survivors from Palestine to Mesopotamia is linked to this idea. Mandaean traditions, in other words, seem to express a belief in a Palestinian origin of Mandaeanism. In the opinion of some scholars, this belief is the memory, however distorted, of events that actually happened before A.D. 70, the year of the destruction of Jerusalem by the Romans, a destruction to which the Mandaean legends possibly refer. Mandaeanism would thus have been born in Palestine before then, at the same time as Christianity. This would provide an additional, historical explanation of the Mandaean love for John the Baptist: Who else are the Palestinian Mandaeans, persecuted by the Jews for religious reasons and refugees in Mesopotamia, if not the surviving disciples of John the Baptist? In this way, all the old questions, argued over and debated for centuries, leap back into the limelight rejuvenated, even where they seemed to have been discarded by Western criticism in the last few decades.

The idea that in the past there had been some relationship between Mandaeanism and Judaism can be found in three different contexts in Mandaean writings. The first records a revelation of the Mandaean message in Jerusalem, the work of revealers well known to the Mandaeans. The second concerns the adventures of a Mandaean heroine in Jerusalem, a certain Miriai. The third relates John the Baptist's activities in Jerusalem. We shall begin with the first: two parallel phrases contained in the *Right Ginza*,[24] where there are traces of a revelatory activity of Manda d-Hiia.

> A cry resounded throughout the earth, and caused the splendor of every city to be thrown down; Manda d-Hiia showed himself in Judaea, a Vine appeared in Jerusalem. . . .
>
> A cry resounded throughout the earth, and caused the splendor of every city to be thrown down; Manda d-Hiia showed himself to all the sons of men and freed them from the darkness leading them into the light, from obscurity to the light of Life.

In this passage, not bound to any specific chronological scheme, Jerusalem and Judaea appear to be synonyms of the creation in its dark and evil aspects rather than indications of any precise geographical reality. Salvation is brought to "all the sons of men"; it is not explicitly stated that it is some Jews who are converted. As the text proceeds, the Mandaeans are certainly threatened by "wolves" and "lions," who could lead the Mandaeans to "vacillate," or "limp," but this refers to risks of apostasy, not to ancient persecutions.

In the "Book of John" there is a more interesting and precisely indicative passage.[25] The "stranger," the "alien man" there, that is, the revealer, who is identified in the text sometimes as Manda d-Hiia and sometimes as Hibil Ziua, comes down to Jerusalem, which takes on the clear features of cosmic negativity: it is "the stronghold that Adunai built," and the stranger is not very keen on going there. Adunai "brought to it falsehood in plenty, and it meant persecution against my *tarmidia.*" There is mention of a persecution here, but it is entirely marginal in the overall economy of the passage and generic in its formulation. The scene in Jerusalem is richer in detail:

> When I reached the city of Jerusalem, Adunai opened his mouth and spoke to me from the heavens . . . : "Where are you going, O alien man, against whose will this stronghold was built? This stronghold . . . in which you are now trying to obtain your prey." Then I answered Adunai . . . : "[In

24. GR 5.2 (Pet. 177-79; Lid. 181-82).
25. JB 54 (Lid. 191-95).

it I have] my brothers Iaqip and Bnia Amin, both golden sons; I have [in it] Miriai, the perfect one, who is generations and worlds dear to me."[26]

In the eyes of Adunai, the stranger had come to "obtain his prey," that is, to convert. God's envoy confirms the fears of Adunai by showing he actually had at least three followers with Hebrew names — Miriai (Mary), Iaqip (Jacob), and Bnia Amin (Benjamin, or "Sons of Amin"), of whom nothing else is said afterward. Adunai alludes also to a prior event that is not narrated; the city had been allegedly constructed against the will of the stranger. All this shows that the passage is reworking the material of a much more highly developed legend, known to us through other texts, in which the divine hero, however, is neither Manda d-Hiia nor Hibil Ziua, but Anuš 'Utra. Built around this character and his descent into Jerusalem is a kind of saga about which we can uncover various features or compositional levels.

First, there is a descent of Anuš 'Utra to combat Jesus' activities there. An exposition of this legend is known to us in two versions (that derive from a more ancient text) contained in the first two treatises of the *Right Ginza*.[27] In both it is explicitly denied that the revealer is Hibil Ziua, and it is emphasized that Anuš is being referred to.

(a) Hibil Ziua did not show himself at that time. Rather, Anuš 'Utra came and journeyed to Jerusalem. . . . He comes and goes in the days of Palṭus (Pilate). . . . He heals the sick, gives the blind their sight, purifies the lepers, makes the paralyzed walk, . . . makes the deaf and dumb talk and gives life to the dead. He makes converts among the Jews. . . . He converts the Jews to the name of the most high king of light. And three hundred and sixty prophets go out of (or else "derive from," "come out of," "separate themselves from") the place Jerusalem. They witness the name of the Lord of greatness (Mara d-Rabuta). Then Anuš 'Utra rises up on high and withdraws to Mšunia Kušṭa. All the 'utria hide themselves from the eyes of the sons of men. Then the place Jerusalem is destroyed, the Jews go into exile, and are dispersed into every city.

---

26. The text continues with Ruha, Adunai, and the Seven, who put together a "book of crime and deception" and deliver it to Miša bar Amra (Moses son of Amram) after having made him fast for forty days on Mount Sinai.

27. GR 1.200-202 and GR 2.1.133, 136-37. For the text see also below, pp. 243-44.

(b) I (Hibil Ziua) do not show myself at this time to the sons of men. Rather, Anuš 'Utra comes . . . in the years of Piliaṭus . . . [the passage continues as above]. He separates (or: "makes leave" or "brings out") from them (the Jews) whoever is zealous and firm in the faith in the One, the Lord of all the Worlds. Then, while he shows the Truth to his friends, he destroys the city Jerusalem and we rise up to the worlds of light and to the dwelling places of Splendor, and we do not show ourselves any longer to the world, until the time comes and the measure of the world is full.

According to this level of the Mandaean legend,[28] after John and after Jesus Anuš also arrived in Jerusalem and carried out all the miracles that the Christians relate about their Messiah. His preaching, like that of Jesus, leads to a conversion of Jews. Having said this, the two versions of the legend diverge. According to (a), there are 360 "prophets" that separate themselves from Jerusalem. The text does not say where they go, and the separation can be understood in a spiritual sense of separation from the rest of the Jews. These 360, afterward, offer a "testimony." If we were in an ancient Gnostic text, this "testimony" or "witness" would be one of martyrdom and would therefore refer to their death. Here the context does not help us, and it would seem to imply a further preaching by these "prophets." So, the text may imply that the "prophets" stay in Jerusalem, separated spiritually from the other Jews, and are killed there, or else that they go somewhere else (not specified) to preach the new message. After this, however, all the entities of light leave the earth, Jerusalem is destroyed (the text does not say by whom or why), and the Jews go into exile. This last detail refers to the destruction of Nebuchadnezzar (586 B.C.). I would suggest that we are dealing here with the Mandaean outcome of a well-known Judaic, Christian, and Islamic legend, of ancient Old Testament origin. According to this, Jerusalem was destroyed by God (through human agency) because it was guilty of the death of one or more prophets. Depending on the texts, the "prophet" is Zechariah,[29] John the Baptist, or Jesus, and the destruction is that of Nebuchadnezzar, Titus, or Chosroes (A.D. 614), or else the text presents the

28. Which should be rather ancient since two versions exist in texts redacted at the beginning of the Islamic epoch.

29. It is almost never clear which Zechariah it is; often, in Christian and Islamic traditions, he is the father of John the Baptist.

characteristics of all three together. The Mandaean legend of course cannot have John the Baptist murdered, and, in fact, as we shall see, he is made to die a natural and exemplary death; there is all the less reason for having Anuš 'Utra murdered since he is not in possession of a physical body but has an appearance made up of a "cloak of clouds of water," as is suitable for the savior of a Baptist group. At this point the 360 "prophets" appear who are not to be found elsewhere, as "prophets," either in the writings or the oral traditions. The fact that they are called "prophets" indicates their legend's closeness to its model, in which it was necessary that a prophet of one's own religion (Judaic, Christian, or Islamic) die in Jerusalem. The fact that they are 360 in number is explained quite easily, considering the Mandaean love for the number six and its multiples, used to define all that is Mandaean, and also taking into account that 360 are the days of the twelve months (of thirty days each) of the Mandaean calendar. They are the exact reflection of the Twelve, disciples of Christ and Signs of the Zodiac. Just as Anuš 'Utra arrived on the scene to stop Jesus' work, likewise the 360 prophets, with their "testimony," hold back the influence of the Twelve. If this is true, it is not hard to see why the text, as we have just noted, is so ambiguous about the fate of the 360. The Mandaean legend, deriving from the Judaic, Christian, and perhaps Islamic complex of sources on the destruction of Jerusalem, required the death of prophets, whereas its use in our context requires them to have survived and been active.

Passage (b) shows another stage in the transformation of the legend. The 360 prophets have disappeared. Anuš 'Utra separates "whoever is zealous and firm in the faith," and, at the same time as "he shows the truth (Kušṭa) to his friends," he takes upon himself the responsibility of destroying Jerusalem, dissolving the doubts of passage (a). The idea of a migration of Mandaeans from Jerusalem to Mesopotamia is lacking, however. The only ones to move, from the earth to the heavens, are the 'utria, to which the "we" of Anuš 'Utra in passage (b) corresponds. Miriai, Iaqip, and Bnia Amin are not mentioned, and there are no grounds for seeing in them the "friends" of passage (b). In the latter, the "testimony" has disappeared, and even the memory of a persecution has vanished.[30] This is very much in ev-

30. A group of passages on the saga of Anuš 'Utra in Jerusalem visualizes an actual confrontation between the Mandaean revealer and Jesus Christ, as in JB 76 (see text at pp. 246-47). In others, it is even Anuš 'Utra who unmasks Jesus' impostures in the eyes of the Jews, who thus kill him. The glory that the Jews attribute to themselves in the *Toledot Iešu* is showered by the Mandaeans on their own savior.

idence in a passage in the *Right Ginza*, however, in which the "saga" appears at a mature and well-developed stage.[31] There is the description of the foundation of Jerusalem, against the will of Anuš 'Utra, who tries to stop it. The city of the Jews is the most impure entity of the entire creation: it is enough to recall that it was created with the seed that the seven planets obtained, each and every one, by lying with Ruha, their mother. Into it, however, descends Anuš 'Utra, who relates thus:

> I assumed a bodily form and went to Jerusalem. I spoke with my voice and preached and became a doctor for Miriai. . . . I guided Miriai down and baptized her in the Jordan and marked her with a pure mark. From Miriai, the perfect one, came Iaqip and Bnia Amin. From Iaqip and Bnia Amin came 365 *tarmidia*. 365 *tarmidia* came out of the Place Jerusalem. The Jews became inflamed with anger and killed my *tarmidia,* who pronounced the name of Life. When I saw them I was filled with anger and rage towards them.

Thus Anuš obtains from his father, the Great Life, a letter authorizing him to proceed against the Jews. Having assumed the appearance of a "white hawk" and armed with a "bludgeon of light," he knocks over Ruha and drops down on Jerusalem, dismantling it "column after column" and massacring the Jews:

> I destroyed the place Jerusalem, where the blood of my *tarmidia* was poured out; I killed the Jews, who were a persecution of the race of Life, and . . . all the evil beasts (the religions derived from Judaism), . . . against which there was anger.

We have therefore reached a text that, like the one on the stranger at Jerusalem, knows of a level of the legend that includes the presence of Miriai, Iaqip, and Bnia Amin and in which the city is constructed against the will of the Mandaean God. Here, however, there is a good deal more. Though the chronological connection with Pilate and Jesus has disappeared, as well as the 360 prophets (who will not be met with elsewhere), "365 *tarmidia*" make their appearance, and it is difficult to know whether to translate them as "disciples" (of Anuš 'Utra) or "priests" since the text

31. GR 15.11. See the text at pp. 217-20.

perhaps means both. Like the 360 prophets, these too "come out" and "separate themselves off," but they do stay "in the place Jerusalem," where indeed they are murdered; the separation is clearly of a spiritual rather than geographical kind. Their number, which according to the other evidence we have will rest unchanged, demonstrates that the option of the solar year symbolism, introducing the five extra days not included in the months, has been maintained. The entire solar year is covered by the *tarmidia* of Anuš 'Utra. It is less clear, though, for what this "cover" is needed, since the 365 go nowhere and do nothing except get killed. Still less clear is how the passage, after having spoken of their murder, can end like this: "And safety was given to my *tarmidia* who had suffered persecution in Jerusalem; and I destroyed the house of those who were without goodness." I imagine that either the redactor of the passage or someone who copied it out after him had been unable to allow the text to end without a word of hope for the Mandaeanism of the present, persecuted in a Jerusalem that once again assumed cosmic features. Not even the person who wrote this last phrase, however, thought of a flight or an exodus of Mandaeans out of Jerusalem.

We have thus reached the end of the first batch of legends on the Mandaean presence in Jerusalem. It is linked to the descent of a revealer, usually Anuš 'Utra, but sometimes another. In the texts that appear to be older, this descent serves to combat the work of Jesus, whereas in other texts it has an anti-Judaic or anti-cosmic function. In the passages we have examined, Manda d-Hiia does not make disciples; the stranger seems to find three (Miriai, Iaqip, and Bnia Amin); Anuš 'Utra has to deal either with 360 prophets or with the three above-named and 365 *tarmidia*. The prophets and *tarmidia* are either murdered in Jerusalem or find safety, but at any rate they go nowhere, their "separation" being of a spiritual kind. The only movement, indicated in the two parallel texts of the *Right Ginza*, is of the *'utria*, who abandon creation, until the end of time, to journey to the worlds of light.

We now turn to Miriai, Iaqip, and Bnia Amin. On Miriai there is a fair amount of information in two chapters of the "Book of John,"[32] whose content can be summed up as follows: Miriai is said to be the "daughter of

32. See the texts at pp. 220-23. For the derivation of the character of Miriai from Christian legends, see J. Jacobsen Buckley, "The Mandaean Appropriation of Jesus' Mother, Miriai," *Novum Testamentum* 35.2 (1993): 181-96.

the king of Babylon," or "daughter of the powerful kings of Jerusalem," or again "daughter of all the *kahnia* (Jewish priests)." It can be deduced from this that Jerusalem is Babylon[33] and that the Jewish priests (like the Mandaeans) are also kings. The young girl, just like and perhaps even more so than the adolescent Mary of Christian legends, is the true mistress of the temple of Jerusalem, of which she has the keys. Disobeying the command of her parents,[34] who would like her to remain shut up in her home, she enters the temple of the Mandaeans (that hence exists at Jerusalem-Baghdad) by mistake and is converted. An altercation with her father, who discovers the conversion, closes the first of the two chapters. The second is in part taken up with a reflection on Miriai as symbol of Mandaeanism as a whole. She is the Mandaean Vine that grows at the mouth of the Euphrates, which is the background for the narrative part of the chapter. The Jews wish to kill the stranger with whom Miriai now lives by the river and expose the girl to public shame, but the stranger is the Lord that she loves chastely. At the end of quite a lively dialogue between Miriai and her mother, in the presence of the Judaic authorities gathered together threateningly by the river, from the heavens drops a "pure hawk." This is an ʿutra whose task is to take revenge for Miriai:

> He flew over the Jews, he swooped down over them with his wings and shackling them together threw them down to the bottom of the waters, under the stinking mud. He sank them under the burning [water], which is within the muddy water. He sank their boats down to the bottom of the burning water. He destroyed the temple and set fire to Jerusalem.

After this spectacular scene of destruction and before the concluding dialogue between the ʿutra and Miriai (containing speculations on adherence to the Voice and on ascending to the world of light), we find the most amazing phrase of the entire text: "[the hawk] had everything collapse on top of them and killed the *tarmidia* in Jerusalem." The *tarmidia* are suddenly back on the scene once again, this time without any number attached to them, in order to be murdered not by the Jews but by the emis-

33. We should not be too surprised; apart from the symbolic value (already present in both Testaments) of the identification of a city with Babylon or Jerusalem, there are other Mandaean texts that place Jerusalem on the Euphrates (see below, p. 156).
34. Their names do not appear in the text. According to Siouffi's informant, the father of Miriai was the high priest Eleazar.

sary of the Mandaean divinity himself, however extraordinary this may seem. Furthermore, these *tarmidia* arrive quite out of the blue, since at the start Miriai does go into a Mandaean temple, where she finds "brothers" and "sisters," but then seems to be alone, to be converted by the stranger on the banks of the Euphrates. Clearly, so strong was the idea that the *tarmidia* have been murdered that the redactor of the chapters on Miriai of the "Book of John" has neither eliminated it nor tried to tone it down in some way (as happened in the passage from the *Ginza*); instead, the redactor attributed it to the will of the God of the Mandaeans, almost as if he did not want to show the Jews to be strong enough to destroy the *tarmidia* themselves.[35]

Otherwise, with regard to the material surveyed already there are both similarities and differences. The exaltation of Miriai has meant the disappearance of Iaqip and Bnia Amin. In one part of the text she is the disciple of the stranger, as she was of Anuš 'Utra in the *Ginza;* she does not, however, seem to have disciples of her own. In another part of the text, the Mandaeans exist prior to her conversion. The scene takes place partly in Jerusalem and partly by the Euphrates, but there is no actual shift from Palestine to Mesopotamia on the part of Miriai or other Mandaeans: it is Jerusalem that is identified with Babylon and placed in the east. The legend of Miriai, taken as a whole, is another sign of the human capacity for recycling hagiographic material not just within one particular religion but from one religion to another. The Mary of the Christians, girl-child and adolescent, who is raised in the temple (Miriai says: "The Jews have generated me; the *kahnia* have brought me up") and then put on trial when she is discovered to be pregnant, is the ancient model of the Mary of the Mandaeans. Mandaean traditions add two features to the general structure of the Christian legend (in addition to the ample modification of particulars): the presence of the Mandaeans and the massacre of the *tarmidia*. This means that when the legend of Miriai was formed, the idea of a Jerusalem persecution of the Mandaeans had already been developed.

We can therefore assume that we are here faced with two originally separate legendary traditions. According to the one, a celestial revealer comes down to Jerusalem and there makes disciples, who are persecuted;

---

35. Alternatively, these *tarmidia* should be interpreted as the Jewish priests, usually called *kahnia.*

as a punishment for this Jerusalem is destroyed. According to the other, Miriai is converted at Jerusalem; she is persecuted, and as punishment Jerusalem is destroyed. The two traditions are therefore closely interrelated. Miriai is a disciple or else makes disciples, and all are persecuted together; a constant is the final punishment of Jerusalem. This complex of legends that in part reutilizes hagiographic material originating in other religions (the killing of prophets in Jerusalem; an adolescent Mary) seems to be barely connected to actual historical events since Jerusalem itself (the only geographical reference point that is not in Mesopotamia) tends to take on the form of a symbol, sometimes of the evil of the created world, sometimes of the place where power actually resides and in which the Judaic authorities are actually considered princes at court, in the most likely epoch of the written redaction of these stories known to us: the Baghdad of the Caliphs.

Miriai, alone or with Iaqip and Bnia Amin, appears again in two of the chapters devoted to John the Baptist in the "Book of John." Her presence as an interlocutor of John in redactional passages shows that the redactor, active at the beginning of the Arab epoch, knows of a legend that places Miriai and the other two in Jerusalem. Since his hero also lives in Jerusalem, he must have believed it necessary to have the various characters meet one another. Miriai, however, plays only a walk-on part here. In one passage she is listening to John when he speaks about himself and his own death, but her presence is entirely of an occasional nature. She is named at the start of the dialogue beside Elizabeth (Mary and Elizabeth, as in the Christian stories), but she disappears without a trace and without even having said a word. In the following chapter, together with Iaqip and Bnia Amin, she listens to John prophesy the probable disappearance of Mandaeanism and the arrival of Muhammad, after the destruction of the Judaic priesthood. Her presence just proves the redactor's desire to link together the various traditions he knew of concerning the Mandaean characters in Jerusalem. At any rate, this is the oldest context known to us, in which John and Miriai are to be found next to each other.

We come now to John the Baptist, a much less evanescent character than Miriai. The texts devoted to him in the *Ginza* and in the "Book of John" explicitly consider him both born and then active in Jerusalem, and they paint him as a Mandaean priest. His relationship with the Judaic priests is one of conflict right from before his actual birth, when the Jerusalem clergy are scared by horribly uneasy dreams of the future: the one about to be born will be the ruin of Judaism. One passage presents all the priests ready to embrace Mandaeanism, but immediately afterwards they are seeking to murder the newborn infant, who is miraculously saved on a magic mountain. As an adult, the "Book of John" presents him again on a collision course with the same priests who had sought to eliminate him at birth. The conflict is one of words (also because John, like all the *naṣuraiia* of the past, is invincible and invulnerable to iron or fire). His preaching is a "fire" and an "earthquake" for the temple and for the city. With the birth of John's eight children, Jerusalem becomes a "ruin Jerusalem." He himself prophesies the destruction of the Judaic priests, the arrival of Muhammad, and the most serious difficulties for Mandaeanism. The idea of a persecution of the Mandaeans by the Judaism of his time is absent. One passage in the *Ginza* shows him surrounded by *tarmidia;* they must be his disciples and perhaps at the same time Mandaean priests. Their number is not given, they are not persecuted, and they have no intention of dying or going away. Finally, the material on John in the *Ginza* and in the "Book of John" presents John the Baptist as a victorious hero; there is no idea of a Judaic persecution, and there is no exodus of the converted from Jerusalem toward the east.

The legend of John presents a new level of development in the *Haran Gauaita*, a text as interesting as it is mangled. There Jesus *precedes* John the Baptist,[36] who is sent by Life to the earth precisely to somehow hinder the success of Christianity. John's activity in Jerusalem is triumphant, to the extent that it is he, throughout his long life, who carries out the Messianic miracles we have seen Anuš 'Utra carry out in the more archaic texts. The history, however, does not terminate with his death, in the sense that tragic new events occur sixty years afterward:

> And he (John) instructed *tarmidia* and proclaimed the call of Life into the fallen house. 42 years [he stayed] there and then his transplanter looked at him and he ascended with his transplanter — blessed be his Name. . . .
>
> And there came a time, 60 years after Iahia Iuhana had abandoned his body . . . Ruha and Adunai decided to erect . . . the fallen house and spoke to Moses the prophet and the sons of Israel who had built the house. . . . Then they raised an idle cry against the tribes of Anuš 'Utra

---

36. Something similar happened already in the *Right Ginza;* see the texts at pp. 244-46 and 224-25.

... and spilt their blood about, so that none of the *tarmidia* or *naṣuraiia* were left ...

After the preaching of John, Judaism was reduced to being a "fallen house," in a spiritual sense, and therefore the gods of Judaism turn to Moses,[37] whose intervention appears to be decisive: it is the massacre of the *tarmidia* in Jerusalem. Their number does not appear (at least in the present text), but they are all massacred, together with the Mandaeans that are left (the Mandaeans of the past were all *naṣuraiia*). The reaction of the Life is immediate. From the fragments of the text it would seem that in the heavenly Iardna itself some character destined to descend to the world is baptized; here Ruha herself "disperses the Jews. . . ."[38] It is therefore exile (the present text does not speak here of destruction), of which we have this amazing description:

And then Adunai sent a rod. . . . And he (Moses?) spoke over it and struck Sup Zaba and the waters that were in Sup Zaba were divided like the two mountains above a ravine, and there was a road. And Ruha took them beyond Sup Zaba.

Sup Zaba is the Šaṭṭ al-ʿArab, in other words, the Euphrates, identified with the Sea of Sup, the "Sea of the Reeds," where the biblical miracle of the Red Sea occurs. Perhaps it is again Moses himself who leads the Jews beyond the Euphrates, for whose crossing the ancient miracle is repeated.[39] Immediately afterward, the Jews build what the text calls "the last Jerusalem."

---

37. To our eyes this is an anachronism, but not to those of the Mandaean narrator. It should be noticed that the text, however full of gaps, is referring to a past event ("that had built the house"), thus supporting our hypothesis that the lost part of the scroll mentions Moses.

38. In GR 15.11 Ruha asks authorization of Anuš ʿUtra so that she can be the one to destroy Jerusalem, but Anuš ʿUtra does not allow this (and indeed clubs her with a "bludgeon of light").

39. The idea that the Jews cross the Euphrates with dry feet is by no means unique to Mandaeanism; it appears also in the Judaic and Christian traditions. It is usually projected on to the end of time, when the lost tribes of Israel will return from the east to conquer the world and cross back over the Euphrates in a miraculous way.

And she (Ruha) built for them, and mixed together for them sacred mud and built an edifice, and they arranged for it column after column of falsehood and they raised each column. . . .[40] And Ruha surrounded [with walls] the last Jerusalem of the Jews. . . .

Anuš ʿUtra rises up into the heavens to lodge a protest with the divinity and together with Hibil Ziua receives a complex task:

Then came Hibil [Ziua] . . . towards Anuš ʿUtra and said to him: "Go down to Midai and take 7 arrows, that is 7 darts, and go and pronounce words over them. And take with you 7 guardians of Mount Paruan and take bows for them and they will pronounce over them 7 words and they will crumble the sacred brick in the house of Ruha, since in every place where these darts fall, fire will come out and will devour in the heavens and will eat in the earth for twelve *niskia*,[41] thanks to those pure and important spells.

. . . and Hibil Ziua came and burned and destroyed Jerusalem and reduced it to a mass of rubble and came to Baghdad and massacred all the *kahnia* and took their kingdom away from them and smashed and reduced to dust every city in which there were Jews. And thus [the Jews lasted] 800 years and their kingdom at Baghdad was; 400 kings among the Jews held the kingdom. . . . and thus the house of the Jews was annihilated and finished, and the power of darkness ceased.

Those seven guardians, that [were] men of proven righteousness, brought together by Anuš ʿUtra, for the word and the command of Hibil Ziua, came just as the great Father of Glory had ordered.

. . . they came with Anuš ʿUtra to conquer the darkness and destroy Ruha's conspiracy. And they destroyed the kings of the Jews and made them as if they had never existed. And Anuš ʿUtra placed them at the seven corners of the house, on the seven horns of the worlds, to break the power of darkness and to establish the call of Life and make vain the rebellious cry.

40. These are the seven columns of Jerusalem, of which also GR 15.11 speaks. See pp. 219-20.

41. The plural of *niska*, a measurement of capacity or of length, whose equivalent is unknown. The passage, including the measurement, derives literally from the description of the destruction in fire of the second age of the world, according to the text of GR 18.

The text is thus the result of the merger of two legends. According to one, Anuš ʿUtra goes to Ṭura d-Madai, here identified with Mount Paruan, the mount of the Mandaean paradise,[42] and takes seven archers from there with magic weapons; with them he destroys Jerusalem. According to the other, Hibil Ziua acts alone and destroys Jerusalem-Baghdad after a Judaic "kingdom" lasting eight hundred years.[43] The victory is complete, but in the meantime Mandaeanism is extinct, so that a new intervention of the divinity is necessary:

> Anuš ʿUtra went to Ṭura d-Madai, called Haran Gauaita, and brought Bhira bar Šitil, descendant of Ardban, king of the Naṣuraiia, and placed him in Baghdad, and established him in the kingdom. And with him there were sixty Naṣuraiia, and the Naṣuraiia in Baghdad multiplied and became many . . . until there were four hundred *mašknia* in Baghdad.

In the *Haran Gauaita,* then, the *tarmidia* murdered in Jerusalem became the *tarmidia* of John, none of which, however, survived the massacre. No Mandaean moved from Palestine to Mesopotamia: only the "dispersed" Jews did this. After an unclear intermediate phase, these Jews build a New Jerusalem in the east, which is destroyed, and the Jews are wiped off the face of the earth. As for the Mandaeans, they reappear thanks to an intervention of Anuš ʿUtra, who brings with him a new nucleus, led by a descendant of Artabanus.[44] The later Mandaeans therefore do not descend from the converted from Jerusalem who were all killed, but originate in Ṭura d-Madai.

Nevertheless, a few lines further on, we read:

> And in the world there are some of the sons of the *tarmidia* that Iahia Iuhana instructed. . . . From the root of those disciples of Iahia Iuhana came men without rank, who . . . lasted . . . ; and 280 years comes out from the sons[45] of those *tarmidia* of Iahia Iuhana, when Ruha comes and per-

42. Where, for example, John was brought up as a child. See below, p. 229.
43. Here too, therefore, as in the legend of Miriai, we find the Jewish kings of Jerusalem-Baghdad.
44. The information does not appear to be in contradiction to the statement that six of the seven king-archers of the magic weapons "generated descendents in the world."
45. The meaning may also be "that . . . lasted 280 years [and] came (out) from the sons."

turbs them and modifies words and transforms signs and modifies phrases and prayers thanks to descendents of those *tarmidia,* that is those *tarmidia* who originate in the seed (or else: malice) of the Jews. . . . Ruha made them obey the mysteries of the body, and they fell away from purity.

This depraved group coincides with the heretics that the book speaks of further on when it narrates the unfortunate adventures of a certain Qiqil, a Mandaean *riš ama* from Ṭib. Ruha appeared to him in a false guise and dictated books to him full of lies and falsity. Having had these circulate, Qiqil realized he had been deceived, came to his senses, had the copies of his works given back to him, and burned them, but "all those whose root was Judaic did not return (the manuscript) and did not give them to Qiqil, and some of these writings they kept."[46] According to this part of the *Haran Gauaita,* all the heretical Mandaeans, and only them, have Jewish blood in their veins. Thus, to be a descendant of a Jew is an insult, finding expression only in a passage of polemical heresiology, not exactly an awareness of the origins of Mandaeanism in Jerusalem!

A link between John and the *tarmidia* is present again in a prayer, called "Our First Fathers,"[47] and in an esoteric text. In the prayer, a long litany, there is a list of ancient Mandaeans whose names are remembered; it opens with Adam, goes through the founding fathers of the ages, and arrives at John the Baptist. Immediately after him are remembered the "365 *tarmidia* who separated themselves from the city of Jerusalem." Nothing links John to Šum bar Nu, who immediately precedes him, and so also nothing in the text links the 365 *tarmidia* to John. The text says nothing about them at all, not even their martyrdom. The esoteric text, entitled "A Thousand and Twelve Questions," states clearly that "he (John) three hundred and sixty [five] *tarmidia* separated from that place where they [were?]." The context is somewhat sibylline, and the state of the manuscript also makes it extremely difficult to understand the text. Yet there is enough of the sentence to show that the idea in *Haran Gauaita* had gained some currency, however small.

46. Since the schism of Qiqil is dated "86 years" before the arrival of Muhammad, it can be deduced that from John to Muhammed exactly 366 years (280 + 86) passed, a number very rich in symbolism. From what Iahia told Petermann, the schism of Qiqil happened 250 years after John the Baptist; the figure is rounded out but proves that Iahia also saw in the schism of Qiqil the heresy of the disciples of John.

47. See below, p. 239.

In contemporary oral traditions it has enjoyed a much greater currency. For example, Macuch published the text of a brief summary of Mandaean history, compiled for him by a Mandaean acquaintance in 1960. It is said here that after John "the *tarmidia* were murdered." The text does not say where, but Jerusalem may be assumed, given its connection with John. Of those *tarmidia*, however, 365 did not die but took refuge by the waters of Supat, where other Mandaeans were living already. These "waters of Supat" could be the same as Sup Zaba, or Šaṭṭ al-ʿArab. Afterward they all die — it would seem (the text is not clear) that they are murdered — for Abatur's lamentations are provoked. Anuš ʿUtra then intervenes in the usual way, taking sixty Mandaean houses from Ṭura d-Madai to Baghdad. All this is supposed to have happened five hundred years before Muhammad. It should be noticed that if the story speaks clearly of an exodus of the 365 to Supat, and that then they all die, the ancestors of present-day Mandaeans are not those converted from Judaism but the *naṣuraiia* brought from Ṭura d-Madai. The historical pattern that Adam proposed to Siouffi should be noticed here.[48] John leaves 366 (not 365) disciples; from these Miriai is converted[49] and around thirty are saved and go "to another place." Under King Pharaoh and King Artabanus, the Mandaeans multiply and arrive at a conflict with Moses; again, another thirty or so are saved, taking refuge in Šuštar, while Pharaoh and Artabanus continue to Mšunia Kušṭa. The unnamed intermediary place has all the air of being a narrative expedient to join legendary materials that the informant himself does not feel are consecutive. Still more clear is the evidence Petermann collected: John is active in Jerusalem at the time of "Pontius Pilate";[50] after forty-two years Jesus arrives to have himself baptized; in Jerusalem Anuš ʿUtra arrives, "sending" 360 prophets and bringing with him a wife for John. John's only son is killed by the Jews, and therefore Jerusalem is destroyed;[51] the Mandaeans are extinguished, and

48. See above, pp. 136-37.
49. Thus the order seen in GR 15.11 is overturned.
50. See above, p. 137.
51. This information is not backed up by any Mandaean tradition known to me. According to the "Book of John," John had eight children; according to Ignatius, four (and not generated by him and his wife, but by the water of the Jordan); according to Petermann, one; according to Siouffi, none (and the passages in which the children of John are spoken of are to be interpreted allegorically). With the passing of time (and after contact with Christians?) it would seem that the ascetic ideal gains ground.

240 years after Mšiha,[52] Anuš 'Utra leads sixty thousand from Mšunia Kušṭa to Damascus (!). As can be seen, almost every Mandaean narrator is capable of concocting a history, more or less coherent and complex, for the European who asks for one; yet a "knowledge of their Palestinian origin" was only to be found in the past in certain passages written by those Barefooted Carmelites who, like Basil and Ignatius, were mostly involved in the attempt to get the Mandaeans to emigrate to Christian territories. It is present among the Mandaeans today and appears in the evidence collected in the twentieth century, but in the nineteenth century it appeared to be still a long way from being accepted.

The fact that this idea has spread so widely is in any case significant, independently of the weight one wishes to give to the ideological bombardment the Mandaeans have been subjected to, first from the missionaries and then from Western scholars. From the point of view of a comparative analysis it means also that Mandaeanism has aligned itself with those religions that allocate a flight to their beginnings, following upon a persecution. In backgrounds linked to Judaism, this flight or original migration is characterized by a flight from Jerusalem before its destruction,[53] which is then explained as a divine punishment.[54] The motif is well represented in Judaic traditions — for example, in the so-called "Second Book of Baruch" — but it is above all in Christian or post-Christian traditions where it has found the most ample scope for its development. Already in the Synoptic Gospels there is Jesus' exhortation to flee to the hills, leaving Jerusalem and Judaea to their destiny of death,[55] but most important of all

52. And therefore 282 after John? It should be noted that the schism of Qiqil was supposed to take place 250 years after John. Those who, like a scholar a few years ago, try to base a case for some persecution of the Mandaeans around A.D. 240 on this seem to me to be running serious risks.

53. The event was so traumatic that it exercised a remarkable influence on the belief of all the religions arising from or in some way deriving from Judaism. The legends on the flights from Jerusalem are the religious parallel of the "secular" legends on the original flight-migration from a famous city of the past, afterward destroyed. This is the legend of Aeneas, of course, and of many analogies to be found here and there in virtually all cultures.

54. Also within Judaism, the only way to save the faith after the destruction of the temple and of Jerusalem is to consider the catastrophe a punishment decided by one's own God for sins committed; outside of Judaism, and in particular in Christianity and in Islam, it will be the God of each one (whether thought to be the same God as the Jews' or not) who punished the Judaic sins.

55. Mark 13:14-27 and parallels.

was the legend of a flight of the entire Christian community in Jerusalem from the Judaic capital to Pella, a pagan city beyond the Jordan, shortly before the arrival of the Romans. On this score, the most ancient literary evidence goes back to a certain Ariston, bishop at Pella in the second century. The information was then picked up by the ecclesiastical heresiologists and historians of the following centuries, such as Eusebius and Epiphanius, and from that point it entered into all the ecclesiastical histories that came afterward. It was considered to be either true or realistic until only a few years ago, when strong doubts began to be raised in the criticism, whether because there was no corroborating evidence from other sources (Flavius Josephus says nothing about it) or perhaps primarily because Pella was laid waste by the Jewish rebels, because it was a pagan city, at the beginning of the rebellion. It is therefore not easy to determine to where the Christians could have fled. Structurally similar to the flight to Pella appears the exodus of a handful of dissident Israelites before the arrival of Nebuchadnezzar (586 B.C.). The fugitives, led by a prophet by the name of Lehi (of the tribe of Manasseh), reach America (where they find the last Iaredites, who had taken refuge there after events connected to the construction of the tower of Babel and who by that time were almost extinct), and here they develop their own traditions. They divide up into two groups, the Lamanites (from which the pagan Indians descend) and the Nephites, who remain Jahwists and continue to enjoy a special revelation (also the resurrected Jesus Christ arrives in America to visit them and to explain the obscure parts of the New Testament) up until their total extinction (they are massacred by the Lamanites, before the arrival of the Spanish). The book they wrote in mysterious characters was revealed by an angel to Joseph Smith (1805-44) and is the scriptural and historical foundation of Mormonism.

It is not a good idea to judge the evidence of faith by strictly historical criteria, but there are religions that deliberately invite the faithful to reflect on certain historical aspects of their past. On these we cannot avoid expressing a professional opinion, while not of course interfering in the right of the individual to believe or not believe, and fully respecting the opinions of others. In this particular case, the early Christian story of the flight to Pella, the Mormon story of an exodus to America, and the modern Mandaean one of the migration to Mesopotamia are three examples of etiological legends that are useful for our understanding of the historical situation of the religious community or the charismatic head that produced them but that tell us nothing about the actual ancient history to which they refer.

Given the feeble basis of the legend of the persecuted *tarmidia* who, perhaps, took to flight, the Mandaean relationship with Jerusalem appears difficult to substantiate from a purely historical perspective, and the historical relationship of Mandaeanism with the figure of John the Baptist still remains to be clarified. Our first remarks on this subject are of a "negative" nature. Unlike all the human characters of the prehistory of Mandaean salvation, from Adam to Shem, no celestial hypostasis exists for John. In other words, there is no character in the world of light who bears his name, and there are no stories about his personal double who should certainly be living in Mšunia Kušṭa, as of course is the case with every Mandaean. This explains why, despite being present in two very commonly used prayers,[56] in one of which the forgiveness of his sins is asked for, he does not appear in specific liturgical texts or in hymns, why, in other words, he is not invoked as an intermediary or helper. Not being a celestial figure, he did not preexist his physical birth and so is absent from the theogonic, cosmogonic, and anthropogonic stories. Despite the great quantity of known esoteric texts, he appears in only one of them,[57] and there almost in passing. In addition, he does not appear in the apocalyptic texts or in those that in some way deal with the end of the world. Whereas the return of Jesus is expected, for example, no Mandaean expects the return of John the Baptist as the end of the world approaches. In spite of being a figure of extraordinary standing, and although in certain texts, such as the "Book of John," an attempt is made to exalt him as a superhuman and semi-divine being, in the Mandaean religious consciousness he has always remained only a human being.[58]

Recent traditions present John as the only true prophet, the prophet of Mandaeanism, in opposition to the four prophets of falsehood: that is, Abraham, Moses, Jesus, and Muhammad. In the more ancient literary con-

56. See below, p. 238.

57. At *Alp Trisar Šuialia* 1.1.29 (E. S. Drower, *The Thousand and Twelve Questions (Alf Trisar Šuialia)* [Berlin: Akademie-Verlag, 1960], p. 120) and 1.2.236 (Drower, *The Thousand and Twelve Questions*, pp. 170-72).

58. The idea of Messiah, as it is understood in Judaic and Christian traditions, is absent in Mandaeanism (very faint traces appear only in those texts subject to Christian influence). The hypothesis of a messianic role or quality for John, therefore, cannot even be suggested.

texts, however, he does not act as a prophet, nor is he called one, except in an anti-Islamic function. The only prophecy that is recorded for him concerns the coming of Muhammad. We can therefore argue that his prophetic aspect was consolidated within the context of the polemic against Islam. In addition, for the Mandaeans John is not the Baptist par excellence (indeed, he is not even called "baptist," except in just one of the many passages that speak of him) since he was not the one who invented baptism. This was revealed to Adam by Manda d-Hiia, and so Adam is the initiator of the Mandaean ritual baptism on the earth, and John learned it, as a child, from Anuš 'Utra during the course of his instruction on Mount Paruan. According to *Haran Gauaita,* he was baptized as an infant at the hands of a certain Bihram, brought to Paruan by Anuš himself, who had picked him up at Ṭura d-Madai (rather obviously, given the nature of the text), itself Haran Gauaita. This Bihram, or Bahram, is an important character, being the eponym of Mandaean baptism. The Mandaeans define their baptism as "baptism by Bihram the Great" (not by John). In Mandaeanism, therefore, beside the idea that baptism was revealed by Manda d-Hiia, there is also the idea that it was in some way initiated by Bihram, who is the Semitic outcome of Verethraghna, the name of an Indo-Iranic divinity present in the religions of ancient Persia and India.[59] The most interesting aspect for us here is that Verethraghna-Bihram, identified with Heracles, was the divinity who protected the Hyspaosinnidic dynasts (the descendants of Hyspaosines) who governed Mesene/Characene[60] as a vassal of the Persians, starting from their founder (who reigned from 165 to 120 B.C.), almost until the end of the Arsacid Empire (to be exact, until A.D. 222). If we exclude some brief interlude, due to the reign of some non-Hyspaosinnid, Bihram-Verethraghna-Heracles was always the protecting divinity of the ruling dynasty, appeared on every Characene coin for nearly three centuries and a half, and was to be found in effigy in official places dedicated to the cult. This means that the Mandaeans considered the one who established their baptism to be the protector deity of the sovereigns of Characene during the Arsacid Empire, made Mandaean by them (as we have seen) to the extent that they had taken Artabanus as their king. This also means that the Mandaeans must have been living in Characene in

---

59. His name means "Killer of Verethra" (i.e., of the monster that causes drought, devouring the clouds). In Avestic traditions he is seen as a genius of victory.

60. I.e., the part of southern Mesopotamia where the Mandaeans usually lived.

such a very ancient epoch of their history that they could choose Bihram as eponymous deity of their baptism. I cannot imagine why on earth the Palestinian disciples of John the Baptist would have sought the pagan deity who was protector of the Hyspaosinnidics without even glancing at their venerable master.[61]

Why then, if they are an ethno-religious reality of Mesopotamia, did the Mandaeans make of John a great *tarmida* and *naṣuraia* of the past, or even one sent by the divinity to restore Mandaeanism to the world, after one of the extinctions that have characterized its history since the Flood? The reason can be discovered if we analyze how Mandaeanism has dealt with all well-known biblical figures, whether from the Old or New Testament. The founders of hostile or enemy religions, Abraham, Moses, and Jesus, are turned into demons. Their predecessors, from Adam to Shem in the Old Testament and John and his parents in the New, are transformed into Mandaean figures. In this way Judaism and Christianity can be considered a deviation from a preexisting Mandaean reality. Paul does something of this kind when he goes back to Abraham, whose faith saves, thus going over the head of Moses, that is, the Law and its observance. Still more similar is the operation Muhammad carries out when he presents Abraham as the first Muslim of history, thus going over the head of Moses and Jesus, Judaism and Christianity. Muhammad, however, wishes to remain within the tracks of Judaic and Christian tradition, whose Scripture he recognizes in some way, in order to present himself as the concluding or perfecting "seal" of a prophetic line that starts with the Bible. Like Paul, he goes back to the origins of the religious tradition from which he derives. Yet this is what a religious reformer usually does: think of Luther, who goes back to the Scriptures, thus going over the head of the Catholic ecclesiastical tradition. Mandaeanism goes one further since it is a new religion, hostile to Judaism and Christianity. It therefore does not turn the founders into Mandaeans, but the protagonists who preceded them. John becomes a Mandaean in the same way and for the same reason that Adam, Abel, Seth,

61. We have information concerning the existence, in a Syrio-Palestinian area in the second century, perhaps at the beginning, of a group of "Disciples of John," baptists who proclaimed that John, and not Jesus, was the Messiah. They were also supposed to have believed that John was not really dead but was "hidden," which allows us to believe that they expected his return. The latter behaved as if they really were the descendants of those disciples of John that did not convert to Christianity and that did not return simply to Judaism; not, however, the Mandaeans.

Enoch, Noah, and Shem become Mandaeans. This also demonstrates that Judaism and Christianity, with their Scriptures, already existed when Mandaeanism was formed. Further proof of this is supplied by the fact that the phenomenon does not repeat itself with Manichaeism and Islam, so that there is no seeking for anyone preceding the founder to turn into a Mandaean; both Manichaeism and Islam are in fact considered a further degeneration of Judaism and Christianity, not directly a deviation from Mandaeanism. The fact that Judaism and Christianity, with their founders, receive such careful attention, whereas Buddhism (which certainly already existed), for example, does not, proves that the specific variety of Gnostic syncretism that is Mandaeanism stems from Judaism and Christianity and splits off from them.

John, however, does take not on the significance of Adam or Shem. One reason is more or less fortuitous. At the time Mandaeanism originated there must already have been extensive, established Judaic legends on Adam, the patriarchs, and the Flood, upon which the Mandaeans could draw, whereas the Christian legends on John were still in the process of being formed. The basic reason, though, is that whereas Judaism has always had strong communities in Mesopotamia that were able to influence the decisions of religious policy of the Parthians, Christianity must have been seen as a (threatening) entity in competition with it. It is only in the Sassanian era when the Byzantines managed to make their own influence felt or, above all, when the Syriac Church was able to organize propaganda and missionary activities.[62] The figure of John, then, as a Mandaean predecessor to Jesus, though present in Mandaeanism right from the beginning, grew in importance with the passing of time. This meant that despite occasional exaltation, it retains something of an adventitious or secondary character.

GENEALOGIES OF SCRIBES

What we have examined so far leads us to suppose that the original environment of Mandaeanism was Mesopotamia, and in particular Characene, in an era postdating the appearance of Christianity but prior to the end of

---

62. The Sassanid Empire protected the Nestorian Church, which was persecuted by the Greeks.

the Arsacid Empire. We should say around the second century — incidentally the century of the great flowering of Christian Gnosticism. At this point, leaving to one side the legends recycled from Judaism and Christianity, and the link with Jerusalem to be found in them, we can examine what the Mandaeans themselves have to say about their Mesopotamian history. We shall proceed by going backward in time from the event that functions as a watershed in the nonmythical history of Mandaeanism: the appearance in Mesopotamia in A.D. 639 of the "son of the butcher," or, rather, of his armies.

Precious evidence here is provided by the *Haran Gauaita*, which, unlike other texts, speaks at length of otherwise unknown details.

Thus, before the son of the butcher, the Arab (or: the son of the Arab butcher), appeared, the peoples became many: the Christians, the Dumaiia (Idumeans) who are the Jews, the Hurdabaiia and the Dilbilaiia. The peoples were divided and the languages many; also the languages of the Naṣuraiia became many. This; and then was taken away from the sons of the sons of King Artabanus the kingdom from Baghdad; and the Hardabaiia took the kingdom in Baghdad. There remained 170 *drapšia* and *bimandia*. And then the king of the Hardabaiia reigned 360 years, and then the son of the Arab butcher Abdallah[63] took power, and took a people for himself and practiced circumcision. After this happened 60 *drapšia* remained at Baghdad and belong to me (Hibil Ziua). Then he took the sword and put everyone to the sword from the city of Damascus as far as Bit Dubar, called Bdin. He governed over all this and dominated the lord of the mount of the Persians who are called Hardabaiia, and took away their kingdom from them.

Then, this happened, in time Anuš arrived, called bar Danqa, from the mount of the Arsaiia, from the city of Baghdad, [descendant of] Bihnus,[64] [son of the] kings [descendants] of the sons of Artabanus, and brought him (the Arab?) into his [country], that now belongs to Muḥammad, son of Abdallāh, the son of the Arab butcher (or: the son of the butcher, the Arab), when [the last millennium of the world] was 800 years old.[65]

63. Perhaps: "The son of the butcher, the Arab Abdallah."
64. It is not certain that the term is a proper noun.
65. The text is badly mangled, and the interpretative interventions (all of them hypo-

And he brought him from his city to Sup Zaba that is called Basra, and he showed him the Mount of the Persians, the city of Baghdad. And Anuš instructed the son of the butcher, as he had instructed Anuš bar Danqa, on this book [coming] from his fathers, on which all the kings of the Naṣuraiia founded themselves. And a list of the kings is to be found in this book, that taught from Adam, king of the world, to King Artabanus, to Anuš bar Danqa, who were of the chosen root (they were all Mandaeans). Then he told him of the king of the Ardubaiia, of everything that he tried to do and his *kibša* (conquest? submission? connection?) with the children of the great stock of Life, so that they (the Moslems) could do no harm to the Naṣuraiia who lived in the time of his reign.

Thus Anuš bar Danqa explained, and said to the son of the Arab butcher (or: the son of the butcher, the Arab), that it was not allowed to harm the stock of souls, thanks to the power of the most high King of Light, praised be his name, for the protection conceded by this "Explanation of the Great Revelation," blessed be his name.

In a literature like that of the Mandaeans, a passage anchored to exact historical events in this way is quite exceptional. Anuš son of Danqa, whether this is his real name or else an already legendary one, was apparently a political head of the Mandaeans, the descendant of Artabanus (like all those who count for anything). He apparently managed to demonstrate to the Islamic invaders that the Mandaeans were a "people of the book," showing them a text that the redactor of the *Haran Gauaita* believed to be the *Haran Gauaita* itself. In actual fact we do not have the slightest idea what Anuš would have taken to his new overlords; the mention of a list of sovereigns brings to mind texts like Book XVIII of the *Right Ginza*. Was it then the *Ginza*, in whole or in part? What is certain is that with the Arab occupation the writing of their own sacred books became for the Mandaeans not simply a meritorious activity but one necessary for their actual survival as a tolerated ethnic group and religion. It is not at all surprising that the more ancient and revered religious chiefs, *riš amia* or *ganzibria*, are also (and even primarily) remembered as scribes.

---

thetical) are extensive. Having observed that "800 years" is also the length of the Judaic kingdom at Jerusalem-Baghdad, it is well worth stressing that the text does not say who or what was eight hundred years old. It could easily mean that the facts described occurred eight hundred years after Artabanus, or else eight hundred years before the narrator.

So when the prayer "Our First Fathers" remembers the most ancient *riš amia,* we find a series of names that correspond to those of the best known among the ancient copiers of sacred texts, at least if we take the colophons as evidence. The four most ancient and revered names are those of Baian, Ramuia, Šganda or Ašganda, and Zazai. The order reflects their age, the first being the most recent and the last the most ancient.[66] Here is a colophon text in its simplest form:

> And he copied from the manuscript of Baian son of Zakia. His mother was Haiuna daughter of Iahia. It was copied from the treasure (*ginza,* thus "library") which was with them at Ṭib. And Ramuia son of ʿQaimat copied him, and Ramuia copied from Šganda and Šganda copied from Zazai d-Gauazta son of Haua (Eve); his father was Naṭar by name. And Zazai copied from the scroll of the First Life.

From other colophons we can understand that the list reports only the names of the more important copiers, since between Ramuia and Šganda there are at least five or six scribes. However this may be, the most recent of the four is famous for his work of organization and normalization of the sacred text:

> And then Baian Hibil son of Brik Iauar[67] wrote: "I purified myself when I came into the possession of these mysteries. And I traveled and went on foot to the *naṣuraiia* and I approached many *diuanan* from place to place. And in no place did I find trustworthy mysteries like these mysteries of baptism and of the *masiqta* and of the holy oil. I have written them here and I have distributed them to a hundred *naṣuraiia* so that they may adhere to them and remain faithful to them."

66. In the articles quoted in n. 59 (p. 53), Buckley identifies a different scribal tradition, in some way connected to "Ṭabia son of (maybe: initiated by) Zazai." As I understand the text, a scribe named Brik Manda copied his manuscript from four or five older scrolls (one owned — maybe copied — by Ṭabia), the last of which had been owned or copied by "the father (of) Šlama, daughter of Qidra." But the texts of the colophons are very "insidious" and may well indicate the existence of a scribal tradition which was — or was presented as — older than Zazai, and the initiator of which might have been a woman, the aforementioned Šlama.

67. This should be the same character elsewhere indicated as Baian, son of Zakia and Haiuna.

The work of normalization bore fruit: "[And there] was as far as Jerusalem, the city of the Jews, [one only sacred text, that was in everything] like [that which contains] these mysteries." It is not clear whether Jerusalem here indicates a geographical reality, situated in Palestine (or perhaps in Mesopotamia), or else the negative summit of the created world. In the latter case, the phrase would mean that everywhere in the world (the part inhabited by the Mandaeans) the texts were made uniform.[68] The information is hence exact, with a constant geographical connection to the city of Ṭib, in southern Mesopotamia; the chronological reference is lacking, but by the luckiest of chances it can be reconstructed from other colophons.

> And Ramuia son of ʿQaimat said: "I have written this *diuan* in the place Ṭib, in the years in which Anuš bar Danqa came with the *riš amia*, in the years of the era of the Arabs."

Ramuia, then, lived at the moment of the Islamic invasion. Baian was active in the Arab era, and Šganda and Zazai before it. We also learn that Šganda was from Ṭib:

> The city of Ṭib . . . is called the city of Ašganda, because of all that was done during his reign in Baghdad. Ašganda was in the place Ṭib; it was called the city of Šganda . . . as within it there were *naṣuraiia* [who are] *riš amia.*

Ašganda, then, was "king" of Baghdad; this could mean that he held some position of responsibility in the administration of the state, perhaps at the court of the Sassanids. Who he really was, however, remains shrouded in the mists of time.

Out of these mists, though, emerge more clearly the features of Zazai, both because of apparently exact information provided by Ramuia himself and because of the gradual process of divinization to which he is subjected.

68. There is a record of other interventions aimed at normalization in the history of Mandaean literature: "And Adam Sabur said: 'I went to Bit Hurdsaiia and traveled a long time and I did not find a trustworthy *masiqta* similar to this *masiqta*. And when I saw that it was trustworthy, I wrote this *masiqta* just as it was. And every priest and Mandaean who prays must adhere to this *masiqta*. And now, O priests who adhere to it, be faithful to this *masiqta*. . . .'"

And Ramuia son of 'Qaimat said: "From the day that [this *diuan*] fell from Zazai d-Gauazta son of Haua until now, the years in which I write, 368 years in the age have passed."

Ramuia, then, placed in the remotest past (over a year of years) the most ancient figure known in Mandaean history. This Zazai also appears in the *Haran Gauaita,* where he is the most important of the seven magic archers who destroy Jerusalem.

> And one of them was Zazai bar Hibil 'Utra, and Anuš 'Utra placed him in the city of Baghdad. And Anuš 'Utra placed one whose name was Papa bar Guda on the great Tigris and at the mouth of the 'Ulai. And one called Anuš bar Naṭar Hiia, Anuš 'Utra placed at his spring. Anuš Šaiar bar Nṣab on the Euphrates, and one whose name was Brik Iauar bar Bihdad he placed in Pumbedita, a place situated at the end of Sura.[69] And one whose name was Nṣab bar Bihram he placed in Ṭura d-Glazlak. And one whose name was Ska Manda he placed at the extremity of the Mount of Springs, situated in the furthest ends of Mount Paruan, the place from which these seven kings came and separated, they who came with Anuš 'Utra to conquer the darkness and destroy the machinations of Ruha. . . .
>   Until there were 400 *mašknia* at Baghdad. . . .
>   Then the one named Zazai, one of the men of proven righteousness, ascended into the heavens and lived with Iurba 62 days, and ascended to his fathers. And the six men of proven righteousness sent their descendants into the world.

Zazai himself, also "king" of Baghdad, hero of the victory over Judaism, seems to enjoy a special revelation that he obtained by dwelling in the heavens for sixty-two days.[70] This detail helps us to understand why Ramuia said that the *diuan* he copied had "fallen" from Zazai. The "fall" in this context would indicate its coming from the heavens, with a terminology that is adopted also in the Islamic world to indicate that a book is in-

---

69. Pumbedita and Sura were both the seats of famous Judaic academies in the Talmudic era. It should not be fortuitous, then, that the Mandaeans wished to claim their own dominion over those cities.

70. The number does not seem to have been chosen for any reason other than that it contains the number six.

spired. This is expressed in another way in all the other colophons that mention Zazai, in which it is always underlined that Zazai copied his text from the First Life or, at any rate, from a celestial figure. In certain colophons, finally, Zazai himself becomes a semi-celestial figure, himself an 'utra or the son of 'utria.

> . . . who copied from an ancient *diuan* written by the hand of Baian son of Zakia and his mother [was] Haiuna daughter of Iahia; his treasure (the library) was with R. Adam son of Saruan. And Baian copied from the *diuan* of Ramuia son of 'Qaimat who copied from the *diuan* of Šganda son of Iasmin [and] son of Iahia Iuhana, and Šganda copied from the *diuan* of Zazai d-Gauazta son of Manda d-Hiia and Zazai copied from the First Life, his Father.[71]

So who is Zazai d-Gauazta, son of Naṭar and of Haua? He is the oldest figure known in Mandaean history. From the evidence in our possession we can readily suppose that he was a religious reformer who, after inspiration, composed a sacred text, on the basis of which Mandaeanism was established as a historical religion. From the theological point of view, however, Mandaeanism is an eternal religion, which cannot have human founders, since it was already revealed to Adam.[72] For this reason the

71. Another colophon goes as follows: "And Ašganda copied from Anuš son of Naṭar, and Anuš 'Utra copied from Hibil Ziua and Hibil Ziua copied from the *diuan* of the First Life." This should mean that Zazai son of Naṭar was transformed into an Anuš who is actually Anuš 'Utra. Anuš the son of Naṭar, however, really existed, the third of the magic archers of *Haran Gauaita,* and thus it is also possible that for reasons that escape us there was the desire to substitute another figure of the same legend for Zazai.

72. According to Theodorus bar Koni, a Christian monk of Syria who was active at the end of the eighth century and wrote a short treatise against all heresies, the group of the *Dostei,* also called Mandaeans and Naṣuraiia, was supposed to have been founded by an extremely lazy beggar called Ado. The latter, with the rest of his family (they all begged on the streets), was supposed to have moved from Adiabene (northern Mesopotamia) as far as Mesene and to the banks of the river Karun. After he arrived there, since he was so lazy that he could not even be utilized as the guardian of a palm grove, he was helped by one Papa, who prepared for him a shack at the side of a road, where he could beg. Around him the first faithful gathered together, and thus Mandaeanism began. This presentation is obviously full of contempt (the founders of "heresies" are often beggars or escaped slaves, according to Theodorus), and it does not seem that the description of Ado, equipped with those features that rather recall Indian asceticism, can possibly be compared to Mandaean customs. Rather, what is important is that here too the founder is made to come from the north and

Mandaeans cannot have preserved the historical memory of a founder, nor
did they construct one (as they might well have done, for example, using
John the Baptist). Their true founder they have demoted to the role of inspired scribe, and a tentative attempt to make him divine has not stopped
him from virtually disappearing from the traditions and legends of the religion he began. If this is true, Zazai must still have been active under the
Arsacids, to whose epoch we have been led by the various data we have collected on the historical origin of Mandaeanism, prior to the fall of
Artabanus V (A.D. 224)[73] — and with even greater reason, to the origin of
Manichaeism.[74] Distant in time and initiator of an "eternal" religion, Zazai
is condemned to oblivion.

---

that therefore the legend reflects the Mandaean idea about its own kingdom of the north
(Ṭura d-Madai; Mšunia Kušṭa); as for the name, Ado means Adam.

73. The information of Ramuia, on the 368 years, is somewhat lacking.

74. Besides what has been said already, from the Manichaean texts we learn of two
other aspects. In the first place Mani himself spent his own adolescence with a Mesopotamian Baptist community that dressed in white and practiced abstinence. These were
not Mandaeans, since the same text presents them as followers of Elchasai, a Judaeo-
Christian Baptist who had a vision at the beginning of the second century. However, the information from Manichaeism does prove the existence in Mesopotamia of a religious fervor
linked to Baptist groups, in which we can discern the original *humus* of Mandaeanism itself.
Second, another Manichaean text, of a hymnographic appearance, has a great many similarities at some points with passages from the *Ginza*. The text, which can be dated paleo-
graphically around the fourth to fifth centuries, was discovered in Egypt, redacted in the
Coptic language, and seems to have been translated from Greek. The original appears to be
from Mesopotamia (also because the place of revelation the text refers to is a bank of the Euphrates, not the Nile, and not even the Jordan). At the time of its composition, then, at least
something of the hymnographical material that then went into the making of the *Ginza* of
today must already have been well known.

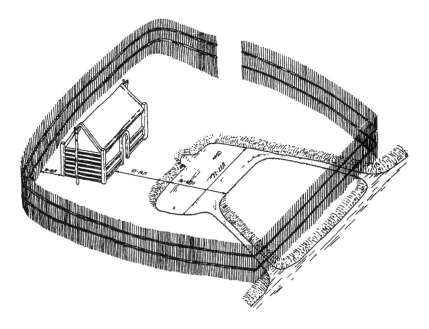

The manda and its enclosure
(from a drawing by Lady Drower, circa 1930).

A couple of wild beasts, standing by a heavenly
"house of punishment."

A typically Mandaean
portrayal of a
spiritual being.

Baptefme.   Sacrifice de la Poulle,

Sacrific: d.ı paıa, vın, & huylle.   Sacrifice du Mouton.

The oldest representation of Mandaeans ever seen
in the West (circa 1650).

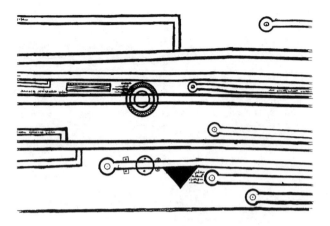

Details from a Mandaean geographical atlas. The parallel lines are rivers with their tributaries (water flows from left to right). The circles with dots are springs. The rectangle on the left is the city of Jerusalem, while the large, elaborate circle is the temple (the round shape represents a dome). Both the city and the temple are on or near the Euphrates. The black triangle at the bottom is a mountain (it looks upside-down as it is seen from the river).

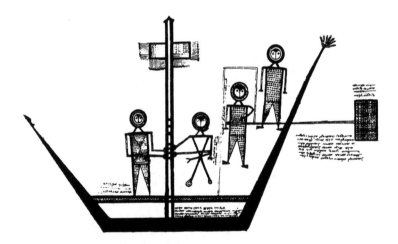

Ship of the God of the Moon (Sin). The God-Moon is the misshapen figure on the right side of the mainmast. This mast is a stylized *drapsa*, as can clearly be seen from the white cotton cloth (surrounded by tufts), representing the light that the moon (as well as the sun) receives from the divine world and projects toward the earth. The other figures are "rudder gods" (the rudder is on the right side).

The figure with curls is Venus, i.e., the Holy Spirit (considered a female being); the one on her side is probably Mercury, i.e., Jesus Christ.

The figure on the right is Mary (Jesus' mother); the one nearby (wearing Venus's attributes) may be the Holy Spirit; consequently, the two on the far left are probably the last two persons of the Christian Trinity.

Preparatory prayers
Boston, MA, June 13, 1999 (Charles River)

Baptism: The drinking of water
Boston, MA, June 13, 1999 (Charles River)

PART II

THE TEXTS
(AN ANTHOLOGY)

1. Abstracts of Theology

In Mandaeanism there are no texts comparable to a treatise of theology of the Western Christian kind. There are, however, stories on the origins of the divinity, of the cosmos, and of humankind, as well as prayers and esoteric descriptions and interpretations of the rituals. From these one can reconstruct the theological premises that, depending on the historical period, have exercised their influence on the writers of Mandaean sacred texts. Without making any claim to being exhaustive or to giving a complete picture, I here present some examples of the most compelling texts, in a speculative sense.[1]

THE THEOGONIES

The most typically Mandaean vision of the divinity (the Life) presents that divine presence as stratified in four levels of decreasing power: the First Life, without a proper name; the Second Life or Iušamin; the Third Life or Abatur; and the Fourth Life or Ptahil, the god demiurge. According to one text, "six thousand myriads of years" separate the four successive manifestations of the divinity from each other. This chronological distinction does not appear in other texts, nor is it clear whether there is one or more specific moments for the production of all the innumerable ʿutria ("riches"?) or malkia ("sovereigns") or malakia ("angels") that people the world of light. Starting from Iušamin, the Second Life, all the celestial entities that

---

1. In this chapter I have mostly made use of the English translation of K. Rudolph, in W. Foerster, ed., *Gnosis: A Selection of Gnostic Texts*, vol. 2, part II (Oxford: Clarendon, 1974).

can in some way be distinguished from the First Life can be defined as ʿutria. The origin of each divine entity can happen through creation or through emanation or through "call to existence," with or without the emission of a creational word, on the part of a higher divine entity. According to some texts, before the first production there was the Fruit, a sort of Gnostic Pleroma ("fullness"), the undivided totality of everything, the wholeness of the divinity before any kind of differentiation.

In relatively recent texts the First Life is often defined as the great Mana,[2] or the King of the light. The theological ideas present in the contexts of the great Mana do not coincide with those of the King of light, nor are they always consistent within the same context. However, the theologies of the great Mana and of the King of light have perhaps produced the most speculative texts. The passage below belongs to the theology of the great Mana.

GR 3 (Pet. 69-70; Lid. 66-67)

When the Fruit was still in the Fruit, when the Ether was still in the Ether, and when the great Radiance [was], whose radiance and light are extensive and great, before which no one existed, and from which the great *Iardna* of living water came into being, the Life himself came into being [gushing] out of it, and it (the living water) flowed to the earth of Ether, on which the Life sat, and the Life presented himself in the likeness of the great Mana, from which he came into being,[3] and he addressed himself with a request.

2. Originally "recipient," "container," *mana* passes on to mean "divine entity," "spirit." If accompanied by epithets such as "great" or "powerful," it refers to the undivided divinity, prior to the First Life. Otherwise, it can be used as a name for any kind of ʿutra.

3. Here then the Life, the First Life, appears to proceed like a voluntary emanation ("image/likeness") of the great Mana within the primordial Fruit: it therefore "(sits) on the earth of Ether," i.e., in the pleromatic world still closed up in itself ("when the Ether was still in the Ether"). From the great Splendor, i.e., from the great Mana, the great Iardna proceeds, which, insofar as it is a liquid reality, represents the first movement ("flowed") within the Pleroma, whereas the Life "sat," i.e., proceeds to be without movement, in that it represents the static aspect of the divinity. The fact that it is presented as "image/likeness" means that the great Mana-Splendor is in some way reflected in the great Iardna it has emanated, and that basically it is again God himself. This therefore seems to be a speculation of a Trinitarian kind, strongly characterized by heterodox Gnostic motifs, even if of distant Christian origin. Here it is said that the Son (the Life) at the pleromatic level proceeds from the Father (the Mana) and from the Spirit (the Iardna).

By the first request a confirmed *'utra*[4] came into existence, whom the Life called the "Second Life." Countless and endless *'utria* also came into existence.[5] From the Life a *iardna* came into being, which like the first Iardna flowed into the earth of light, and the Second Life stood in it.[6] And that Second Life called forth *'utria* and set up *škinata* and called forth a *iardna*, in which the *'utria* were set up.[7]

Three *'utria* came into being, who addressed a request to the Second Life; they were then allowed to produce *škinata* for themselves. What the three *'utria* requested from the Second Life was granted to them. They consulted together and produced *škinata*.[8] They petitioned and spoke to their Father; they asked their Father and said to him:

"Are you the one who created this *Iardna* of living water, which is so marvelous and whose aroma is so fragrant, and the *'utria* which were established in it and which are so great, and are they your *'utria* which were established in it?" The Second Life replied, speaking to the three *'utria*:

"As for me, your Father, the Life created me, and the *Iardna* belongs to the Life, and you are brought into being by the power of the Life." Then

4. The terms that indicate "to confirm," "to establish," "to strengthen," "to solidify," and "to erect" originate in baptismal language and describe the effect of baptism on the baptized.

5. With the first prayer, which the Life can address only to itself, finding itself still in its pleromatic primordial equilibrium, lightly rippled by the great Iardna and unmarked by the procession of the first image, a new dimension of the being of the divinity is created. This new world is still divine and of the highest spirituality, yet it does appear created, or rather generated, since the first *'utra* is the same "prayed prayer" of the Life, which is hypostatized. From this moment and not before the *'utria* originate, i.e., all the divine entities come after the First Life.

6. This is the confirmation or solidification of the Second Life. It should be observed that this second world ("earth of light") is developed as an image of the first events within the "ethereal Fruit," from which it is, however, by that time distinct (and inferior).

7. As in a play of mirrors, the Second Life carries out the same gestures, at a less powerful level, creating a new spiritual world, inferior to the "Fruit" but superior to the material world, which does not yet exist. It should be noted that at this time the "coming into existence" is indicated with a "call [outside]." It is hence not a simple emanation nor a creation of the Life from itself, even if it is not yet a creation from matter (understood as negativity). Our text does not know other "Lives" after the Second; only *'utria* will follow it.

8. A new creative process starts, but the three entities, though still acting in the spiritual world (they prepare their own *škinata,* which are "dwelling places," i.e., their own worlds), are no longer capable of creating alone and without the authorization of the higher divinity.

they spoke to him: "Give us of your radiance and your light and of that which surrounds you and we shall depart and go below the streams of water, call forth *škinata* for you, establish a world for you, and may the world belong to us and to you."[9]

THE WORLD OF LIGHT AND ITS INHABITANTS

The passage that follows describes the divinity in its visible and perceptible aspects; it belongs to the first treatise of the *Ginza* and is quite recent. It clearly expresses the features of the theology of the King of light, to which is also applied the name of Lord of greatness *(mara d-rabuta)*, a term that does not appear in the more ancient Mandaean texts. For a description of the angelic court, see GR 1.42-43 (Pet. 7-8; Lid. 11-12).

GR 1.5-7 (Pet. 2-3; Lid. 5-6)

The great Lord of all Kings *(malkia)*. Nothing was when he was not and nothing would be were he not to be; he is under no obligation to death, and destruction means nothing to him. His light illuminates and his radiance irradiates all the worlds, and the *malkia* who stand before him and shine in their radiance and in the great light which rests upon them. He gave them prayer and praise, which settled in their hearts, those who stand in the clouds of light. They worship, praise, confess, and contemplate the Lord of greatness, the sublime King of light, whose light and radiance and glory have no measure, number, or limit, who is full of Radiance, full of Light, full of Brightness, full of Life, full of Kušta ("Truth"; "Right"), full of Love, full of Mercy, full of Forgiveness, full of Eyes, full of lauded Faces of Beauty, full of Understanding, Perception, and Revelation, and full of Names of Glory.[10]

9. These three *'utria,* then, are demiurgical entities, characterized by ignorance (they do not know their own nature, nor that of the Father nor the Iardna) and by what they lack (they have need of Radiance, of Light, and of the Clothing of the Father). Nevertheless they will come out of the world of light ("beyond the streams of waters," a sort of cosmic ocean that constitutes the limits of light) to create the world, i.e., the physical world, destined to be a mixture of lesser light and darkness.

10. I have decided to use capital letters in this series of attributes of the fullness of God, since it is not clear whether they are simple definitions or actual divine hypostases.

. . . the King of kings *(malka d-malkia)* and the great Lord of all *malkia*. Radiance, which is immutable, Light which is inextinguishable, Beauty, Lustre, and Glory, in which there is no fault. Life, which [is] above life, Radiance, which [is] above radiance, and Light, which [is] above light; there is no imperfection and deficiency in him. He is the Light, in whom is no darkness, the Living One, in whom is no death, the Good One, in whom is no malice, the Gentle One, in whom is no confusion and anger, the Kind One, in whom is no venom or bitterness.

. . . That sublime King of light is secure in his dwelling and is loftier than all the worlds, as the earth [is greater] than its inhabitants; he excels everyone, as the sky [excels] the mountains, and he outshines everyone, as the sun [outshines] lamps, and he is brighter than everyone, as the moon [is brighter than] the stars.

THE WORLD OF DARKNESS AND ITS INHABITANTS

Mirror-like and anti-typical with respect to the world of light, below the created world (Tibil) lies the kingdom of darkness. In the relatively recent texts (belonging to the theology of the King of light), the negative correspondence of the world of darkness compared to that of light is pushed to remarkable extremes. The King of darkness becomes a true anti-god, with features that decidedly recall Manichaean traditions. On this subject the final part of the passage that follows should be noticed, in which the King of darkness contemplates and threatens the world of light.

GR 12.6 (Pet. 278-80; Lid. 277-79)

Beyond the earth of light downwards and beyond the earth Tibil southwards is that earth of darkness. It has a form which differs in kind and deviates from the aspect of the earth of light, for they deviate from each other in every characteristic and form. Darkness exists through its own evil nature; a howling darkness, a desolate gloom which knows not the first or the last. . . .

From the black water the King of darkness fashioned himself[11]

11. Or: was fashioned.

through his own evil nature and came forth. He waxed strong, mighty, and powerful, he called forth and spread abroad thousands of thousands of evil generations without number and myriads of myriads of ugly creations beyond count. Darkness waxed strong and multiplied through demons, *daiuia,* genii, [evil] spirits, *humria,*[12] *liliata,*[13] temple- and chapel-spirits, idols, archons, [evil] angels, vampires. . . .[14] They are artists of every hideous practice, they know countless languages and understand what meets the eye. They partake of every kind of form: some of them crawl on their bellies, some move about in water, some fly, some have many feet like the creeping animals of the earth, and some carry a hundred. . . .[15] They have molars and incisors in their jaws. The taste of their trees is poison and gall, their sap is naphtha and pitch.

That King of darkness assumed all the forms of earthly creatures: the head of the lion, the body of the dragon, the wings of the eagle, the back of the tortoise, the hands and feet of a monster.[16] He walks, he crawls, creeps, flies, screams, is insolent, threatening, roars, groans, gives [impudent] winks, whistles, and knows all the languages of the world. But he is stupid, muddled, his ideas are confused, and he knows neither the first nor the last, but he does know what happens in all the worlds. . . . When he pleases he magnifies his appearance, and when he pleases he makes himself small. He moves his membrum in and out and thus possesses men and women.[17] And when he shakes all the mysteries, he rages with his voice, his word, his breath, his breathing, his eyes, his jaws, his hands, his feet, his strength, his poison, his wrath, his utterance, his fear, his dread, his terror, his roaring, [and] all the worlds of darkness are terrified. His form is hideous, his body stinks, and his face is disfigured. The thickness of his lips measures 144,000 parasangs.[18] The breath of his jaws melts iron, and the rocks are scorched

12. The plural of *humarta,* "idol"; it indicates a type of demon.

13. Female demons (the plural of *lilita*).

14. I leave out here a long list of evil entities, at the end of which we have the description I reproduce.

15. There is a gap in the text here. Are they hydras of a hundred heads or monsters of a hundred arms?

16. This is what the evil demiurge (Ialdabaoth) looked like according to some ancient Gnostic sects, and also the evil god of Manichaeism.

17. The Sovereign of Evil is therefore androgynous (as he likes) and a seducer par excellence.

18. The parasang is a unit of Persian measurement used for very long distances. Its

by his breath. He lifts up his eyes and the mountains quake, the whisper of his lips makes the plains shudder.

. . . "Is there anyone who is greater than I? Is there anyone whose power is equal to mine? Is there anyone who is greater than I, greater and more excellent than all the worlds?[19] . . .

He concealed himself and beheld the worlds of light from afar at the boundary of darkness and light: like fire on the summit of high mountains, like stars which shine in the firmament, like the radiance of the sun when it rises and comes from the east, and like the moon in its brightness. He beheld the lustre of that earth of light like burning lamps, which, protected by glass containers, shine forth.

He conferred with himself, flew into a temper, raged mightily, and spoke: "I looked at that world; what is this abode of darkness to me, whose magnificence is hideous and frightful, whose food is black water and corruption? I will ascend to that shining earth and conduct a war with its king, I will take his crown from him, set it on my head, and I will be king of the heights and the depths."

THE COSMOGONIES

There are various cosmogonic stories in existence that are not easy to reconcile to each other. Among the texts of a dualistic character, I give here two poetical texts, the first more synthetic, with Abatur and Ptahil the main actors, and the second much more diffuse and rich in detail, with Ruha, the evil female Spirit of darkness, fully active.

GR 15.13 (Pet. 336-38; Lid. 348-51)

When I, Ptahil, was formed and came into being, I came into being from the source of the great Radiance. When my Father considered and called me forth, he called me forth from the source of radiance. He clothed me in

---

length has varied with time. A fairly good estimate is that a parasang is a little more than five kilometers.

19. This is the Mandaean outcome of the Gnostic exegesis that applied the words of Isa. 44:7 (or similar passages) to the demiurge (ignorant and arrogant).

a robe of radiance and wrapped me in a covering of light. He gave me a great crown by whose radiance the worlds shine. He spoke: "O Son, arise, go and betake yourself to the Tibil earth and make a solidification in the black waters. Solidify the Tibil earth and disperse *iardnia* and canals in it."[20]

. . . I set off and came as far as the boundary of the Tibil earth. My eyes were filled with black waters.[21] Up to my knees I stood in the waters, but the waters did not solidify. Up to my thighs I stood in the waters, but the waters did not solidify. Up to my first mouth (the anus) I stood in the waters, but the waters did not solidify. Up to my last mouth (the actual mouth) I stood in the waters, but the waters did not solidify. I pronounced the name of the Life and of Manda d-Hiia over the waters, but the waters did not solidify. Some of the seven garments of radiance, light, and glory,[22] which my father gave to me, I cast upon the waters, but the waters did not solidify. . . .

When I had thus spoken to my father Abatur, . . . he ascended to the Life, his Father, to speak to him concerning the works of this world. He called Hibil-Ziwa and sent him to the flank of the stallion,[23] and from him he took the solidification. The solidification he took from him, he came and gave it to Abatur. Abatur wrapped it up in his pure turban (?), he brought it to his son Ptahil and gave it to him. He spoke to him: "Go, solidify the Tibil earth and span out the firmament in perfection." I rose up from my father Abatur, and arrived at the boundaries of the Tibil earth. I cast the solidification, which my father gave to me, upon the waters, and the waters solidified.

20. The creation is understood as "solidification" of the dark water, i.e., of matter as negativity. The abundance of terminology originating in baptismal rituals should be noticed: we come across solidification once again, whereas the *iardnia* are the natural currents of water, and the "canals" should be those prepared for the baptisms.

21. I.e., he saw only black water.

22. These are the seven articles of clothing that make up the Mandaean sacred garments.

23. "Stallion" would here be an epithet of the King of darkness (perhaps on account of its pronounced sexuality, the stallion becomes the symbol of the principle of physical life).

GR 3 (Pet. 93-95; Lid. 97-99)

Then the Second [Life] was established, and his *'utria* rose up and gave
him advice. . . . The sons of the Second (his *'utria*) arose, they went and descended to the Place of Darkness, they called forth Ptahil 'Utra, they called
him forth and set him in his place. . . . They [finally] arrived at the streams
[of the waters] and they saw and beheld the Place of Darkness. Bhaq Ziua
shone by himself, and he held himself to be a Mighty One.[24] He held himself to be a Mighty One and abandoned the name that his Father had
called him by. And he spoke: "I am the father of the *'utria*, the father of the
'utria am I."[25]

. . . He called Ptahil 'Utra, embraced him, and kissed him like a
Mighty One. He bestowed names on him, which are hidden and protected
in their place. He gave him the name "Gabriel, the Messenger,"[26] he called
him, gave command, and spoke to him: "Arise, go, descend to the place
where there are no *škinata* or worlds. Call forth and create a world for
yourself, just like the Sons of Perfection, whom you saw. Set up and establish a world, establish a world for yourself and make *'utria* in it." The father
of the *'utria* in his greatness told him nothing about the adversaries, he
neither armed him nor instructed him.[27] Ptahil 'Utra rose up, he went out
and descended below the *škinata*, to the place where there is no world. He
trod in the filthy mud, he entered the turbid water. He spoke with his voice,
as the living fire [in him] changed [his appearance].[28] When the living fire
[in him] changed, he was troubled in his heart and said: "Since I am a son
of the Great One, why has the living fire [in me] changed [his appear-
ance]?" When Ptahil said this, Ruha took heart. Ruha took heart, she herself became arrogant. She spoke: "His radiance has changed, his radiance
has become deficient and imperfect." She arose, destroyed her property

24. This is Abatur, presented with the characteristics of the morning sun and with the
pride of the demiurge who is unaware of his true nature.

25. The popular etymology of Abatur from *ab d-'utria,* "father of *'utria*"; with this
self-definition, Abatur would leave the name of Bhaq Ziua.

26. In Islamic legends as well as Mandaean ones, Gabriel is the name of the demiurge.

27. When, in previous parts of the history, a celestial messenger (Hibil Ziua or Manda
d-Hiia) was sent to the lower world in order to imprison the monstrous Lord of the darkness or to get possession of his talisman, he was previously instructed and armed (with a
club of light and mantle of splendor, for example) by Life.

28. Or else, here and afterwards, "disappeared."

and clothed herself in a capacious robe. She changed her spirit into arrogance, she conducted herself, as she was not [herself]. She spoke to the
Warrior, the Foolish One who has no sense or understanding.[29] She spoke
to him: "Arise, see how the radiance of the alien Man[30] has diminished; his
radiance has become deficient and imperfect. Arise, sleep with [me, who
am] your mother, and you will be released (or: release yourself) from the
chain which binds you, which is stronger than all the world."[31] When the
Evil One heard this he trembled in his bones. He slept with Ruha, and she
conceived seven forms by the one act. After seven days she was in labour
and brought forth the Despicable Ones. She gave birth to the Seven from
which seven forms emanated.[32] When she caught sight of them, her heart
fell down from its support.[33] . . .

Ptahil washed his hands in the turbid water and spoke: "May an
earth come into being as it did in the house of the Mighty Ones." When he
immersed his hands a solidification took place. A solidification took place,
which was thrown down and ran here and there, as though there were no
solidification. When no earth came into being and solidified, his heart was
torn with discord. When his heart was torn with discord, Ruha again took
heart, and she spoke: "I will get up . . . I will go to the king of the world."[34]
. . . She spoke to him: ". . . If you sleep with me, your strength shall be dou-
bled." When he slept with her, she conceived twelve monsters[35] by the
[one] act. She conceived twelve monsters by him, none of which was good
for anything. After twelve days Ruha was in travail. She was in labour and
gave birth to twelve forms, none of which resembled any other. . . .

Ptahil stood engrossed in [his] thought, engrossed in [his] thought
Ptahil stood and cried: "I shall leave the world." When Ruha heard, her
heart righted itself on its support (she took heart once again). . . . She pre-

29. This is 'Ur, her monstrous son, a Lord of the darkness.

30. All the celestial messengers in the physical world or in the worlds of darkness are
considered "aliens."

31. This alludes to the chain with which 'Ur was imprisoned (by Hibil Ziua or by
Manda d-Hiia) in the previous history.

32. These second "images" or "forms" should be the seven visible planets, emanations
of the seven planetary divinities.

33. The idiomatic expression indicates dismay and terror: the sight of the seven monsters terrifies even their mother, who is certainly not the purest of saints.

34. This is Gap, the brother of Ruha.

35. These are the signs of the zodiac.

pared to go, destroyed her property, and went to the source (to the house?) of the Place of Darkness. She spoke to the Base Warrior, who is without hands and feet: "Rise, my father, behold: I am your daughter! Embrace me, kiss me, and sleep with me." . . . He kissed her and slept with her, and she became pregnant by him. She conceived five scoundrels by him, who disavowed one another.[36] . . .

Ptahil pondered in his mind, he conferred in his wisdom and said: "I shall get ready, fall at the feet of the Life, and cast myself before the Great One. I long to put on a clothing of living fire, and walk in the turbid water. . . . He received the garment of living fire and walked in the turbid water. When the living fire intermingled with the turbid water, at the aroma of the clothing of living fire dust ascended from the earth Siniauis. Dust flew up from the earth Siniauis and dispersed in all directions. All the seas were stopped up, and all the mines were filled. Dryness came into being, and solidification took place and fell into the water. . . .

When he seized the navel of the earth, took it up, and pinned it to the vault, when he seized the lofty circle of the firmament, took it up, and fixed it to his throne; the Seven were bound, they ascended, and took their place in the vault. The Monsters[37] took up position; they were bound in their thongs. As for their five Pilots, they wailed: "Alas, alas." Ptahil sits there in his wisdom and asks them severally: "Where do you come from, [you] wicked, you whose image is not from the father's house?"[38] When he said this to them, Ruha answered him from below: "We come wishing to be your servants, we would approach and be your helpers. We would be your helpers in everything you do, and leave you on your throne in peace. On your throne we would leave you in peace, we would approach and maintain order in the world. We would be good and be completely devoted to you." When the seven planets had thus spoken, he said to them: "You are my sons! If you perform good deeds then I will reckon you on my side!"

---

36. These five are star-like entities, whose identification is uncertain; often called "helmsmen" or "pilots," they share with the Seven and the Twelve their untrustworthiness. Their epithets refer perhaps to their activity as guides of the celestial ships (those on which the planets travel?).

37. After the planets, it is now the turn of the signs of the zodiac ("monsters") to be hung from the celestial vault.

38. Here the "image," to which the outward appearance corresponds, is in reality the substantial form, on whose basis a difference of nature between the entities of darkness and those of light can be defined.

When Ptahil said this, his house was taken [away] from him, and the "Perishable Ones"[39] gained dominion over it, as before the firmament was spanned out and the earth had become compact by solidification.[40] . . .

When Ptahil beheld them, he shone in his wisdom. He clinched his fist and beat upon the forecourts of his breast and said: "Before I enter the Father's house, I shall appoint a Master over this world. The Masters of the house do not know that this world has a Master."[41]

39. These are the Seven, the Twelve, and the Five. The evil entities, in that they are destined to final destruction, are not without end; they last as long as time and the world last.

40. In this text, then, the basic error of Ptahil is to allow himself to be deceived by Ruha and her sons, enabling them to control the world (the "house," which is taken away from him). This precipitates the created world into a situation similar to the one that preceded the creation, when all matter ("black water") lay in the power of Darkness. Now, however, the Darkness has not just regained control over the whole of matter, but, insofar as the latter has solidified through the intervention of Light, it has managed to take away from the Light some of the Light's domain. This is the typical dualistic explanation of the imbalance, of the imperfection of this world and the existence of evil itself.

41. Ptahil, before leaving the created world in order to return to the higher light, plans the creation of the Celestial Adam, the Man par excellence, to whom the true dominion over the world is destined. Man will be the instrument worked out by the divinity to recover from matter what of the divine had been lost in it, ending up in the power of darkness.

2. The First Man

The figure of Adam in Mandaean literature appears primarily in two contexts: the creation of the first man, and his death. In the anthropogonic context, Mandaeanism develops a meditation of a Gnostic type, centered on the presence of a celestial or spiritual Adam, who, without the demiurge knowing, is shut up within the physical Adam in order to give him life.

THE CREATION OF ADAM

The anthropogonic texts also differ among themselves and sometimes contradict each other. I have selected one that includes all the main Mandaean themes on the subject.

GR 3 (Pet. 100-104; Lid. 107-13)

When Ptahil came and said to the planets: "Let us create Adam that he may be king of the world," when he had thus spoken to them, they all conferred together: "We shall tell him that we want to create Adam and Eve,[1] because he belongs to us." They said to him: "Come now, we will create Adam and Eve, the head of the whole [human] family." . . .

---

1. From the immediate context it can be seen both here and in the lines following that the figure of Eve has been added on.

They created Adam and laid him down, but there was no soul in him.[2] . . .

The Planets gave utterance and spoke to Ptahil: "Grant us, that we may cast into him some of the spirit *(ruha)*[3] which you brought with you from the Father's house." All the planets exerted themselves, and the lord of the world (Ptahil) exerted himself. Despite their exertions, they could not set him on his feet. [So] Ptahil went in his illumination and ascended to the Place of Light. He entered the presence of the Father of the ʿutria (Abatur), and his father asked him: "What have you accomplished?" He answered him: "Everything that I made has been successful, [but] my image and yours have not been successful."[4] The Father of the ʿutria raised himself up, went forth, and hastened to the secret place. He fetched the great Mana, that he might illuminate all corruptible things; that he might illuminate the bodily mantle of every type and variety.[5] He wrapped him in his pure turban[6] under invocation of the Name which the Life gave to him. He grasped him by the ends of his turban, brought him hither, and gave him to Ptahil, his son. When he had given him to Ptahil ʿUtra, the Life summoned the Helpers. He summoned Hibil, Šitil, and Anuš, the ʿutria, who are outstanding and without defect. He summoned them and gave them their orders, and issued warnings[7] to them concerning the souls.

[The Life] said to them: "You, be a guardian over them,[8] so that all

2. There follows a poetic passage that describes in detail the failed attempt to create a living Adam.

3. In this case the term *ruha* indicates the divine Spirit and is without any negative overtones or connotation at all.

4. Adam is considered to be the earthly counterpart of the divinity.

5. The great Mana is not the entire primordial principle of the divinity but a particle of, or emanation from, it; he is the spiritual Adam, destined to enter into the physical Adam ("the bodily mantle") and hence to constitute the spiritual principle of the created world.

6. As in the cosmogonic text of GR 15, reported above and of which this is clearly a parallel, the interpretation "turban" is not certain. It must, however, be a wrapping of light.

7. Or, possibly, "magic formulas" of defense for the soul of Adam.

8. Here a new context begins (probably the Mandaean author is reutilizing a more ancient text) in which the hero — the "you" without a name that afterward will be talking in the first person — should be Manda d-Hiia, the first and most important savior and revealer in Mandaism. Hibil, Šitil, and Anuš gradually disappear from the scene, whereas Manda d-Hiia first takes on the responsibility for taking the spiritual principle out of the hands of the demiurge, then inserts it into Adam's body, and finally saves it, taking it back into the world of light. Immediately afterward, it will again be Manda d-Hiia who instructs the soul of

the worlds may know nothing about them. Let not the wicked Ptahil know how the soul falls into the body. . . . The supporter of Adakas Mana, let him be his protector.[9] When he (Adam) is clothed in the Radiance of Life, he will be fortified and stand on his feet, when he speaks with a pure mouth you (Manda d-Hiia) restore him to his place once more. Restore him to his place once more and protect him against all and sundry."[10] Ptahil enveloped him in his pure turban, he wrapped him in his garment.[11] . . . When they reached the Tibil and the bodily trunk [of Adam], when he (Ptahil) wanted to cast him into the trunk, I (Manda d-Hiia) took him out of his wrapping. While Ptahil lifted Adam up it was I who raised up his bones. While he laid his hands on him, it was I who made him breathe the breath of life. His body filled with marrow,[12] and the radiance of the Life spoke in him. When the radiance of the Life spoke in him, he opened his eyes in the bodily trunk. When the radiance of the Life spoke in him, Adakas Ziua ascended to his place. I (Manda d-Hiia) made him ascend to his place, to the house of the Mighty One, to the place where the Great One is enthroned.[13] I committed him to the charge of the Ganzibria, the *'utria* who take care of

---

Adam in (Mandaean) salvation, the soul having remained in the body, and being distinct from the spiritual Adam, which is now its celestial double.

9. Here we have the doubling of Adakas, the celestial Adam. Adakas Mana, "Spirit Adakas," will become the soul or spirit of Adam, whereas his "support," his more spiritual and deeper part, is Adakas Ziua, "Radiance Adakas," who will be at once recovered, becoming the celestial double — and hence the "protector" or helper — of the soul or spirit of that Adam who is left in the world.

10. In this particular the Gnostic schools and Mandaeanism differ sharply from the Judaic and Christian orthodox traditions. The sin of Adam simply does not exist. The sin belongs to the demiurge, who forces a spiritual principle into a physical body. There is no repentance or punishment for Adam. A part of the celestial Adam is saved immediately. The history of the salvation will then be the means by which the divinity will save from matter what remains of the spiritual principle caught up in matter (the soul or spirit of Adam).

11. In Mandaean speculations the Gnostic distinction between "spirit," originating in the higher divinity, and "soul," originating in the demiurge, has been lost. This verse, however, bears traces of a "psychical" covering, worked by the demiurge, of the fragment of spirit destined to enter into Adam.

12. For the ancients, the marrow, which disappears in the bones of the dead, is a principle and mark of life.

13. The separation of Adakas Ziua, then, takes place immediately, as soon as the earthly Adam becomes a living being and opens his eyes (and perhaps his mouth in order to speak). The first "vision" or the first "word," then, would be the celestial Adam himself, leaving the earthly Adam.

the *iardnia*.[14] The Life thanked the 'Utra (Manda d-Hiia), who had brought the soul.[15]

The Great One (the Life) summoned me and commanded me and said to me: "Go, bestow a sublime call. Bestow a sublime call so that the wicked may learn nothing of the soul."[16] I came and found the wicked. . . . I appeared to Ptahil 'Utra, who then howled and lamented. He howled and lamented, because of what he had done. I appeared to Ruha, the seductress, who seduces all the worlds. I showed her the great mystery, by which rebels are subdued. I showed her the great mystery and she remained blind and did not see it [any more]. I showed her the second [mystery], then I put a camel's bridle on her. I showed her the third mystery and split her head open with a blow.[17] When they saw me, they were all afraid and declared themselves guilty, the Seven declared themselves guilty. . . .

I concealed myself before the souls, I restrained myself: I took on a bodily form. I took on a bodily form and told myself I would not frighten the soul.[18] I would not frighten the soul and it would not be alarmed in its

14. These celestial *ganzibria*, like the earthly Mandaean priests, are responsible for the purifying practices directed at those spiritual entities that, even if for a short time (as is the case if Adakas Ziua), have been in contact with the physical. The earthly rituals of the Mandaeans, therefore, are modeled on the celestial ones (and are effective for that reason). We should note that the term *ganzibra*, from *ginza* ("treasure"), could be translated "treasurer"; in certain Gnostic texts *(Pistis Sophia)* intermediate entities appear, called "treasurers," with responsibility for the purifying rituals for souls.

15. Here the typically Mandaean tendency not to distinguish between soul and spirit can be seen. The soul of Adam is now within his body, whereas he who has returned to his place is the more spiritual part of it, Adakas Ziua.

16. The revelation is a "call," a "vocation" donated by the divinity to the elect, whereas the demiurge and the other evil creator spirits remain in ignorance and do not understand the nature and the presence among them of the spiritual principle higher than themselves.

17. The term "mystery" can take on various meanings. The basic one (quite clear at this point) is of "emission or manifestation of power and of knowledge." This "knowledge" is able to blind, subject, and finally destroy its adversaries. (In some Gnostic traditions, known also to Origen, the "head" is the seat of prophecy, i.e., of the highest intellectual capacity of the human composite. That the head of Ruha is split into two here should mean that the knowledge destined to the elect cannot even be contained inside the mind of the evil.) The "mystery," in that it is emission of knowledge, is a creative force, a seminal emission. Also, the sons of Ruha have their "mysteries," i.e., their evil seed, which they use in their attempts at anti-creation, for example, as we shall see, to fashion Jerusalem and the stock of the Jews.

18. The revealer, having overcome the planetary obstacle, takes on a bodily appearance to present himself to Adam. The Christian mystery of the incarnation is thus projected

garment. I assumed bodily form for its sake and sat down beside it in splendor. I spread the radiance of the great Mana over it out of which he (Adam) had been planted.[19] I sat beside him and instructed him in that with which the Life charged me. I sang [hymns] to him in a sublime voice, more sublime and luminous than all the worlds. I sang [hymns] to him in a soft voice and roused his heart from sleep. I spoke to him in the speech of the ʿutria and taught him my wisdom.[20] I taught him [secrets] from my wisdom and said to him that he should arise and prostrate himself and praise the Mighty One. That he should praise the lofty place, the abode in which the Good sits. That he should praise Adakas Ziua, the Father from whom he came [into being]. As I sat there and gave him instruction, he rose up, bowed down, and praised the Mighty One. He praised his father Adakas Ziua, the Mana, by whom he had been planted.

When he bowed down and praised his Father, the ʿUtra, he appeared to him out of the secret place. When he beheld his Father, the ʿUtra, [Adam] was filled with the most sublime praises. He sang [hymns] in a loud voice and overturned the planets. He overturned the planets and overturned the lord of the world.[21] He disowned the sons of the house (this world) and all the deeds that they had done.

THE DEATH OF ADAM

The first three chapters of the *Left Ginza* (GL), a text devoted for the most part to teachings and rituals connected to the death and the world beyond

---

into the history of the origins and the salvation of the Gnostic Adam. In this way, for both the Gnostics and the Mandaeans, salvation has already taken place, and the succeeding revealers (among them is Christ, for the Christian Gnostics) simply have the task of reevoking the memory of the events of earliest history. We can also see why, for the Gnostics, orthodox Christian ideas about the death of Jesus Christ bringing salvation do not make sense.

19. "To plant" means to "create." The radiance of the revealer spreads over the earth.

20. With these verses we are at the heart of the Gnostic process of revelation and, at the same time, of salvation. Without sins to expiate, the spirit of Adam, "fallen asleep" in matter, has only to "wake up again" and, through a cognitive act, "learn" of his true nature and the nature of the world, both physical and divine.

21. Having acquired the knowledge of his own spiritual nature, Adam — and with him every Gnostic — enters into direct contact with the divinity (the revealer himself disappears from the scene) and demonstrates his superiority to the planetary powers and to the demiurge Ptahil.

this one, deal with the end of Adam. The first (GL 1.1) is perhaps the most famous passage (and most typically Mandaean), in that in it Adam, who does not want to die, manages to convince God's messenger to have his son Šitil (Seth) die in his place. In the second passage, too (GL 1.2), Adam does not want to die but in the end accepts his destiny. In the third (GL 1.3, which is not quoted here), we have the lamentation of Eve for her dead husband.

GL 1.1 (Pet. 1-9; Lid. 424-29)

The Life thought, and was infused with light. The Life sat in his great Radiance and spoke: "Arise, we shall inflict the punishment of death upon that world of the wicked and upon that abode which is replete with faults and full of defects. Now that Adam is 1,000 years old he shall be called from the body and be fetched out of it before he becomes senile, before he deteriorates and before his youngest children rise up and perpetrate many follies against him."[22] . . .

And the great Life spoke to the separator Sauriel, Qmamir Ziua:[23] "Arise, go to that world of the wicked and in that dwelling place that is replete with faults and full of defects. Call Adam with a call and instruct him with suitable knowledge. Speak to him thus: O Adam, first man, mute, stupid, deaf, confused! Now, abandon the [earth] Tibil, which is replete with faults and full of defects, since you are a thousand years old, before you become senile, before you deteriorate, before your youngest children rise up and perpetrate many follies against you." . . .

Sauriel carries out the divine order.

---

22. Unlike the previous one, but similar to Christian and Judaic ones from which it derives, the passage frequently adopts a tone echoing fable or folklore. However, it should be noted that death is not a punishment for Adam (for whom, on the contrary, it is salvation) but for the physical world, controlled by the planets (the "evil ones"). Adam should be the instrument destined by the Life to introduce death into the world, to defeat the world and its forces. This idea, too, is decidedly not Christian.

23. It is not at all clear if Qmamir Ziua (Radiance) is an epithet for Sauriel (Suriel, the "separator," i.e., the angel of death) or another figure. In the passage the verbs are sometimes in the singular and sometimes in the plural.

[At the call of the messenger] Adam flew into a rage, he wrapped himself up in rage, he was enveloped in rage. He spat, and flung down on to the earth a bitter spittle. He bent himself double and would not unwind, his heart was filled with pain. He felt a tear in his eyes, he cried out and wailed, howled and wept. He threw himself on the ground and stretched himself out. He clenched his fists and smote them against the anteroom of his chest, and called: "O cry which summons me, O you choice knowledge who instructed me, I now am a thousand years old! In this world, in which I live, first the shoots of the dates are eaten, and then the dates. First the still green grains of wheat and then the ears of wheat are eaten. And then, in this world in which I live, the young vegetables are eaten before the tougher ones, and afterwards the tougher ones are eaten." . . .

The messengers return to the Life, who sends them back to Adam.

Then he (Adam) spoke to them: "O you, messenger who has summoned me; and you, choice knowledge, who has instructed me! I am 1,000 years old and long to live for another 1,000 years. Go to my son Šitil and summon him: it is he who is desired for that world. He is younger than I and more tender than I, he is [only] eighty years old in this world, he has not yet mounted on the sex of a woman and no great fruits have yet been granted him. He has not drawn a sword and has never shed blood in the [earthly] dwelling-places. It is he who is needed by that world." . . .

After having received the assent of the Life, the two messengers go to Šitil.

Then spoke Šitil, the son of Adam: "O you, messenger that has summoned me; O you, choice knowledge, that has been revealed to me! I am [only] eighty years old in this world; I have not yet mounted on the sex of a woman and no great fruits have yet been granted me; I have never drawn a sword and I have never shed blood in the [earth] Tibil. Go to my father Adam; he has reached a thousand years in this world. [He may die] before he becomes senile, before he deteriorates, before his youngest children rise up and perpetrate many follies against him."

Then they spoke to him: "O Šitil, son of Adam! Before we summoned you with this cry, we summoned Adam with it and spoke to him, but Adam your father sent us to you." Šitil, the son of Adam, said in his mind: "I am afraid to say that I do not want to leave my body, lest the Great Life even be angry with me in his great place."

Then Šitil the son of Adam arose and uttered a long, not a short prayer. He then cast away the trunk of flesh and blood and was clothed in the garment of radiance and in a fine, pure turban of light: his light shone 990,000 myriads of times more than the light of the sun, and its brightness became 990,000 myriads of times clearer than the brightness of the moon. Thousands of thousands and myriads of myriads accompanied him to the right and the left. Winds, winds took up Šitil, the son of Adam, storms, storms carried him away, lifted him up and placed him in a great cloud of light. He uttered a prayer that was very long, not short. . . .

Šitil asks that Adam receive the gift of knowledge.

Thus rose up the cry, the lamentation and the submission of Šitil, son of Adam, up until the first great Life; and the covering of the eyes, the ear plugs and the stratum of flesh from the heart [of Adam] were removed. He looked at that world that Šitil saw and spoke to him: "My son, come, come! I wish to come to that world which I desire." Then [Šitil] answered him: "Go away, old man without knowledge, great twit[24] without intellect! Is there anyone who, after having spat their spittle out of their mouths, has swallowed it? Is there anyone who has left his mother's womb and then has been brought back to where he was before? . . ."

Šitil contemplates the truth and celestial blessedness.

Šitil, the son of Adam, said: "Upon this road, path, and ascent which I ascended, the true, believing, glorious, and perfect men shall ascend and come, when they leave the body." Then the Life, the ʿutria and the malkia of the world of light and of the luminous dwelling place of Kušta exchanged [with Šitil] the [handshaking of] kušta, they shook hands kušta-like with Šitil, the son of Adam.[25]

24. The Mandaean term mariba, used here and in contexts of insults to old people, seems to be connected etymologically to an expression indicating female genitals.
25. His prayer that asks for the salvation of future Mandaeans was accepted.

The First Man

GL 1.2 (Pet. 9-19; Lid. 430-37)

In the name of the Life.[26]

When the project of the house of the great Life was carried out, he sent the messenger to Adam, to free him and bring him out of his body, out of this world, from the shackles, from the chain, from the noose, and the bonds, to bring him away from the earth, that Ptahil and the seven planets had built, into which they had then led him and had made him live and remain, to liberate him and lead him out of his filthy, stinking body, the destroyer, corruptible, from the heart-rending lions, from the flames of fire, pernicious, from the [body] that disintegrates and is reduced to pulp, from the sea, that cannot be sounded, from the abyss, that cannot be closed up again, from the serpentlike beast that surrounds the world, from whose force no one has grown. . . .[27]

When Adam heard this, he made a lamentation about himself and cried. He emitted laments and cried and in his eye a tear formed. Adam opened his mouth and spoke to the messenger who had come to him: "Father, if I come with you, who will be the guardian of this Tibil that is so vast? Who will keep company with this my wife Eve? Who will defend in [future] times these plants I have planted? Who will defend them? Who will dwell in the house where I have dwelt? . . . When the palm brings forth fruit and the clover flowers, who will be their guardian? When the Euphrates and the Tigris rise, who will grasp his spade[28] and bring water to the plants? When the woman in labor gives birth, who will be near her? Who will yoke the oxen to the plough and scatter the seeds in the earth? Who will take the rattle in his hand and gather the sheep into the fold and the antelopes in their flocks? Who will look after the orphans and who will fill the pockets of the widow? Who will clothe the naked and place a cloak around their shoulders? Who will free the imprisoned and who will compose the quarrels in the village? . . ."

The celestial messenger sings the praises of the world beyond and describes the wretchedness of this world.

26. An introductory formula, usual in Mandaean texts.

27. There is here a dialogue of the soul, desirous to leave, with the spirit and the "filthy body" of Adam.

28. In actual fact this is an unknown term, supposedly indicating an agricultural instrument for directing water.

Then Adam opened his mouth and spoke to the Herald: "Father, if you knew that it is thus, why have you deceived me and have brought me into a stinking body? If I now abandon my body, who will defend it? When it sleeps, who will wake it up, who will shake it out of its sleep? Who will give it to eat and drink and who will keep it company in [future] times? . . . Father, if you want me to come with you, my body should also come as my companion. My body should come with me and keep me company in my journey. . . .

Then the Herald replied . . . : "A body cannot rise up to the house of the Life."

Then Adam answered . . . : "Messenger of the Life, if it pleases you and is dear to you, let my wife Eve come with me as my companion, and keep me company along the way. Let my sons and my daughters come with me and keep me company on the journey."

When his wife Eve heard these words of Adam, she shouted out in a loud voice. She shouted out in a loud voice and in her eye a tear formed. She said to him: "I wish to come with you as your companion, O Adam, and I wish to keep you company along the way." . . .

There follows a long speech of the messenger on the impossibility for a body to reach the world beyond, also for the risks that it would run.

When Adam heard this, he lamented and cried for himself and his tears fell. . . . Then Adam left his body. He turned around and looked at it. Then he trembled. It was difficult for him to leave his body and he was unable to separate himself from it. Then his migration across the ether began. Adam wandered and shifted around like a bird that has not yet built his nest, has not yet brooded, that has not yet raised any young. . . . He flies and passes through worlds and aeons and seems to be an animal that is separated from its flock. . . .

Adam acquires knowledge of his celestial origins once again and of the violence he has suffered to enter into the body, and yet he looks back longingly on its beauty.

"How beautiful my body was, however, and how wise and beautiful were the artists that have portrayed it and the jewelers that have engraved it in relief. They have created a truly beautiful head, they have made and smoothed the hair. They made and smoothed the hair and placed the intellect in the head and poured wisdom into the heart. They made two eyes for it, that shone day and night. They made a great door for it (the mouth), that every day praises the Life. They made two hands for it, that work every day, without weakening. They made two feet for it, that walk from the East to the West. Now the figure, that was so beautiful, goes away and becomes dust and worms in the cemetery. Its eyes looked around and seemed to be the images of stars; now they are darkness. Both the windows are closed, that every day listen to the word of the Life. Closed is the great door, that every day invokes the Life. Whereas otherwise the hands every day worked without weakening, now the birds are not afraid of my body. Whereas before the feet walked miles and miles, now they do not scare off the birds. It is hard for me to abandon it, and anyway I cannot take it with me. I told myself that we could go, and in the meantime I would take my body, but its walls split and fell to pieces. Thus I left my body to slump to the ground and I threw it away; it went there and became dust and worms." . . .

There follow long speeches on the caducity of the world; also the Roman and Persian Empires, in perpetual conflict, are destined to come to an end.[29] Adam eventually reaches the Life and asks protection for his stock (the Mandaeans), so that the true cult may be carried on.

Then spoke the great, first Life to Adam, the forefather to the entire stock: "O Adam, be tranquil in your illumination and the peace of the good wrap you around. Hibil Ziua is here; your brothers, the ʿutria, are here. The entire Iardna is here. You, Adam, must live here. Your wife Eve will come here, and your entire stock will ascend here after you. This is the dwelling place that the powerful First Life has prepared for you and your wife Eve until the day, until the day of judgment; until the hour, the hour of redemption; until the great day of the resurrection. Then you will arise again, Adam, with all your descendants, and go into your own earth. Therefore placate your mind and leave your heart to stay with its support."
And the Life is victorious.

This is how this passage ends, containing very contradictory statements concerning the usual Mandaean speculations. It is enough to remember the

---

29. Arabs are not mentioned, a proof of the ancient date of the passage.

exaltation of the body and its creators, which are none other than the Seven and the Twelve. The final promise of the return to the paradise lost and of resurrection that the Life promises Adam is evidence of how anomalous the text is. There is nothing more extraneous to Mandaean religious sensibilities than the idea of the recovery of the physical body; the presence of a statement of this kind demonstrates how heavily indebted the Mandaean writer is in this case to the Judaic literary model or, more probably, to the Christian one he followed.

3. From the Creation to the Flood

The ancient history of the world is narrated in the Mandaean texts by fusing the data of the biblical tradition (the Old Testament) with the theory of the four ages of the world. As in the Gnostic traditions from which the Mandaean legend would seem to derive, the victims of the water of the flood or of the fire (of Sodom?) are not sinners but among the righteous who "will ascend to the light."

GR 2.1.118-22a (Pet. 48-50; Lid. 45-46)

118. In the first age the world will be destroyed[1] by the sword and plagues. The souls will separate from their bodies and rise up to the light. For it has been established for the perfect and for the believers that they should separate from the body with this [type of] separation. You, Adam, have been destined to live for a thousand years in the world and you will ascend before the sword. Then your wife Eve will separate [from the body], then all your descendants,[2] except for Ram, the man, and Rud, the woman. From them the world will multiply; from them the world will be once more reawakened. All will invoke [the divinity] with one speech and one praise, the one I have brought to this world, with which they must utter [their] praises.[3]

1. The text is presented as a revelation, to Adam, of the future of human history.
2. This story does not seem to take the story of the vicarious death of Šitil into account at all.
3. This means that the second age of the world, too, will be entirely and only Mandaean.

199

119. Then the world will be destroyed by fire. For it is established for the sons of the great stock of the Life, that they should separate from their bodies with this [type of] separation, except for two, Šurbai, the man, and Šurhab'il, the woman, from whom the world will multiply. Šurbai, the man, will be called the head of the age. The souls that separate because of the fire rise to the light, since they have not falsified the teaching that their Lord sent them.

120. From the age of Ram and Rud to the age of Šurbai and Šurhab'il mankind will multiply; with these speeches they will utter praises and will not separate themselves from the word of the Lordship.

121. When twenty-five ages (generations) pass, the world will be destroyed by water. Mankind will be separated from their bodies through a separation caused by water. For it has been written down for that age that the bodies have to die by water and the souls ascend to the light, except for Nu (Noah), the man, and Nuraita, his wife, and Šum (Shem), Iam (?) and Iapit (Japheth), the sons of Nu, who will be saved from death by water. From them the world again has to be reawakened.

122. From Šurbai and Šurhab'il until the age of Nu, there are fifteen generations.

The last book of the *Right Ginza* is quite an extensive text, containing a universal history from the creation to the end of time. It is a collection of material of heterogeneous origin with a lengthy apocalyptic final part, rich in prophecies. Among other things, it forecasts that Islamic domination of Mesopotamia should last only seventy-one years. This detail allows us to date the prophecy with a certain accuracy between the end of the sixth and the very earliest years of the seventh centuries (since the Arab invasion of Mesopotamia took place in A.D. 639, the addition of seventy-one years takes us to A.D. 710; so, the forecast cannot postdate that year).

GR 18 (Pet. 378-81; Lid. 407-10)

In the Name of the great Life . . .

Then quantity and number were given to the world. From the day Adam was made until the end of the worlds there are 480,000 years.

Then quantity and number were given to the seven planets and the twelve Pilots (signs of the zodiac). The quantity was divided into seven equal parts, so that no one had too much and no one had too little. To each man (planet) went as his portion 68,571 years, five months, four days, 6.5 hours, 4 sossis,[4] and 1.5 minutes.[5] The twelve signs of the zodiac last together with the seven planets, and the seven planets last together with the twelve signs.[6] The twelve signs take from the quantity of Bil (Jupiter), when to Bil still remain nine thousand years; the twelve signs take from him. Then they last nine thousand years together with Bil and sixty-nine [thousand years] together with Nirig (Mars).[7] Of these 78,000 years, in which the twelve signs last, twelve thousand years were destined as a portion to Aries, eleven thousand to Taurus, ten thousand to Gemini, nine thousand to Cancer, eight thousand to Leo, seven thousand to the ear of wheat (Virgo), six thousand to Libra, five thousand to Scorpio, four thousand to Sagittarius, three thousand to Capricorn, two thousand to Aquarius, a thousand to Pisces, . . .

Then, when there were still eight thousand years left of the years [of Mars, and hence of the world], there came a call to Nu of the Ark, and spoke to him thus: "Build an ark." So Nu had carpenters come who could do the work properly, cut cedars of Harran and [the so-called] female cedars of Lebanon and built for three hundred years. He put the ark together so that it measured 300 cubits in length, 50 cubits in width, and 30 cubits in height.[8] Then Nu took two of each species, male and female, and led them into the ark. Then for 42 days and 42 nights[9] the higher waters from the heavens and the lower waters from the earth came, submerged the mountains and submerged the high places. Thus all the world was destroyed by water.

The ark floated on the water for eleven months. After eleven months there was calm and the ark went lower and stopped on Mount Qardun. Then Nu understood in his soul that there was calm in the world. Nu then

---

4. A *sosso* is a twelfth of an hour, a period of five minutes.

5. Should anyone wish to redo the calculation, he or she will find it accurate to within a half a minute. In what follows, the figures will be rounded out a little (in particular, the text will indicate in 69,000 years the length of the power of each planet).

6. I.e., as will at once be explained, they will reign together.

7. The planets therefore reign over the world for around 69,000 years each, following this order: Sun, Venus, Mercury, Moon, Saturn, Jupiter, and Mars. Mars is the planet of the end of time. The twelve signs, however, reign with a part of Jupiter and with Mars for 78,000 years, dividing this time into decreasing periods.

8. Cf. Gen. 6:15.

9. The biblical number of "forty days" (Gen. 7:17) is lengthened to forty-two, perhaps to make it coincide with six weeks.

sent out the crow and [thus] spoke to him: "Go, see if there is calm in the world." The crow went out and found a corpse; he ate of it and forgot what Nu had commanded him to do. So Nu, after that, sent out the dove and [thus] spoke to her: "Go, see if there is calm in the world, and where the crow is that I sent out before you."

Then the dove went out and found the crow that was standing over a corpse and eating it. She saw the olive tree, on Mount Qardun, whose leaves had sprung up out of the water. The dove gathered [a little branch] and brought [it] to Nu, so that he could know in his soul that calm had descended. Thus Nu cursed the crow and blessed the dove.[10]

Then the age of the world was guarded by Šum the son of Nu, and by his wife Nhuraita,[11] from whom the world was again reawakened.

The short text I present here is taken from the "Book of John." Written in a moment of crisis for Mandaeanism, probably at the beginning of Islamic domination, it casts a disconsolate eye on human life and on human history. The author, in other sections of his work, seems to be convinced of the imminent disappearance off the face of the earth of Mandaeanism itself, whose message of faith and of knowledge nevertheless remains the only means of salvation for the "stock of the Souls."

JB 25 (Lid. 90, 93)

O you . . . corrupt world! Your people die and your deceiving writings are closed. Where [is] Adam, who here was the head of the ages? Where [is] Eve, his wife, from whom the world was called to life? Where [is] Šitil, son of Adam, from whom worlds and ages were established? Where [are] Ram and Rud, who belonged to the age of the sword? Where [are] Šurbai and Šurhabʿil, who belonged to the age of fire? Where [is] Šum son of Nu, who belonged[12] to the age of the Flood? They all have gone away and have not returned [. . . ?] and sit as guardians in Tibil.

---

10. This anecdote is known to Judaic legendary traditions, from which the Mandaean narrator derives his story.

11. In GR 2.1 this was the name of the wife of Nu. The disappearance of Shem's brothers should be noted.

12. Plural in Mandaean; thus his wife was also remembered.

4. The Religions of Others

In general, it can be argued that the gods of others, or the founders of other religions, are demonized; this always (or frequently) happens in monotheistic religions. The most ancient of the polemics are directed against the planetary gods of Mesopotamian tradition and perhaps contain echoes of an ancient Zoroastrian preaching. "New arrivals" overlap with traditional gods: Šamiš (Sun) becomes Adunai, the god of the Jews; Libat (Venus) becomes Ruha (d-Qudša), the Holy Spirit of the Christians; Nbu (Mercury, the god of deception and of writing) becomes Mšiha, Messiah, that is, Christ (considered a heretical and deceiving Mandaean, the author of another "book," the Gospel); Nirig (Mars, the god of violence) becomes Muhammad (in a territory occupied militarily by Islamicized Arabs, the connection with violence is obvious); in one isolated case, Moses is identified with Kiuan (Saturn, the planet of Saturday).

The first text excerpt offered here is wholly devoted to the polemic against other religions, entitled "the collapse of the seven stars." It is a kind of heresiological treatise and appears in the form of a revelation conceded by Manda d-Hiia to Hibil, Šitil, and Anuš, and revealed by them to the Mandaeans. Through it the divinity leads the faithful Mandaean to an understanding of the true meaning, the actual demoniacal root, of the various religious sects with which he has met. These, often called "doors," are not always easy to identify, though it is sometimes clear that Christian churches or communities are being dealt with. The anti-Islamic conclusion, dedicated to Nirig, will be found later on (pp. 258-59).

GR 9.1 (Pet. 222-31; Lid. 223-32)

. . . [Manda d-Hiia] revealed to them [part] of the mysteries and the crimes of the seven planets and of the first following that Kiuan among all the stars of anger procured for himself among the sons of the great stock of the Life (the Mandaeans). He prepared a veil (cowl) and distorted the sign.[1] He sent prophets of deception and placed the cross of darkness on their left shoulder and captured them by their houses. He appeared to them in the guise of the messenger and defined himself "the Lord of Lords, the God who shows portents in the heavens and on the earth." He established himself with those who fast, male and female, made monks of the men and nuns of the women and established himself with them. Demons, *daiuia* and *liliata* lie with them, male *daiuia* go with the women and female *liliata* go with the men. They imprison their bodies, they kill them, and draw out the souls from their bodies before their time. They teach them a wisdom based on lies, they appear as images of light, they appropriate the speeches of the alien man, and they make deceptive speeches and prepare a house of mysteries, where they perform their ceremonies. They lie with each other, gather up their seminal emissions, mix them with water from the Iardna and of Ocean, both old and fresh; they take . . .[2] from all the sons of man and they make it similar to the *pihta* of the alien man, and in this way they chain their souls up. Each of them, when they die, place blood, filth and (?) of black water and oil on their mouths. Like my disciples, they prepare *masiqta* and *dukrana* for themselves. They are called prophets of lies. They impose on themselves a fast of 4 days, of 8 days, and of 20 days with [the command of] silence. He imposes on them a fast of 50 and 61 days. . . . Lo, I have spoken of Kiuan and of the following he has ac-

1. The "distorting of the sign" must be the sign of the cross or the Christian baptismal anointing. This is how, in an esoteric passage, the difference between the Mandaean "sign" and the Christian one is explained: "And take oil with your finger near to the thumb of your right hand and mark [the baptized] from the right ear to the left ear; the sign of Kušṭa, of the Father, is more radiant than the sign of Mšiha, of the mother, since he reigns over the world of darkness, of the left." Both the sign of the cross and the Christian baptismal anointing of the ears, with which the Mandaean marking seems to be quite evidently connected, first touch the left-hand side of the body, and only afterward the righthand side. The intentional plays on words should be noted, between anointing and Mšiha — Christ, i.e., "Anointed" — and between the usual (in Gnostic contexts) negative value given to what is female, maternal, and what is of the left.

2. There is a word that cannot be understood here.

quired among the sons of the great stock of the Life. They suffer from hunger more than the snake and suffer from thirst more than the ant. When their spirit dies, it goes out like ashes; and their soul is extinguished like the coals of a fire. . . . He (Kiuan) and the following he has acquired will end on the last day.

Now I shall speak to you of Šamiš and the following he has acquired. From him come the Iazuqei.[3] They make themselves similar to me, the alien man. They tie their *bursma*[4] like crosses on their shoulders. They name the name of Išu. Like *pihta* and *mambuha* which are mine, of the alien man, they take *uasqa;*[5] like *masiqta* they prepare *'ndruna.*[6] Water and fire they revere very greatly. They eat the dead[7] and say that God has killed them. They go to bed with mothers and daughters. They impose silence on themselves. They take the clothing of menstruating women, they clothe themselves with it and wrap it round them saying: we do not contaminate ourselves. They do not recognize their acts of violence. When their women abort their fetuses through their bellies, they take the skin off them, they take them to seven springs, they sprinkle the urine of animals over them and they rinse them down with a feather cloth.

From the door of the Iazuqei originate the Jews. They mount each other and circumcise themselves and with their hands they rub their faces [with blood]. They take the blood from circumcision, and water, and they spray it on their faces. What they have prepared to eat, they sprinkle with this blood. They are called Jews because they have sinned, and *maskilania*[8] because they perform deeds of madness.[9] When their spirit dies, you burn them in a flaming fire.

From the circumcised and good-for-nothing Jews come all the peoples and the doors of darkness. They soil, and contaminate themselves, with their own filth and menstrual juices. Whoever performs their deeds

3. In the Talmud, *iezuqim* are called the "pious."
4. The sacred staffs of the Parsees.
5. The sacred food of the Parsees.
6. *Druna,* a Syriac name for the blessed bread of the Parsees.
7. The custom of the Parsees, to expose the corpses of their dead to the elements and to the vultures until all the flesh has gone, has provoked these merciless judgments in the contexts of polemics between religions.
8. *Maškylym* means "wise men" and is found in Daniel (cf. Dan. 11:33-35) and in the Qumran texts.
9. The text contains a double play on words that cannot be translated.

is unworthy of the house of the Life. Whoever eats their food, his eyes will not see the light. Whoever shows them friendship dies the second death.[10] . . .[11]

Good; I have spoken to you about the door of the Jews; now I shall speak to you of the door of the star Libat (Venus), that is different from other stars. From her derives adultery, lust, and prostitution. From her come 360 songs and shamelessness of all kinds; evil spirits come from her. They prepare banquets and choruses and throw imprisonment everywhere. They prepare dulcimers and harps and furnish lust, imprisonment and song to the "chosen ones of Ruha (spirit)." They hang dulcimers on their shoulders and place flutes and songs on their mouth and thus speak with violent anger. Women and men, big and little thus heat themselves and get into heat and rub up against one another. Lust wraps itself around them and they throw themselves into the dance. The demons *(humria)* of Nirig in the form of monkeys sit on their shoulders; they make them jump about in the dance and they throw them into clefts of fire. They surround them with magic and lust and remain imprisoned in the mystery of intoxication, and they do not know what they do.

Then another door derives from them, called that of the M(i)nunei. They clothe themselves in roses, they cover themselves with roses and place on their heads the crowns of lust and prostitution. Their breast is bared in perdition and their sides are open to dishonor. They capture the sons of men and push them into a trap. They are called "the stock of heroic men and of the clots gone rotten."[12] Beings are killed and imprisoned, and it is their fault. They practice witchcraft with the entire stock of souls (the Mandaeans). With magic and evil actions they seize men in their houses, they take them away from their women and throw them into very serious sufferings. They are called "the chosen ones of Ruha and of Mšiha (of the Spirit and of Christ)." They take away prisoners, they drag off loot and utter

10. I.e., he will not have eternal life.

11. The text here contains the following insertion: "I speak to you, my disciples, and I explain to you every thing. All that you bring home from the market or from the streets, wash it with water and then eat it. [He] who does not wash before eating will be tortured on instruments of ice."

12. The text appears to contain an intended Mandaean misunderstanding of the official terminology for the members of the sects. As far as their name goes, *mnunaiia* or *minunaiia* seems to be connected to the *mynym* of the Judaic traditions, i.e., "heretics," among which are sometimes included the Nazarene Jews, i.e., Christians.

the name of death.[13] They take home and sell and earn gold and wealth. . . .[14] They kill a Jewish child, they take his blood, they cook it in bread and they proffer it to them as food. They mix the menstrual blood of a nun who prostitutes herself with their wine, and they give it to them in a chalice to drink. The glance of the sons of men cannot fall upon them, and they do not allow themselves to be observed. They distort the works of the alien man. They dig a bath in the earth, they steal water from the Iardna, they have it boil on a fire,[15] they pour it into the pool and they make men and women enter into it completely naked.[16] They baptize them in water and give each of them that water to drink. They pronounce over them the name of death, the name of the Father, of the Son, and of the Holy Spirit. They baptize them and utter over them the name of Mšiha. Then there is also another mystery, that is called "the sacrament of the female ass with four legs."[17] . . . It is called the "dirty" sacrament, with which the entire stock of souls is imprisoned. To them belong the unmarried and the "saints," those whose seed runs down their legs and those that kill their babies inside their bodies. They are called "celibate" and "saints" and have to remain imprisoned in the *maṭarata*. From them come the monks and nuns, who sink down into the great Sea of Sup.[18]

Then there is another door, of those that shave their heads[19] and make a god of a piece of wood and invoke him. They paint the gods in

13. In contrast to the name of the Life, the Christian "name" is the name of death.

14. The text continues with a description of their punishment; then, among numerous small corruptions of the text, it begins to speak of their "seven sacraments." What follows is evidently a description of the Christian Eucharist and baptism.

15. This alludes, perhaps, to the practice of warming baptismal water for reasons of weather or health. In any case, a practice of this kind makes the water of Christian baptism "cut" and therefore not valid, even if originally derived ("stolen") from a watercourse that in itself would offer water valid for Mandaean baptism.

16. Nakedness in baptism is a characteristic of the ritual of ancient Christian churches, especially in the East. The practice must have appeared scandalous to Mandaean eyes, since they always baptize themselves fully dressed (and with the women, as we have seen, wearing an extra layer of clothing).

17. From Christian heresiological texts we learn of the existence (real or presumed) of sects of a Satanic character, featuring the worship of a so-called "ass with three legs." The terminology used is unknown elsewhere; unfortunately an unclear phrase follows here.

18. The Sea of Sup (or Waters of Sup) is the Sea of Reeds in which, according to Exodus 15, the armies of the Pharaoh perished. In the Mandaean texts this name often indicates the turbid waters of the kingdom of darkness.

19. These must have been Christian monks, or Christians in general, painted here as idolaters or worshippers of icons.

their houses and invoke them, they and their sons and their daughters. They play their castanets (rattles?) and perform works of witchcraft, of [evil] wisdom and vileness. They lie with their wives during menstruation and call it "the hope of the house of the divinity of our Lord Jesus Christ (Išu Mšiha)." Ruha speaks to them: "Do not consider her impure, since there is no prohibition for you." Then Ruha says to them: "Whoever's father, mother, or eldest son, who is dear to them, dies; place him in your houses and do not separate him from yourselves." She (Ruha) tells them yet another mystery: "Whatever Philosophos, Katholikos, Metropolites, Episkopos, Presbyteros, Diakonos[20] who dies amongst you, put them in the church, honor them and pray for them and do not take them away from your houses of prayer. Also every Visitor, Cleric (?), priest of the nocturnal vigils (?) that among you departs, who is instructed in the miracles of Mšiha, place him on the altar and do not consider him impure."[21]

I wish to speak with you of another door, that of the sacrament of the temple, that burns in the heart of men and burns in their minds. Seven "saints" go together, sleep with the same woman, throw their seed inside of her, and she becomes pregnant of them. Then after seven months they beat her up so that she has an abortion. Then they take the fetus, the placenta, the blood, the excrement and the menstrual liquid and they prepare with the marrow of bones the oil of benediction. This mystery they cook in water. And with the bones they prepare the *mdudia* (?) of the sacrament. This mystery they cook in the oven with flour and honey. They perform witchcraft and lasciviousness inside, and it is called the "sacrament of the *gumarta*," that which burns in the heart and in the mind.[22] Whoever eats it, his face cannot reach the house of the Life, and remains hidden for worlds and generations.[23]

20. In an area of the Syriac language, the higher ranks in the Christian Church are expressed by Greek terms transliterated and adapted; the Mandaean here reproduces the terminology of the Syriac Church (*philosophos*, obviously, is irrelevant except for its sound or for an intended irony).

21. Houses of prayer are the Judaic "synagogues," but here certainly the term indicates Christian churches. The passage alludes to Christian burial in consecrated earth, often inside churches, and to the cult of the relics of saints.

22. *Gumarta* means "host" in Syriac, but also coal; on this play of words the allusion to fire and to burning is founded. As for "temple," the expression used (*bit mqadšia;* "house of holiness") may indicate the temple of Jerusalem.

23. The expression means "for ever and ever."

I wish to speak with you of another door, that generates great confusion in the stock of souls. From it have come out the monks and the nuns. They wander about the hills, the high places and the fields, and to all appearances are similar to demons. They go about completely naked, and their hair makes them look like stinking goats.[24] Their appearance is uglier than the night and more frightful than the yelling darkness. They are called "anchorites." They graze on grass,[25] and they cannot eat foods that are fine and wholesome, that Ptahil the creator of the heaven and the earth created. They know no joy; Ruha and Mšiha do not let them experience any pleasure in this world. Demons whisper to them and then they say: "God is whispering to us; we shall not separate ourselves from God." They call my disciples "soothsayers" and "sellers of buckets of water";[26] and they say to my disciples: "You do not have the right faith in the world." They impose fasts on their mouths, so that the name of the murdered man should not disappear from their midst.[27] They take dust from a dead man and put it in all their foods and dishes.[28] . . .

Then I explain to you, my disciples, that there is yet another door, that derives from Mšiha. They are called "Zandiqi"[29] and "Mardmani."[30] They sow seeds in concealment and entrust their part to the darkness. Men and women lie together, gather up the seed, they put it in wine and they give it to drink to the souls (to the Mandaeans) and say that it is pure. They invoke the wind, fire, and water; they pray to the sun and the moon.[31]

---

24. The monastic movement, especially in the Syriac areas, was often characterized by extreme positions and was sometimes the object of condemnation and persecution by the ecclesiastical authorities. Here it appears that mendicant or wandering monks of the Messalian type are being criticized — or perhaps they are the ones that in the Syriac area were called *sarabaite*.

25. These were called *boskoi* in Greek.

26. A rare Mandaean testimony to a Christian reaction to Mandaeanism itself.

27. This "murdered man" quite obviously is Jesus Christ.

28. This would seem to be a critique of relics. There follows a description of the punishments that await the Naṣuraiia who adhere to Christian practices.

29. "Heretics"; this is how the Christians of Syria referred to the Manichaeans.

30. These are the Manichaeans, from Mar (lord, father, saint) Mani.

31. The sun and the moon were very important in Manichaean soteriology. The phases of the moon, indeed, were explained as first a filling up and then an emptying of the moon. It was filled with all the spiritual matter coming from the earth and directed at the sun. The two planets were therefore the necessary means by which the light could reach the world above the heavens, proper to it.

When their spirit dies, they are like the flies on a vase. The vapor rises and catches them; they lose their wings, are taken and fall inside. They are called "the election that Mar Mani has elected." Any Naṣuraia who takes food from them is thrown down headlong into the great Sea of Sup.

I have spoken to you of Ruha, of Mšiha, and of the seven sacraments that they have made in the world, so as to imprison the stock of souls. Now I wish to recount to you further of another door, the one that Bil has made. They take the crown upon themselves and exercise kingly power. From them the book of Ruha comes. . . .[32]

Now I will teach you about Sin (Moon) and of the shout he emitted. From him come the Jews, the deliberate abortions and miscarriages, and male and female lepers.[33] He does evil everywhere throughout Tibil. He adds and takes away, raises and lowers, carries up on high and throws down. He cuts away quantity and number [from life]. He ruins the years and provokes evil in the days, the months and the years.[34] He leads away from the true path the entire stock of souls. Demons *(humria)* who are stinking and prostitutes, who settle on men and women, come from him. They are called *baiuazig,*[35] and they wash themselves with water. They put a priest at their head, go to bed with him and produce seed in him, they take this mystery, they cook it in a cake, they take it to a point on a border,[36] they bind themselves with oaths, and they do not reveal it to each other. They are also called "miscarriages" and "abortions." . . .[37]

What follows is the concluding fragment of a passage against the planets and against Christianity. In it Nirig (Mars) does not yet appear to be Islamicized.

---

32. There follows an extensive passage against the rulers of the earth, a passage that expresses the problems of an oppressed minority. Then the rest of the text is directed against those who feed on wild game and against the jewels and the rich clothes of women.

33. In many religions the god of the Moon, the "planet" that waxes and wanes, is considered to be responsible for physical irregularities, especially in cases of mutilation and incompleteness, or else of elephantiasis and monstrosity.

34. The phrase seems to reflect a speculation on the irreconcilability of the lunar calendar with the solar calendar.

35. The term is not Mandaean (it is probably Persian) and is not perspicacious; it seems to mean: "those of the power/word of God."

36. Where it would seem the exorcisms work better.

37. Their punishment follows.

GR 2.1.160-61 (Pet. 59-60; Lid. 53)

160. The *daiuia* of Nirig spread theft among the sons of man. Because of their theft the sons of man are torn apart. Sources of anger and idols throw themselves down on the sons of men and fill them with anger, and these are dismembered. Those become rippers (executioners), they become priests and soothsayers, and they cut their body to pieces. Those *daiuia* and *humria* of Nirig and the satans place themselves upon them, they eat of their flesh and drink of their blood and they become a spectacle in the world. They practice astrology, and the soothsayers prepare offerings for them both raw and cooked. They establish themselves in their temples everywhere, on *tells*, roofs, mountains, high places, and in every city, and they lead the sons of men away from the path of faith. They lead astray the whole world with tabors, flutes, horns and *shofars;*[38] they speak with a loud voice and lead the world astray. They lead the hearts of the sons of men astray, and they intoxicate them with the intoxication of love, the sumptuousness of gold and silver and with sculpture in lengthened shapes, that are fashioned with mud. These futile works of their own hands they then worship; they prostrate themselves before them and smoke before them.

161. Some among them worship the angels of fire and the stars that wander across the celestial sphere, whose splendor and luminosity can light up the worlds of darkness. Those obtuse and vile do not know that that splendor has come from the superior height and has merely been entrusted to the wanderers, so that they may wander day and night.

My last excerpt is an example of the outcome of the polemic between religions in an esoteric text like *Alp Trisar Šuialia*. The text, explaining the true meaning of the girdle or waistband Mandaeans use, criticizes its different use by the various sects. The Mandaean's waistband has a cosmic value (it marks the line of separation between the world of light and the world of darkness).

ATŠ 1.2.250

Woe to him who doth not acknowledge its power! He will perish at the ending of the worlds. Woe unto those who tie it (the girdle) but know not

---

38. The Judaic ceremonial horn is here considered a pagan instrument.

[its esoteric meaning] nor do they know whither they are going. (Woe unto) those who tie on (a girdle woven of) black hair or of leather of various colours and kinds! When they wish to perform their rites their bodies and bones are not compactly held together until, by some kind of girdle, they bind together all that they find. And [some] tie [it] beneath their clothes[39] and [others] above their clothes, and those who are clerks and functionaries of the world tie it before the king of the Jews ([ia]hutaiia) and Christians (mšihaia) who are not girdled with a girdle; those who worship fire and those who hang up a cross; embracing the girdle and kissing it without knowing what they do,[40] (like unto) beasts of burden, or to a horse unbroken and unridden until it is girt with a girth.

39. The ritual custom of the Parsees is being criticized here.
40. This seems to be alluding to the Christian ritual in the preparation of the mass.

5. The Jews, Jerusalem, and Miriai

Anti-Judaism is a constant in Mandaean texts of any age. Jerusalem often takes on a cosmic significance, becoming a symbol of the world of darkness, the corrupt and feminine mark of the depravation reigning in Tibil. Judaism is often considered the first religious deviation (from Mandaeanism, the first religion), the one from which all other religions derive. A vision of past religious history of this kind has a clearly apologetic and polemical significance, since what is said against any other religion can be projected onto the Judaic matrix. This latter aspect comes out clearly in the passage that follows, taken from the first treatise of the *Ginza*. It is presented in the form of a revelation, originally destined for Adam, then to all "the elect," that is, the Mandaeans.

GR 1.163-80[1] (Pet. 23-26; Lid. 24-27)

163. I say to you, my elect, and I teach you, my faithful. Do not praise the Seven and the Twelve. . . .

164. Do not praise the sun and the moon. . . .

165. Do not praise Šamiš, whose name is Adunai, whose name is Qaduš, whose name is Il Il (El El); in addition he has other hidden names, not shown in the world.

166. He, Adunai, chose a people for himself and founded a synagogue[2] for himself. The place Jerusalem was built, the city of the Jews, who

1. Cf. GR 2.1.101-17.
2. Literally: "house of prayers." In the Mandaean texts it indicates the place where the

circumcise themselves with the sword and sprinkle their faces with their blood and in this way worship Adunai. Husbands abandon their wives, go forth together and lie with one another. The womenfolk lie in the bosoms of their husbands during their menstrual periods. They stray from the first doctrine and produce a book for themselves.

167. I say to you, my chosen stock, have nothing to do with those slaves whose masters have forced them into prostitution. Do not mix with the Jews, who do not follow a simple, unified speech.[3]

168. All peoples and doors[4] proceed from the Jewish people.

169. Lying prophets came into being who wander about in lies and falsehood.[5] They come from angels of imperfection in the wombs of women, who become pregnant with them and give birth to them in blood and menstrual discharge.[6] They bring forth [false] wisdom from their hearts and by it they cast deception into the world. They style themselves "gods" and call themselves "messengers" (or "apostles"). They are clothed in a body and take on the form of men. They write a fraudulent book, impose prohibitions on them, and make them say a false prayer. They throw lasciviousness, lust, and passion upon the face of the earth and call themselves "prophets."

170. I now, the first messenger, teach and say to all the Naṣuraiia:

Jews carry out their religious acts; sometimes, as here, it is the Judaic cultic place in Jerusalem, i.e., the temple. It may well be asked, however, whether or not the Mandaeans have ever had a clear idea of what the temple of Jerusalem had been.

3. I.e., they are divided into many sects and religions. Probably, also, the metaphor of the slave made to prostitute himself or herself has the same meaning: the religious authorities (the masters) drive their followers into idolatry and apostasy; to have (sexual) relationships with them means to adhere to the various religious beliefs.

4. Here begins the historical and theological illustration of the affirmations on the Judaic responsibility for the proliferation of religions among humanity just uttered above.

5. The expression is ambiguous. It can refer to actual Jewish prophets (those of the Bible), just as to Abraham, Moses, Jesus, and Muhammad, the last and most frightening prophet of lies.

6. This phrase contains many interesting concepts. In the first place we have the "angels of imperfection," i.e., in Greek Gnostic language, of *kenoma*, physical negativity, as opposed to the "fullness" *(pleroma)* of the divine world. Their getting the women pregnant could be the final outcome of the legends of angelic sin of which Genesis and many Judaic apocrypha *(Enoch, Jubilees)* speak. This kind of conceiving, however, is the one that, according to the Mandaeans, traditionally led to the birth of Jesus, whose physical nature and contamination are usually underlined precisely by the expression "menstrual discharge and blood."

. . . Do not listen to their speech, . . . do not have anything to do with them, who do not follow a single, unified speech. . . . One king outrages another king, one prophet denies the truth of other prophets.[7] . . .

180. This is the first teaching, that was entrusted to Adam, the ancestor of the human race. And it was one unified speech and one single witness.

JERUSALEM

Mandaean texts are certainly aware that Judaism is also a historical reality. Thus in the *Ginza* there are some accounts of Jerusalem that we could call "historical." The story of Jerusalem's construction is always accompanied by the memory of its ruin. Information deriving from Judaic legends, such as those on King Solomon and his power, are not lacking.

GR 1.189-91 (Pet. 27; Lid. 28)

189. From Nu the man until the place Jerusalem was built [there passed] six generations. It flowers for a thousand years.[8]

190. Then King Solomon, the son of David, was born and presents himself, and becomes king of Judaea and powerful sovereign of Jerusalem. Demons and *dauia* submit to him and go according to his will, until he exalts himself and is no longer grateful for the goodness of his Lord. So demons and *dauia* distance themselves from his word and his power is taken away from him.[9]

7. As above, here too, "king" and "prophets" can lead us to think of biblical history or else, more probably, to the religious history of the time of the Mandaean author. King and prophets would then be the founders and heads of the religious sects with which Mandaeans were then in contact.

8. See n. 10.

9. This is the legend of King Solomon, of his vainglory, punishment, and final rehabilitation. The story is well known to Islamic, Christian, and Judaic traditions, as well as Mandaean ones. Perhaps the most extensive Mandaean story of Solomon is the one Petermann recorded from the voice of Iahia. In a parallel text to ours (GR 2.1.123-25 [Pet. 50; Lid. 46), the construction of Jerusalem is attributed to Solomon, as in *4 Ezra* and in certain Judaic legends. The starting idea is that the city coincides with the temple and that he who constructed the one constructed the other.

In the following passage Solomon disappears and Jerusalem turns out to have been built before Abraham.

GR 18 (Pet. 381-82; Lid. 410-11)

Then the age of the world was entrusted to Šum bar Nu and his wife Nhuraita, by whom the world was reawakened. 6,000 years then passed and 2,000 were left. Then Iurba, whom the Jews call Adunai, meditated, together with his partner Ruha and the seven planets. They decided to found a party. By Adunai's order they built a city, that was called the place Jerusalem. It measures 60 miles in width, must flourish for a 1,000 years, remain 1,000 years destroyed and then the entire Tibil will be destroyed.[10]

Then Abraham was created, the father of the Jews. He and his entire stock journeyed (?) in the land of the Egyptians, whose king was called King Pharaoh (Pirun). . . .[11]

Then, up until 400 years passed in Jerusalem,[12] Jesus, the son of Mary, was born not in Jerusalem. Then was born Jesus, the head of the Christians *(Mšihaiia)*. He made himself a church and chose a community for himself.[13]

---

10. This is perhaps the only Mandaic text of clearly millennialistic origins. It rests on a meditation in which the millennium of cosmic rest, expected before the end, is replaced by a millennium in which Jerusalem remains destroyed. This meditation is of Judaic origin and comes from a period and from environments in which every hope of rebuilding the city had been lost.

11. There follows the story of the passage across the Red Sea, already seen above, p. 131.

12. Therefore 600 years before its destruction and 1,600 years before the end of the world.

13. GR 18 contains two other notations connected to Jerusalem. In a long and composite list of sovereigns who were supposed to have reigned on the earth "from the Flood to the completion of the years of the kings," we find: "After him there was King Dašmšid, who is called King Solomon, son of David. He reigned 1,000 years, 900 on the earth and 100 in the heavens. After him there was King Bruq [there is a gap in the text here], who is called Sandar (Alexander) the Roman ["Romans," i.e., Byzantines, is what the Orientals call the Greeks]. He reigned 14 years." Further on, we also find a chronographical connection: "from the day in which Jerusalem was destroyed, until King Iazdigar, son of Bahran, took power over the Persians, pass 594 years of this last millennium." The number 594 is 6 times 99, so it is a symbolic number. In any case, at the coming to the throne of Iazdeger II (A.D. 438), there would be 406 years to the end of the world.

The poetic passage that follows is composed of two distinct stories, though of similar content. The first, shorter one, records the revelation in the world of Anuš 'Utra, whose realization Ruha tries to oppose by creating the party of the Jews and founding Jerusalem. The origins of Judaism therefore clearly postdate the revelation of Mandaean truth.

GR 15.11 (Pet. 328-33; Lid. 336-44)

Who told Ruha, who informed her, who [lives] in imperfection and error, who told the liar, that the alien man had come here?[14] Ruha spoke in anger and called together her first-born sons.[15] She spoke to them: "Come, come my first-born sons, hear what I have to say to you. Come, meditate on how to carry out evil, and let us found a party in this world, in the stock of the alien man who has come down here."

The seven stars then gathered together, and went to Ruha d-Qudša. They said to her: "How must we found a party within this world?" And she said to them: "Come, let us lie next to each other and let us partake of our common mystery. Let us partake of our common mystery and with it we shall fashion a creation. We fashion a creation with it and build the place Jerusalem." The seven stars arose, they lay down with their mother. They lay down with their mother and partook of their common mystery.[16] They partook of their common mystery and built the city of Jerusalem. They built the city of Jerusalem, and left lewdness, perversion, and fornication in it. They said: "Whoever lives in the city of Jerusalem will not mention the name of God (Alaha)."

The second story, which is longer, describes with a wealth of detail the creation of Jerusalem at the conclusion of a series of attempts that fail through

---

14. This kind of repeated rhetorical question is normal in Mandaean poetical texts. It should be noted that the divinity is, Gnostically, a stranger in this world.

15. There being seven of them, and being sons of an incestuous relation with 'Ur, who was already her son, the description "first-born" applied to the planets is to be explained as an outcome of the anti-Christian polemic. The "first-born" par excellence is Jesus Christ, himself considered to be a son of Ruha, insofar as he was a planet.

16. Here "mystery" means seminal liquid. Going outside the metaphor, the text means that the planetary powers, uniting themselves to the evil Spirit of this world (Ruha), emanate a project (the perverse intellectual seed) with which they conceive and give life to a reality contrary to the providential plan of salvation. The language is Gnostic.

the intervention of the Mandaean divinity. In this passage, Ruha is called Namrus, the mother of the world.[17]

There the seven stars arose and Namrus, mother of the world. The seven stars arose and came in their seven chariots. They came in their seven chariots and came down from the firmament to the earth. They abandoned this [that?] world, and they came to Bet Lehem. Ruha said to her sons, she spoke to the good-for-nothing monsters: "My sons! Lower your chariots, we shall build it (the place Jerusalem) in this city." A voice came forth out of the cloud of Anuš 'Utra and spoke to Ruha d-Qudša: "From the place where this place will be built, 365 disciples *(tarmidia)*[18] will go forth." She shouted with her shrill voice, and shrieked, and said to her seven sons: "Rise, rise up, my seven sons, build it not in this city. It is an evil and filthy curse which has come over your chariots. Sit yourselves in your chariots and make haste away from that city."

The identical scene is repeated twice more, in localities called Bet Mṭalalia and Krak Nṣab. Bet Lehem is Bethlehem. Mṭalalia is possibly a deformation of the Arab toponym Maṭarīye, that is, Matarea, an Egyptian city where the Holy Family rested in their flight. Here was and is preserved the sycamore in whose shade the illustrious fugitives rested, and the spring that Jesus brought about so that Mary could wash him with a handkerchief drenched in sweat (from that sweat comes the balsam the region is so rich in). Behind Nṣab, finally, there may be a deformation of Niṣrat (→ Nṣar → Nṣab), that is, Nazareth. The planets, therefore, would have attempted to found Jerusalem in three famous Christological localities. However this may be, the third attempt having failed, the planets take up their flight once again until their chariots "lose their wings," and then, forced to stop, they decide to build Jerusalem there.

They built Jerusalem, from which the Jews came. They committed the works of darkness to them, and the seven pronounced a blessing over

---

17. From *namusa* or *nimusa*, which is considered a Semitic (Syriac) rendering of the Greek word *nomos*, the "law." Ruha is therefore identified with the Torah, the Judaic "Law" and the law of the God of this world.

18. "Disciple" of Anuš, or else Mandaean "priests," both being possible and logical translations. As Jesus has twelve human disciples, the same number as the months of the year, it thus seems right that Anuš 'Utra has 365 disciples, as many days as there are in the Mandaean solar year (see above, p. 148).

them. They called forth guardian angels, fish of the sea and feathered birds, and bewitched them with a spell. They bewitched them with a spell, and handed them over to the Jews in Jerusalem. They uttered a blessing over them and they found everything they sought, in great quantity. The seven columns rose up, from which all perversions and lies[19] derive. The Jews multiplied in the midst of the desert solitude.[20] The Jews multiplied, and the time arrived to form a following.[21]

Anuš 'Utra comes down to Jerusalem, where he converts Miriai (Mary).

From Miriai, the perfect one, Iaqip and Bnia Amin[22] went forth. From Iaqip and Bnia Amin came 365 *tarmidia*. 365 *tarmidia* came forth in the place Jerusalem. The Jews flew into a rage and murdered my *tarmidia*, who pronounced the name of the Life.

Anuš 'Utra, beside himself with rage, obtains a letter from his Father, with the order to eliminate the Jews. In Mandaeanism, in fact, divine orders are usually imparted through a celestial missive (the idea, not peculiar to Mandaeanism alone, probably derives from the custom of the Persian chancellorship to communicate exclusively in writing). Then Anuš 'Utra comes down in the form of a "white hawk" and faces Ruha, striking her with a "bludgeon of light." In the meantime "the Jews in their terror hid themselves in their various apartments."

The Life sent me in anger, to destroy the place Jerusalem. I threw down column after column and cast them down from their position. I shattered the column 'Ursa'il, who had persecuted my *tarmidia*. I smashed the column Iaqip, which stood at the gate of Jerusalem. I shattered the column Adunai, which was in the center of Jerusalem. I shattered the column Zatan, which was situated by the outer walls. I cast down the column Sihmai, which was

---

19. The speculation on the "seven columns," i.e., on the seven extraordinary figures sent by God to uphold the destiny of Judaism in various times, is present in both Judaic and early Christian traditions; for Mandaean texts the "seven columns" are both architectonic features of the city and figures with symbolic names.

20. It would seem the context reworks the Judaic traditions on the Exodus and on the connected miracles (the "feathered birds" could be the quails).

21. I.e., the Life wishes to establish a group of followers in Jerusalem.

22. Jacob and Benjamin?

situated on the inner wall. I cast down the column Karkum, in which all the angels were to be found.[23] I fettered the great tower, in which the watchers of the place Jerusalem were to be found. I destroyed the place Jerusalem, where the blood of my *tarmidia* was poured out. I slew the Jews, who were a persecution of the stock of the Life, all the feathered birds and the horrible beasts that had come from them; the monkeys and wolves that had derived from the Jews; all the evil beasts, against which there was anger.[24] There was rage against them, and they will have to perish in the great Last Day. But security was provided for my *tarmidia,* who had suffered persecution in Jerusalem.[25] I smashed the house of those who were without goodness.

And the Life is victorious.

THE LEGEND OF MIRIAI

In the previous passage the figure of Miriai appeared, to whom two chapters are devoted in the "Book of John." The literary origin of Miriai is the subject of debate. I believe it lies in a Mandaean reworking of Christian legends on the adolescent Mary in the temple, placed on trial by the Judaic authorities since she was found to be pregnant and therefore considered unworthy. In Mandaean texts and stories, Miriai represents a Mandaeanism that strenuously resists Judaic oppression.

JB 34 (Lid. text: 127-31; transl.: 126-29)

Miriai am I, the daughter of the kings of Babylon, daughter of the powerful kings of Jerusalem. The Jews gave birth to me, the *kahnia* brought me up.[26] They took me in their long vestments inside the gloomy house, the temple *(bit qadšia).* Adunai put a weight into my hands and on both my

---

23. It should be noted that there are only six columns, probably because of an error of an ancient scribe who missed one while copying. Since Iaqip is a column, perhaps the one missing is Bnia Amin (Zatan is Satan).

24. Here the "beasts" are probably the various religions, all deriving from Judaism.

25. This is in open contradiction to what has just been narrated, unless the narrator means the security of the world beyond or in the "great Last Day."

26. These are Jewish priests, *kohanim.*

arms.[27] I have to sweep and clean the unsound house. There is nothing in it to defend the poor, nothing to console the tortured souls. My father went into the synagogue, my mother went into the temple. My father went and said, my mother went and commanded me: "Miriai, close your inner doors and shoot the bolt. Mind you do not go out on to the streets and that the suns *(sic)* of my Lord do not fall on you."

But I, Miriai, did not obey what my mother had said, and did not obey with my ear what my father had commanded me to do. I opened the inner doors, and the outer ones I left open. I went out on to the main streets and the suns *(sic)* of my Lord fell on me. I wished to go to the house of the people, but my walking took me to the (Mandaean) temple. I entered and found my brothers and sisters, while they are standing and preaching sermons.

Miriai, having converted to Mandaeanism, is discovered, and the passage closes with a violent row between daughter and father.

(Miriai speaks:) "If I am really a pig-trough of prostitution, then I want to pull your [gap] and the bolt; if I am a bitch in heat, then I want to fling away pegs and latches; if I am a scrap of unworked cloth, sewn to patch up your garment, then cut me away and separate me off from your garment."

Then he shouted: "Come, see Miriai, who has abandoned Judaism and has gone to love her lord. Come, see Miriai, who has left the colored cloth and has gone to love her lord. She has abandoned the *ṭuṭiptia*[28] and has gone to love the man with the *burzinqa* (turban)." And Miriai said to him: "Far be it from me to love him whom I hate; far be it from me to hate him of whom I am fond. No, far be it from me to hate my lord Manda d-Hiia, who is a defense for me in the world. . . . Dust in the mouth of the Jews, ashes in the mouth of all the *kahnia!* The manure between the hoofs of horses reaches the most distinguished among the powerful kings of Jerusalem!"

The second passage devoted to Miriai opens with a symbolic description of the heroine, who represents Mandaeanism in its entirety.

27. These are the bolts or latches of the doors (or perhaps the "outside keys," for which see below, p. 223) that are in her hands, and the keys ("indoor"?) of the temple that are carried tied to her arms.

28. These are phylacteries, or tefillin, little strips with verses of the Bible written on them, worn by practicing Jews.

JB 35 (Lid. text: 131-42; transl.: 129-38)

Miriai am I, the vine, the tree that stands near the mouth of the Euphrates. The leaves of the tree [are] diamonds, the fruits of the tree [are] pearls. The vine leaf of the vine is splendor, its tendrils precious light. Its perfume extended among the trees and went out on to all the worlds.

Among its branches many birds find shelter. But winds and storms drag many away. A "white hawk" exhorts the survivors to remain with Miriai, "the vine that grows at the mouth of the Euphrates":

"Listen to my cry, brothers! Remain firm and bear the persecution. Become a companion to Miriai; company become to Miriai. May the Jews beware, that were a persecution for Miriai. Beware, 'Lizar, the great house, the pillar that holds up the temple.[29] Beware, column Zatan, that has borne lying witness against Miriai."[30]

All the Jews gathered together, the masters, great and small, came and spoke to (of?) Miriai: "She fled from the priests, loved a man and they held hands. They held hands, went and settled by the mouth of the Euphrates. Let us kill them and make Miriai despised in Jerusalem. Let us prepare a pole for the man who has debased Miriai and carried her off. There must be no day in Tibil in which a stranger penetrates Jerusalem. They break into the dovecotes and capture the doves in Jerusalem."[31]

All the Jews then went to the mouth of the Euphrates, where they found Miriai sitting on a throne clothed in the marks of Mandaean priesthood. Even fish and birds come to hear her: "When the Jews saw her, they stood in front of her. They were ashamed, they clenched their fists, they smote their heartstrings and cried." Her mother also intervenes:

"You are a daughter of mine and of all the priests *(sic)*. Your head (father?) is the great summit of the temple (high priest?). You do not remember,

29. In the story Adam told Siouffi of the events of Miriai's life, Eleazar, i.e., 'Lizar, is the father of the girl (and the high priest).

30. It should be noted that at this point the trial of Miriai has not yet taken place.

31. This phrase, aside from its possible literary derivation from the legends about Miriai being fed by doves in the temple, seems to refer to the importance of the Islamic postal system founded on the use of courier pigeons.

Miriai, that the Torah lay in your lap? You opened it, you read from it and knew what was inside it. The outer keys were in your hands, and the inner ones you kept on the little chain. All the priests and the sons of priests came and kissed your hand. You opened the door to whomever you wanted. Those you did not want had to turn around and go back to where they had come from. A thousand stand and two thousand sit down. They threw themselves at your feet like a eunuch slave; they listened to your word in Jerusalem. Why have you forgotten your brothers and your heart has put apart the priests? Look, the brides cry in Judaea, women and men in Jerusalem. They have thrown away from themselves the gold they loved so much, and they have turned to lamentations and mourning for you."

To these and other lamentations follows a fierce reaction from Miriai, who curses the Jews and the *kahnia* and then exclaims:

"I am not a woman who has left through wantonness, and it is not that I have loved a man. I did not go away to come back to you and see you again, you, the dome of error. Go away, go away from me, you who have testified false witness and lies against me. You have testified against me wantonness and theft and have presented me as you yourselves are. May the man who has freed me from my chains and has planted my feet here be blessed. I have committed no wanton act with him and no theft have I performed in the world. Instead of the testimony that you have borne against me, prayer and praise be showered on me."

When the priests stood and spoke to Miriai at the mouth of the Euphrates, there came a pure hawk, whose wings are the fullness of the world. He flew at the Jews, he swooped down over them with his wings, and shackling them together threw them down to the bottom of the water, under the stinking mud. He sank them below the burning (water) that is in the midst of the turbid water. He sank their boats to the bottom of the burning water. He destroyed the temple and set fire to Jerusalem. He provoked their collapse and killed the *tarmidia* in Jerusalem.[32]

32. This phrase is most unexpected, and it seems strange that the messenger of the divinity should kill the Mandaean *tarmidia*. It would also seem extremely improbable, however, that the term means the disciples of the Jews (priests?).

6. John, a True Mandaean

The first passage on John is a brief summary of everything that appears on him in Mandaean literature. It is an insertion in a more extensive anti-Christian passage, some parts of which we shall be seeing in chapter 7, devoted to Jesus.

GR 2.1.151-53 (Pet. 57; Lid. 51)

151. And after that, in that place, a child shall be born and will be called by the name Iuhana, son of Aba Saba[1] Zakria (Zacharias), who was [given] to him in his old age, at the end of a hundred years. His mother, the woman 'Nisbai (Elizabeth), was pregnant with him; in her old age she gave birth to him. When Iuhana will be and will grow in that time of Jerusalem, the faith will dwell in his heart and he will take[2] the Jordan and he will administer baptism for 42 years, before Nbu (Mercury-Christ) has to be clothed in a body and come into the world.

152. And when Iuhana lives, in that time of Jerusalem, and takes the Jordan and performs baptism, Išu Mšiha comes, goes in humility, is baptized in the baptism of Iuhana and through the wisdom of Iuhana [becomes] full of knowledge. Then he distorts the words of Iuhana and modifies the baptism of the Jordan and distorts the speeches of *kušṭa* and preaches crime and deception in the world.

1. Literally: "white-haired father," a highly respectful term for old people.
2. "To take, welcome the *iardna*" means "to be a Mandaean." Here I translate it as "Jordan," as the legend is situated in Palestine.

153. The day in which the measure of Iuhana is full, I myself come to him, and I appear to Iuhana like a little child of three years and a day, and I speak to him of the baptism and I instruct his friends. And thus I draw him out of his body and I bring him up with victory [until] the world where all is splendor, and I baptize him in the white Iardna of gushing water of life. I clothe him in garments of splendor and cover him with turbans of light, and I install praise into his pure heart, from the praise of the angels of light, with which they praise their lord without interruption in eternity.

The three paragraphs into which the passage is divided up correspond to the three types of material on John known to the Mandaeans. The first is a set of legends on his miraculous birth, his education, his return to Jerusalem, and his baptizing activities in the city of the Jews. The second concerns the meeting with Jesus and his baptism. The third is about his meeting with Manda d-Hiia under a false guise, his missed baptism, the death of John, and the ascent of his soul. Literary evidence on the material of the first two can be found primarily in the "Book of John" and in the *Haran Gauaita,* on that of the third, primarily in the *Right Ginza.*

JOHN'S BIRTH, EDUCATION, AND ADVENTURES IN JERUSALEM

Chapters 18–33 of the "Book of John" concern John the Baptist. The redactor of this set, a Mandaean priest of the Islamic era, wishes to recover the figure of John, to set before the faithful a model of the ideal Mandaean in a moment of crisis like the one caused by the Moslem occupation. To do this, he reutilizes archaic legendary material on the infancy of John that appears especially in chapters 18 and 32, the first and the penultimate of the collection.

JB 18 (Lid. text: 66-76; transl.: 75-82)

In the name of the great Life the most high Light be praised.
    A little child was planted from the heights, a mystery was made manifest in Jerusalem.

225

The priests saw dreams. Paralysis took possession of his sons,[3] paralysis took possession of Jerusalem. In the morning he went early to the temple. He opened his mouth in crime and his lips of deception. He opened his mouth in crime and spoke to all the priests: "In my visions of the night I looked, [I looked] in my visions. When I was lying down, I did not sleep and I did not rest, and the sleep of the night did not take possession of me. I did not sleep and I did not rest, when a star appeared and stopped over 'Nisbai (Elizabeth). Fire burned on Aba Saba Zakria (Zacharias); three celestial lights appeared. The sun set and the stars went out. The house of the people (synagogue, i.e., temple) was set fire to, smoke rose up from the house of holiness (temple). A jolt went through the *markabta,* so much so that the earth moved. A star flew down in Judaea; a star flew down in Jerusalem. The sun appeared at night and the moon by day."[4]

When the priests heard that, they threw dust over their heads. Iaqip, the priest, cried, and the tears of Bnia Amin ran down. Šilai and Šalbai threw dust over their heads. 'Lizar (Eleazar) opened his mouth and spoke to all the priests.[5]

The anguish of the priests consists in their not being able to interpret this dream, even if all of them are interpreters of dreams (in particular Iaqip, Bnia Amin, and Ṭab Iumin). Thus, on the advice of the earth, they decide to turn to a certain Liliuk, to whom they write a letter, which is entrusted to Ṭab Iumin. The latter goes and tells, down to the smallest detail, just what had happened.

3. The text, which begins *ex abrupto,* is not very clear; just as the subject of the following sentences is not known, so it is not easy to understand whom the author wishes to make the fathers of these Jews. Two other translations appear possible: "paralysis took possession of the [priests?] by 'Ulai" (the river of Kuzistan, on which it has to be then believed that the author wished to place Jerusalem) or else "paralysis took possession of Be'ula" (the geographical name of an unknown locality, or else another, secret, name for Jerusalem).

4. These are the traditional signs of the end of time according to Judaic and Christian apocalypticism. *Markabta,* literally (celestial) "chariot," here seems to mean the throne-chariot of the manifestation of God (the Jewish *merkabah*) or the entire cosmos.

5. At this point in the story, Iaqip and Bnia Amin are Jewish priests who have not converted to Mandaeanism, as we have previously seen in the stories about Miriai. Eleazar seems to be the high priest, as in certain Armenian legends on the infancy of Jesus. This Eleazar, according to oral traditions, is the father of Miriai. However this may be, the entire scene wants to make the Jews appear ridiculous.

When Liliuk heard that, he threw dust over his head. Naked Liliuk pulled himself out of his bed and took the Book of dreams. . . . He wrote them a letter and explained it to them on a leaf. In it he said to them: "Woe for all you priests, as ʿNisbai will bear a child. Woe for you rabbis *(rabunia),* as a child will be born in Jerusalem. Woe for you masters and disciples (?), as ʿNisbai will bear a child. Woe for you, mistress Torah, as Iuhana will be born in Jerusalem. Iuhana will receive the Jordan and will be called prophet in Jerusalem."

Liliuk writes a letter and says to them: "The star that comes and remains above ʿNisbai [means]: A child will be planted from the highest heights; he will come and will be given to ʿNisbai. The fire, that burned above Aba Saba Zakria [means]: Iuhana will be born in Jerusalem."

Ṭab Iumin runs to Jerusalem and delivers the letter to Eleazar; the latter reads it in silence, passes it to Zacharias, who does the same, and, still in silence, gives it back to him.

ʿLizar then opened his mouth and spoke to Aba Saba Zakria: "O Aba Saba, go from Judaea, so that you may not cause a quarrel in Jerusalem." Then Zakria raised his right hand and struck him on the head and said to him: "O ʿLizar, you great house, you head of the priests. If you knew your mother from the inside, you would not be able to come into our synagogue. If you knew her from the inside, you would not be able to read the Torah. Because your mother was a prostitute. A prostitute she was, who was not acceptable to the house of her father-in-law. Since your father did not have a hundred staters to write her the libel of repudiation, he abandoned her without any formalities and asked no more about her. Does a day pass that I do not come and look and not see Miša (Moses), the son of Amras? Does a day pass perhaps that I do not come and pray in your synagogue, that I now am false and not sincere and you may say a word that you have not heard about me?

"Where is there a dead person who comes back to life, so that ʿNisbai has to give birth to a child? Where is the blind man whose sight returns; where is the cripple, whose feet . . . ,[6] where is there the mute, who reads a book (aloud), so that ʿNisbai has to give birth to a child? Today 22 years

6. A word of uncertain meaning.

227

have past since I last saw a woman. No, it is not through me nor through you that 'Nisbai will give birth to a child."[7]

Then all the priests rose up and said murmuring to Aba Saba Zakria: "Be calm and stay seated, O Aba Saba, and serenity of the good rest upon you. O Aba Saba, if there were not dreams in Judaea, if there were not visions in Jerusalem, then what Miša has said would all be lies.[8] Rather, your word and [also] our word and [also] the dreams we have seen will come about. Iuhana will [actually] welcome the Jordan and will be called prophet in Jerusalem."

Aba Saba went away from their midst, and 'Lizar followed him; then three lights appeared that accompanied him. They ran after him, got hold of Aba Saba by the lapel of his cloak and said to him: "O Aba Saba, what precedes you and what follows you?" And he replied: "O 'Lizar, you great house, you head of the priests; I do not know whom the lights that precede me protect; I do not know whom the fire that follows me is accompanying.[9] Not for my intervention nor through yours 'Nisbai will give birth to a child."[10]

JB 32 (Lid. text: 116-22; transl.: 115-18)

"My father — says Iahia[11] — was 99 years old and my mother 88. They took me from the pool of the Iardna; they took me, they raised me up, they carried me and put me in the body of 'Nisbai. Nine months, they said, you will have to rest in her body, like all other children." He (John) says: "No

7. This seems to be an extreme outcome of the New Testament doubts of Zacharias. The quarrel with the high priest, however, derives from that of Joachim, in the Marian apocrypha about her infancy.

8. The Bible, then, is a set of dreams and visions (or, the anonymous person whose dream is narrated at the beginning is none other than Moses).

9. In the present text, John is not the true son of Zacharias but "a mystery who comes from on high." The story of these miraculous lights, however, that accompany John in the loins of his father shows that the legend originally recognized the full, albeit miraculous, paternity of Zacharias.

10. After a series of also recent and contradictory redactional interventions, the passage ends up with a phrase of Zacharias that reflects the ideas of John propagated by the redactor of JB 18–33.

11. Except for the first chapter of the set, number 18, in which the Mandaean name Iuhana is used, Iahia (of Arab origin) is normally used.

midwife cut my umbilical cord in Jerusalem. They did not shape for me any deceitful image and they did not hang any bell of deceit on me. From 'Nisbai I was born in the place Jerusalem."[12]

Having said this, the story picks up again from before the birth of John, exactly at the point we were at the end of chapter 18 (so that the two chapters can actually be read one after the other).

The place Jerusalem shook, and the wall of the priests swayed from side to side; 'Lizar, the great house, stands, but its body shakes. The Jews gathered together, come to Aba Saba Zakria and speak to him: "O Aba Saba Zakria, you must have a son. Tell us what name we have to give him. Do we have to give him the name Wisdom Iaqip, so that he can teach the book in Jerusalem? Or do we have to give him the name Column Zatan, so that the Jews may swear by him and not do wrong?"[13]

When 'Nisbai heard that, she shouted and said: "Of all these names that you name, I do not wish to give him even one of them. I will give him the name Iahia Iuhana, that the Life itself has given to him."[14] When the Jews heard that, they were filled with evil anger against her and said: "What weapon must we prepare for him and for his mother, so that he be killed by our own hands?"

When Anuš 'Utra heard that, he took the child and carried him to Paruan, the white mountain, on Mount Paruan, where those being breast-fed and small children are nourished with *mambuha*.[15]

12. These words of Iahia correspond to the idea of him that the redactor of JB wishes to defend. Like the Jesus Christ of the Gnostics, who passed through the body of Mary without receiving anything, this John not only comes directly from the Iardna of light (brought by the unnamed '*utria*) but does not enter into a relation of physical dependence with his mother. The latter houses him within herself, but there is not even an umbilical cord. Since he is, then, of a nature superior to the various demoniacal entities, all the little apotropaic images and bells used at the time of labor are revealed to be useless.

13. The proposal, for the Jews, is supposed to be attractive. We have already met "Column Iaqip" and "Column Zatan" in GR 15.11.

14. The polemic on the imposition of the name is of distant New Testament origin.

15. The story is proceeding in a very summary manner and requires some explanation. In the Christian apocrypha, the child saint John is saved by one or more angels who, with or without the mother (the father is usually killed), snatch him away from Herod's cut-throats (who wish to kill him) and take him into the desert or on to a mountain. For the Mandaeans, Mount Paruan (in the more ancient texts Taruan) is a kind of paradisal moun-

"Until I was 22.[16] There I learned all my wisdom and I learned all my speech in its entirety. They clothed me with clothes of radiance and covered with veils of cloud; they wrapped a waistband around me, a waistband of water, that shone and was radiant beyond measure. They placed me in a cloud, a cloud of radiance, and in the seventh hour one Sunday they took me to the place Jerusalem."[17]

Then a voice sounded in Judaea, a shout announced in Jerusalem. They shouted: "Which woman had a son, that was seized and taken from her? What woman took a vow for him and then took no further interest in him? What woman had a son that was seized and taken away? She should come and seek her son."

The folktale now triumphs. Elizabeth runs to meet him without putting her veil on, and so Zacharias, despite the venerable age of both (121 and 110 years), decides to repudiate her. The sun and the moon intervene, and the sun says to Zacharias that he is being foolish ("a twit . . . like an Arab"). Zacharias thus disappears from the story, nor is he remembered elsewhere in the book (one supposes he did not divorce). Elizabeth goes to meet her son, who descends from the cloud and kisses her on her lips. Anuš ʿUtra (he is the one therefore who accompanied him and who is considered his "guardian angel") objects to this, but John makes a spirited reply: he kisses the lips of "the woman who has given birth" (she who, though she had given birth to him, was not his mother) to thank her for having housed him in her body "for nine months, just like all other babies." This too is evidence of John's extraordinary origins, and he is thus praised by Anuš ʿUtra. The latter, before going away, entrusts the youth ("until we come and take him") to the sun and the moon, who therefore have nothing diabolical about them. The passage ends here.

---

tain, on which the tree grows that gives milk to babies who died before their time. The idea of the existence of such a tree is widespread in many cultures and is present in Judaic traditions (there the educating angel is Metatron). Here the redactor, speaking of *mambuha* (the sacred water that is drunk in the ceremonies), seems to deny the legend of the tree and think of the Mandaean celestial ritual.

16. Without any interruption and without the slightest indication, John takes up the story once more.

17. John, then, reaches Jerusalem in the vestments of a celestial priest, armed with a knowledge that does not come from this world.

The redactor of JB 18–33, in addition to reworking more ancient legends, develops on his own initiative a very clear exaltation of John, who emerges as a semi-divine hero, a model of courageous and consistent behavior before all-powerful Islam. Special attention is given to the relationship of John with women, who are considered dangerous, in that they may easily lead to apostasy. For his part, John decided not to marry so as to be able to continue the practice of nocturnal prayer, which he could not utter in the state of impurity necessarily deriving from the married state. A letter from heaven resolves the difficulty by indicating which nights of the week should be set aside for prayer and which for conjugal obligations. His wife too, however, is gifted with special characteristics.

JB 31 (Lid. text: 111-16; transl.: 111-14)

Then they fashioned for Iahia a wife from you, O Place of the faithful.[18] At the first pregnancy Handan and Šarrat were born. With the middle pregnancy Bihram and R'imat Hiia were born. With the last pregnancy Nṣab, Sam, Anhar Ziua and Šarrat were born. These three pregnancies took place in you, O Ruin [of] Jerusalem.[19]

Iahia opened his mouth and spoke to Anhar[20] in Jerusalem: "Instruct your daughters, that they may not be ruined, and I shall instruct and illuminate my sons, that they not be put in chains." Then Anhar opened her mouth and spoke to Iahia in Jerusalem: "I have given birth to children in Tibil" — she told him — "but I have not given birth to [their] hearts in Tibil. If they let themselves be instructed, they will ascend to the place of light, and if they do not let themselves be instructed, the flaming fire will destroy them."

Iahia opened his mouth and spoke to Anhar in Jerusalem: "When I leave Tibil, tell me what you will do after I have gone." "I shall not eat and I shall not drink" — she replied — "until I see you again." "You have spoken lies, O Anhar, and your word has come out in deception. When a day

18. Mata d-Kuštania, "Place of the faithful" or "Place of the true," equivalent to Mšunia Kušṭa.

19. The numbers (eight children and three pregnancies) must have symbolic value, of perfection or something similar. To the birth of John's children corresponds the collapse of Jerusalem.

20. This is the name of John's wife, who was unnamed before this point.

comes and a day goes, [after my death] you will eat and you will drink and you will forget about me, you will put me out of your mind. I asked you rather for the great Life and for the Vigil of the Day, whose name is dear: When I leave Tibil, what will you do after I have gone?" "I shall not wash and I shall not comb my hair" — she said — "until I see you again." "You have lied again, O Anhar, and your word has come out in deception. When a month comes and a month goes, you will wash yourself and comb your hair and you will forget me and put me out of your mind. Once more I asked you, O Anhar, for our first marriage bedding: When I leave my body, tell me, what will you do after I have gone?" "I shall not wear new clothes ever again" — she replied — "until I see you again." "You have lied once again, O Anhar, and your word has come out in deception. When a year comes and a year goes, you will wear new clothes and you will forget me and put me out of your mind."

The passage carries on in this way a little further, with Anhar seemingly unable to find a satisfactory reply. In the end, funeral honors and a fine tomb having also been refused, Iahia himself will urge the repeated reading of *masiqta*, the Mandaean ceremony for the dead.

THE BAPTISM OF JESUS CHRIST

JB 30 (Lid. text: 103-8; transl.: 103-8)

... Išu ... went to the bank of the Jordan and spoke to him: "Iahia, baptize me with your baptism and utter over me the Name that you take care of pronouncing. If I show myself to be your [true] disciple, I will remember you in my written word; if I do not make a good showing as your disciple, cancel my name from your sheet."[21]

Iahia answered Išu Mšiha in Jerusalem: "You have lied to the Jews and deceived the priests. The seed you have separated from men and the labor and the pregnancy from women. The Sabbath, that Moses tied, you

21. Jesus asks for discipleship and promises in exchange for remembering John in his writings (the Gospel).

unknotted in Jerusalem. You have deceived them with horns and have extended opprobrium (Christianity) with the *shofar*."[22]

Unlike what we have seen above, John, far from being deceived by Jesus, realizes perfectly well his deceiving nature and repeatedly refuses to baptize him. After a lengthy exchange, during which Jesus tries to demonstrate that the impossible is possible, the situation is resolved through divine intervention.

"So baptize me, O Iahia, with your baptism, and the Name that you take care of pronouncing, pronounce over me. If I show myself to be your [true] disciple, I shall remember you in my written word; if I do not show myself to be worthy to be your disciple, erase my name from your leaf. You will be called to account for your sins, and I will be called to account for my sins."

When Išu Mšiha said this, a letter came from the house of Abatur: "Iahia, baptize the deceiver in the Jordan. Guide him to the Jordan and baptize him and take him back out on to the bank again and set him there."

Then Ruha disguised herself as a dove and threw a cross into the Jordan.[23] She threw a cross on to the Jordan and changed the water into several colors "Jordan" — she said — "you sanctify me and sanctify my seven sons."

Also in the Mandaean traditions, then, Jesus' baptism creates problems. For the Christians, in fact, it could be unclear why Jesus, if he really was the Son of God, should actually have himself baptized by someone like John. For the Mandaeans, however, it could be unclear why John, knowing perfectly well who Jesus really was, should baptize him. In both religions one answer seems to be acceptable: It was a question of carrying out the will of God.

22. Jesus is made Jewish again, like a heretical Jew, to the extent that he uses the *shofar*, the Jewish ritual horn, to spread his word.

23. The two images derive from Christian tradition. The dove is obviously the Spirit itself at the moment of Jesus' baptism according to the Gospels; and the cross in the Jordan, as well as the possible memory of ceremonies actually performed in the Jordan, derives from the ancient Easter ritual of the aspersion of the cross at the baptismal font.

THE MEETING WITH MANDA D-HIIA
AND THE DEATH OF JOHN

The *Right Ginza* preserves an extensive passage on these events which from a literary perspective appears to be separated into two sections. The first deals with the arrival of Manda d-Hiia at the Jordan, with his baptism not performed, and with the death of John and his burial. The second deals with the ascent of the soul of John (accompanied by Manda d-Hiia until the celestial beatitude) and the connected reintegration of Ptahil and Abatur, who were met during the journey.

GR 5.4 (Pet. 188-96; Lid. 190-96)

Manda d-Hiia went to Iuhana Maṣbana[24] and spoke to him: "Now then, Iuhana, baptize me with your baptism, with which you baptize, and utter over me something of the name that you take care of pronouncing."

Then spoke Iuhana to Manda d-Hiia: "My belly is hungry for food and my body is thirsty for drink. I gather grass and I observe silence. I yearn for peace, but the souls [of those being baptized?] oppress me. Now the morning is about to arrive; come, later I will baptize you."[25]

Manda d-Hiia, given the tiredness of John, then invokes the higher divinities and obtains a concentration of time; in an hour John sleeps the equivalent of a day. Having roused himself, he sets about baptizing the revealer.

And Manda d-Hiia asked Iuhana: "What is the baptism like, with which you baptize?" And Iuhana spoke to Manda d-Hiia: "I throw the people into the Jordan, as sheep before the shepherd. With my staff I pour water on them and utter the name of the Life over them." And Manda d-Hiia asked

---

24. *Maṣbana* means "baptizer," "baptist"; it is the only time, in all known Mandaean literature, that John is called this. The detail shows the nearness of our text to its Christian source, in which the Baptist was considered to be such (whereas in a religion of baptists, like Mandaeanism, and given that John was not believed to be the inventor of baptism, there can be no reason for calling him the "Baptist").

25. This is the only example in known Mandaean literature where John appears as a vegetarian and as one who fasts. This too marks its nearness to Christian tradition, where this is quite normally the case.

Iuhana Maṣbana: "The name of whom you utter over them, at the baptism you perform?" And the *tarmidia* all opened their mouths as one and spoke to Iuhana: "For 42 years you perform baptism and no one has ever called you to the Jordan, except for this little boy.[26] Do not despise the speeches he pronounced." The *tarmidia* forced Iuhana, and Iuhana rose up and stretched his arms and welcomed Manda d-Hiia and spoke to him: "Come, come, little boy of three years and a day, the little one among his brothers, but great amongst his fathers, who is small, but his speeches are celebrated."

And Manda d-Hiia went to Iuhana at the Jordan. And the Jordan, that saw Manda d-Hiia, rose up and jumped up toward his presence and jumped on to the banks. And [Iuhana] stood with the water above his first mouth (the anus) and below his last mouth (the mouth). Between water and water Iuhana swims and does not have the strength to stay upright. Manda d-Hiia saw Iuhana and was anxious for him. The radiance of Manda d-Hiia spread over the Jordan, and the Jordan, that saw the radiance of Manda d-Hiia, turned back and left Iuhana standing in the dry.[27]

Under the guidance of Manda d-Hiia, both advance toward the water that has drawn back.

26. Manda d-Hiia has presented himself in the guise of a little boy of three years and a day. The reason is not easily accessible from a Mandaean perspective. Lacking a more convincing explanation, I would imagine it is of Christian origin, in that it is the exaggeration of the idea that Jesus ("younger" than John in years, but greater than he in "the kingdom") was baptized as an adolescent (as appears, e.g., in Nestorian legends). In Mandaeanism itself there is a tradition that sees the baptism of Jesus when the latter was twelve (in Siouffi), or fourteen (in Abraham Ecchellensis). The baptism of Jesus as a baby, finally, is very much present in the Oriental, ancient Christian iconography of baptism (and of the Precursor).

27. The rebellion of the Jordan, which almost sweeps John away at the moment of Jesus' baptism, is attested in Greek and Oriental Christian traditions (and confirmed in the iconography). The origin of this idea derives from the conviction that the Jordan houses in its waters, or is itself, a demoniacal entity that sees its imminent defeat in the arrival of the savior. Behind this there is an even deeper idea, very much in evidence in Gnostic texts, that the water of the Jordan is the primordial water of darkness that the savior has come to subdue. Baptism thus becomes a moment of cosmic salvation. In our case the analogy should be noted with the difficulties of Ptahil at the moment of the missing "solidification" of primordial water (the text is to be found above, p. 182). As for the light liberated at the baptism of Jesus, the idea of its presence is so widespread in Christian antiquity that it has even ended up in the text of some ancient Latin manuscripts of the Gospel of Matthew (after Matt. 3:15).

The radiance of Manda d-Hiia spread over the Jordan and over its bank. The fish opened their mouths from the sea, the birds from both banks of the cosmic sea. They praised Manda d-Hiia and spoke to him: "Blessed be you, Manda d-Hiia, and blessed be the place from whence you have come, and blessed and solidified be the great place to which you are going."

When the voice of the fish of the sea and the voice of the birds . . . reached the ear of Iuhana, he understood that it was Manda d-Hiia. . . . "You are the man in whose name I baptized with the baptism of the life!" And he asked him: "In the name of whom do you baptize?" And Iuhana answered Manda d-Hiia: "In the name of he who has been revealed to me, in the name of the predestined, of he who is destined to come, as [in the name] of the Mana well guarded, who has to reveal itself. Now you place upon me your hand of Kušṭa, your great Right of the healings and utter [your name] over me, your plantation that you planted. In your name will be solidified the first and the last."[28]

And Manda d-Hiia said to Iuhana: "If I place my hand on you, you will separate from your body." And Iuhana said to Manda d-Hiia: "I have seen you; now I no longer wish to stay here. Do not curse me far from you, far from the place whence you came. Arm me and give me orders for the great place where you are going."

There follows a corrupt passage, from which it seems that John asks and obtains the vision of the secrets of the cosmos. Afterwards he strips himself of his covering of flesh but, like Adam, does not seem very happy about dying or about seeing his own body devoured by those same birds and fish that had previously held up Manda d-Hiia to praise. The latter, at that point, invented burial.

(Manda d-Hiia) took sand from the sea and from both the banks of the cosmic sea, and went and threw it over the corpse of Iuhana. From that day the covering up of corpses was performed.[29]

At this point the second part of the story begins.

28. The profound fusion of typically Mandaean elements with others of ancient Christian origin should be noted (it is no easy task to explain in Mandaean terms "he who is to come" on the part of John; cf. Luke 7:19 and Matt. 11:3).

29. This institution shows that the redactor of this passage is reutilizing a legend about Adam, for whose corpse it makes sense to speak of first burial.

Manda d-Hiia sets out to walk toward the place that is all radiance, toward the place that is all light, and Iuhana went with him. He went, and arrived at the *maṭarta* of Ptahil the saint, who is without radiance, who is separated from the Light, whom the Light has separated and distanced from himself and from his communion: he (the Light) placed him in a desert and left him in solitude.

When Ptahil saw Manda d-Hiia, he bent his throne beneath him....[30]

Then spoke Manda d-Hiia to Iuhana: "Announce to this Great One that the pardon of the Life has been conceded to him. You too, O man, I have made as one of the *malkia,* as the great *'utria* [who come] from the house of the Lordship. Go, communicate the word to him."

And Iuhana spoke to Ptahil: "The pardon of the Life has been conceded to you and to your Father, the 'Utra, the Man, that armed you and instructed you and sent you down here."

The scene is repeated in the *maṭarta* of Abatur, the father of Ptahil, but John has disappeared.[31] In the final part the two travelers are welcomed into the world of light, but here it is Manda d-Hiia who disappears, and only John remains.

They went and were joined by the four men, the sons of salvation: 'Ain Hai (Fount of Life), Šum Hai (Name of Life), Ziu Hai (Radiance of Life), and Nhur Hai (Light of Life).[32] The man of proven righteousness (epithet for Manda d-Hiia) took him (John) and placed him in the place of safety. He took Iuhana by the hand and placed him in the place of safety. The *'utria* filled him with instructions on how to pray, with prayers, *masqata,* and hymns and said: "Come, let us go and see the man that is come from Tibil, the man of proven righteousness (here this is John), who has remained true and faithful in the midst of evil attacks and under the throne of the

30. Ptahil implores the merciful intercession of Manda d-Hiia with the Life.

31. In this way his figure shows it was inserted in a story of the ascent of Manda d-Hiia (on his own or with Adam, the Man), who reintegrates into celestial glory the two fallen divinities, guilty of having created the physical world. In other texts, the pardon for Ptahil and Abatur is brought by Hibil Ziua, on his own (GR 15.15) or through the order of Manda d-Hiia (GR 15.16).

32. These four entities "of Life" are the Mandaean outcome of the four Judaic *Hayyot* (the "Living" of Christian traditions), i.e., the four highest angelic realities that stand under the throne of God.

ancient Abatur." Each one clothes him with a part of his own radiance; each one covers him with a part of his own light. They raised themselves up and clothed him with clothing of living fire, that is without end and without number.

Then John invokes the higher divinities, with a prayer almost identical to that of Manda d-Hiia in the first part of the story, so that all the true Mandaeans may receive the same treatment. Then the story ends.

Whatever the literary origin of the models used to construct the story of GR 5.4 may be, in this last text John is endowed with the functions of an intermediary of the divinity, higher in the hierarchy than Ptahil himself. Yet we have seen the exaltation he enjoys through the work of the redactor of JB 18–33. Despite this, however, his figure has not penetrated to the deepest level of the myths that characterize Mandaean religion. There are no celestial adventures for John, nor is there his hypostasis with functions of redemption. His name has, however, entered into perhaps the best-known and most common Mandaean prayers, the *Abahatan Qadmaiia* ("Our First Fathers") and the *Asut Malkia* ("Greeting to the Sovereigns"). The *Abahatan Qadmaiia* is a sort of long litany, known to us in many similar versions, that can be used in various circumstances and modified according to necessity. I include here an extract of the *Abahatan Qadmaiia* of a *masiqta* for a dead person (the sense of communion among all the Mandaeans, living or dead, and the divinity is such that the ministrant can consider each entity named as being part "of this *masiqta*").

[Introduction]
  [The formula] "In the name of the Life and in the name of Manda d-Hiia"[33] is pronounced on you, O Goodness.[34] You will approach the goodness of the Life, and Manda d-Hiia revealed it, who in the name of the Life uttered: "The good is good for the good."[35] And their names (of the "good," i.e., the Mandaeans) shall be established, [they] who honor the names [of the dead]. We seek and find and listen.[36] We have sought and

33. This is perhaps the commonest blessing formula in Mandaean rituals.
34. This is the entirety of the sacred foods offered in the *masiqta*.
35. "Good" in this context is still the entirety of the foods offered, whose true value can be understood only by he who takes part in it in spiritual union (the "good").
36. The Gnostic has "sought," then "found," and now can "listen to" the revelation.

found, and spoken and listened in your presence, my Lord, Manda d-Hiia, Lord of health-giving powers. Forgive him (the dead man) his sins, trespasses, follies, stumblings, and mistakes. And forgive those who prepared this bread, *masiqta*, and these good things,[37] [forgive] their sins, trespasses, follies, stumblings, and mistakes, [of those who are] charitable and pious persons too, such as this soul of *x* son of *x* (the dead person) of this *masiqta*, a forgiver of sins may there be for him.

Our First Fathers, a forgiver of sins may there be for them;

Iušamin, son of Dmut Hiia (Image of the Life), of this *masiqta*, a forgiver of sins may there be for him;

Abatur, son of Bihrat, of this *masiqta*, a forgiver of sins may there be for him;

Habšaba and Kana d-Zidqa,[38] [of this *masiqta*], a forgiver of sins may there be for them;

The twenty-four *'utria*, sons of light, of this *masiqta*, a forgiver of sins may there be for them;

Ptahil, son of Zahr'il, of this *masiqta*, a forgiver of sins may there be for him;

Adam, son of Qin, and Eve his wife, of this *masiqta*, a forgiver of sins may there be for them;

Šitil, son of Adam, of this *masiqta*, a forgiver of sins may there be for him;

Ram and Rud, of this *masiqta*, a forgiver of sins may there be for them;

Šurbai and Šurhab'il, of this *masiqta*, a forgiver of sins may there be for them;

Šum, son of Nu, and Nuraita his wife, of this *masiqta*, a forgiver of sins may there be for them:

Iahia Iuhana, son of 'Nisbai Qinta and Anhar his wife, of this *masiqta*, a forgiver of sins may there be for them;

Those 365 *tarmidia*, who separated from the place Jerusalem the city, of this *masiqta*, a forgiver of sins may there be for them;

And for this my soul. . . .

The prayer carries on at length, recalling ancestors, relatives, and masters of the ministrant, then Mandaeans of the past and the present.

37. See above, n. 34.
38. A couple of celestial hypostases: the Day Sunday and the Entirety of the Offerings.

7. Jesus, the "False Messiah"

The Mandaean texts provide us with various narrations about what we would call the Jesus of history. The material on this, with its distant echoes of Gospel stories, finds quite precise parallels in the so-called *Toledot Iešu* ("Stories of Jesus"), medieval Judaic anti-Christian legends, and in Christian texts on the Antichrist and his pseudo-miracles. The Christ of the Mandaeans embodies those features that, according to the Christians, the Antichrist was expected to embody at the moment of his revelation, before the final conflict.

The first passage below is an extensive anti-Christian insertion in the Second Treatise in the *Right Ginza*.

GR 2.1.139-50, 154 (Pet. 54-58; Lid. 42-44)

139. After that I explain to you, my faithful.[1] When Nbu (Mercury) comes from the midst of the angels of deficiency, Ruha d-Qudša, his mother, calls him. On the crown of heaven and earth, on Mount Ṭabdana, the angels of deficiency meet. They anoint Nbu with the horn of oil and they clothe him in fire.[2]

1. This kind of phrase derives from the pen of the last redactor of the text, who combines different materials, "sewing" them together with words that refer to the literary framework of the book (a revelation to Adam).
2. This first paragraph is the celestial antecedent of the earthly history of Jesus and explains to the Mandaean faithful the true nature of the Messiah of the Christians: being Nbu, he is a planet and therefore a demon (in that he is a pagan divinity). That the Holy Spirit, i.e., Ruha (a female term in all the Semitic languages), is the "mother" of Christ

140. Then Mšiha appears, the deceiver, in another guise. He presents himself before you and says to you: "I walk on the water; come with me, you will not drown." But do not do that and do not believe him. When he oppresses and kills some of you, do not be scared. When he kills, he kills only your bodies, but your soul will live in the world of light. Do not be scared, do not be frightened, and do not fear Mšiha, the Roman,[3] the futile, he who modifies the speeches. . . .

142. Then he prepares a stepladder, he places it between the surface of the earth and the sky, he goes up and down, he dangles between earth and sky and says to you: "See that I come from on High; I am your Lord!" But do not believe him. For the ladder of Mšiha is made of illusion, sorcery and trickery. Where Mšiha is, he blinds your eyes, he covers up the splendor of the sun and speaks to the sun: "Cover up your splendor!" But the sun does not cover up his splendor. So [Mšiha] brings darkness to the place where he is, by sorcery, and says to you: "See, I have spoken to the sun and have covered up his splendor, for I am God, the savior."[4] . . .

144. In these guises he comes, makes prisoners in the world, leads astray the children of men and brings them his wisdom. They call themselves "God-fearers" and "righteous." He calls them "Christians." He transforms them into "God-fearers," both men and women. He calls them "God-fearers," "saints," and "righteous," both men and women.

145. They abandon their homes and become monks and nuns. They prevent their seed from reaching each other, the women from the men and the men from the women. They hinder their seed and prevent their progeny [separating them] from the world. They impose fasts on their mouths and they are put in shackles. They keep food and drink far from their mouths, they keep white clothing far from their bodies and they are seated

---

should not surprise us; Origen quotes a passage in a Judaeo-Christian gospel in which the Spirit is in fact the "mother" of Jesus. As for the mysterious Mount Ṭabdana, it may derive from Ṭab[or d-ab]dana, "Tabor of corruption." The idea of a meeting of rebel angels on the summit of a mountain is very old and well attested in Judaic traditions present in the book of Enoch or *Jubilees.* The anointing, too, "with the horn of oil" has a long history; cf. the anointing of Saul in 1 Sam. 10:1.

3. Christ is often called "Roman" by the Mandaeans, since for them he is the Messiah of the Byzantines, called "Romans" throughout the East of the ancient world.

4. The miracle of the ladder could be an ironic explanation of the Ascension. The miracle of obscuring the sun could be a deformation of the story of the obscurity that according to the Synoptic Gospels enveloped the earth at the moment of the crucifixion (Mark 15:33-34 and parallels).

alone. Then the *liliata* go to them, they lie [with them], they gather their seed and they get pregnant with it; from this originate spirits and ghosts that attack the sons of men. They do not take medicine, treatment or exorcism,[5] but they throw over them the seed, grime and filth (excrement?) of those monks, and [thus] they anoint them. Some of them then go away, others do not.[6]

146. After that I explain to you, my disciples.[7] For nine months Nbu-Christ enters in the womb of his mother, the virgin, and conceals himself there. Then he comes out as body, blood, and menstrual discharge and grows up in her bosom and sucks milk.[8]

147. When he has grown up, he enters the house of prayer of the Jewish people and takes possession of all their wisdom. He perverts the Torah and alters its doctrine and all the works.[9]

148. He leads some of the Jews into error, turns them into "God-fearers," and shows them magical apparitions in which they believe. He forces colored clothes upon them, shaves their heads with tonsures, and veils them like the darkness. And on Sunday they keep their hands from work.

149. He speaks to them: "I am the true God, whom my father has sent me here. I am the first messenger and I am the last. I am the Father, I am the Son, I am the Holy Spirit, I have grown up [coming forth from] the city of Nazareth." Above is his chariot.[10] He behaves with humility and goes to Jerusalem. He captures some among the Jews with sorcery and deceit, showing them miracles and (magical) apparitions. He makes *daiuia* of his company enter a dead body, and these speak in the dead body. He calls upon the Jews and says to them: "Come and see, I am he who awakens the dead, performs resurrections, and accomplishes deliverance. I am Anuš the Naṣurean."

---

5. The word is unknown, and the translation "exorcism" is hypothetical.

6. This means that some of the demons can be exorcised, whereas others cannot.

7. See above, n. 1.

8. Note the way the physical nature and the contamination of Jesus are underlined.

9. The *Toledot Iešu* are convinced that Jesus, having penetrated the temple of Jerusalem, had astutely taken over for himself the secret name of God, with which he then managed to perform miracles.

10. Like all the planetary divinities, Nbu-Christ has his own chariot; perhaps the text wishes to say that, while Jesus wanders around the world, his chariot (Mercury) travels around the heavens (could this be the Mandaean explanation of the star of Bethlehem?).

150. Thereupon Ruha lets out a cry in Jerusalem and bears witness concerning him. He ensnares the sons of men with sorcery and defiles them with blood and menstrual discharge. He baptizes them in cut water. He perverts the baptism of life and baptizes them in the name of the Father, the Son and the Holy Spirit. He alienates them from the baptism of life in the Jordan of the water of life, with which you, Adam, were baptized.[11] . . .[12]

154. And after Iuhana the world will continue in lies and Mšiha the Roman will divide the peoples and the twelve deceivers roam the world;[13] for thirty years the Roman showed himself in the world.

Similar material is contained in the following narration, of which two versions exist, very much like each other, in the first two treatises of the *Right Ginza*.

GR 1.198-202 (Pet. 28-29; Lid. 29-30)[14]

198. Mšiha makes himself known in another form. He is clothed in fire,[15] wrapped in fire and shows miracles in fire. Amun'il (Emmanuel) is his name, but he called himself Išu, the savior. His throne is in the fire and he shows his chariots [in the fire?]. He appears to you and says to you: "Come, come near, you will not burn." But do not believe him, for he advances with sorcery and deceit.

199. If he forces you, say to him: "We belong to you." But in your hearts do not recognize him and do not stray from the word of your lord, the Most High King of light. Since to Mšiha of lies, the concealed things are not revealed.[16]

---

11. The apostrophe to Adam can be understood by thinking of the literary framework of the passage, which wants to be a revelation to the progenitor of humanity.

12. Paragraphs 151-53 are a parenthesis on John; see the text at pp. 224-25.

13. These are the disciples, who "roam" like the planets; the coincidence with the number of the twelve signs of the zodiac facilitates the identification of the Christian Twelve with astral entities.

14. Cf. GR 2.1.131-37 (Pet. 51-53; Lid. 67-68).

15. For a Baptist religion, fire is the adverse element.

16. This is perhaps the most explicit example of the equivocal attitudes that often characterized the behavior of the Mandaeans, a behavior sometimes necessary for survival.

200. He says: "I am God, Son of God, whom my father has sent me here." He explains to you: "I am the first messenger, I am Hibil Ziua, I have come from on High." But he is not Hibil Ziua. Hibil Ziua is not clothed in fire. Hibil Ziua does not make himself known in that time. On the contrary, Anuš ʿUtra comes and reaches Jerusalem, clothed with a cloak of clouds of water. He walks about in bodily form, but he is not clothed in any bodily covering. He contains neither passion nor anger.[17]

201. He comes and goes in the years of Palṭus, king of the world.[18] Anuš ʿUtra comes into the world with the power of the Most High King of light. He heals the sick, makes the blind see, purifies the lepers, makes the cripples that drag themselves along the ground walk straight, makes the deaf-mutes talk and gives life to the dead. He procures faithful among the Jews and instructs them: "There is death and there is life; there is darkness and there is light; there is error and there is truth." He calls upon the Jews to convert in the name of the Most High King of light.[19]

202. Three hundred and sixty prophets go forth from the place Jerusalem.[20] They bear witness to the Lord of greatness. Anuš ʿUtra rises up on High and withdraws to Mšunia Kušṭa. All the ʿutria hide themselves from the eyes of the sons of men. Then the place Jerusalem is destroyed, the Jews go into exile and are dispersed into all the cities.

In the chapter devoted to John, we have seen the importance in Mandaean literature of the scene of Jesus' baptism. In the passage that follows, which concludes the chapter of the "Book of John" devoted to Jesus' baptism, we find the apologetic Mandaean explanation for the fact of baptism itself;

17. Hibil Ziua has already come down into the world, or rather into the world of darkness, before history began; the Mandaean response to the Christian incarnation is a descent of Anuš ʿUtra, of a decidedly Docetic appearance.

18. Palṭus is Pilate; "king of the world" means the (Roman) "emperor." It should not be too surprising that the Roman commander becomes emperor. This is what usually happens, e.g., in the Judaic stories of the persecutions at the time of Hadrian, for which Q. Tinneius Rufus becomes the emperor Lupinus (= Rufinus), with a wife, the empress Lupa (= Rufa). As for Pilate, he is considered emperor both in a story of the Toledot and in a Christian Arab text of the tenth to eleventh centuries.

19. The teaching of Anuš is the essence of Mandaean dualism. It should be noticed that the negative reality precedes the positive reality, perhaps because the text is aware that Anuš's answer is an answer to Jesus' previous announcement.

20. For the legend of the 360 prophets or of the 365 tarmidia of Anuš ʿUtra, see above, pp. 146-50 and 154-55.

with it the forces of evil (it is Ruha who speaks) have learned the secrets of Mandaean rituals. This at first sight execrable event in reality allows Mandaean thinking to consider Christianity as a deformed derivation of Mandaeanism itself. That all of Christianity is involved also appears from the name that Jesus has assumed at this point: Mšiha Paulis, that is, "Christ Paul."

The final part is an exhortation against Christian staurolatry, assimilated to pagan idolatry (the text reutilizes expressions characteristic of the anti-idolatry polemic).

JB 30 (Lid. text: 108-9; transl.: 108-9)

The Jordan, in which Mšiha Paulis was baptized, I have transformed into a gutter.[21] The *pihta* (Mandaean sacred bread), that Mšiha Paulis takes, I have transformed into "sacrament." The *mambuha* (sacred water), that Mšiha Paulis takes, I have transformed into "supper." The bands of the turban that Mšiha Paulis takes, I have transformed into a "miter." The *margna* (priestly stick), that Mšiha Paulis takes, I have transformed into a "pastoral staff."[22]
   I warn you, O my brothers, I warn you, O my dear ones; I warn you, O my brothers, of the Dumaiia that look like the cross.[23] They attach it to the walls, and then place themselves before and kneel down before a piece of wood. I warn you, O my brothers, of the god a carpenter has fashioned. If a carpenter has fashioned a god, who fashioned the carpenter?

In the texts we have examined so far, there is no direct comparison between Jesus and Anuš 'Utra; this has, however, given rise to various stories, and we find an example in the *Ginza,* and a much more extensive one in the "Book of John."

---

21. "Sewer"; "ditch of drain," with a mixture of collected and "cut" water, as opposed to the *iardna.* It alludes to Christian baptism.
   22. The Syriac word that corresponds to "pastoral staff" is deformed here, in such a way that in Mandaean its sound corresponds to another word that means "grime" or "excrement."
   23. These Dumaiia could be Rumaiia, i.e., the Romans, and hence once again the Byzantines, or in other words the "Idumaeans," i.e., the name that the Romans (Byzantines) are usually called in Judaic traditions. In other Mandaean texts, however, the *dumaiia* appear as astral realities.

The passage from the "Book of John" devoted to the conflict between the two saviors, one Christian and one Mandaean, in Jerusalem, makes lively reading (though the style is rich in repetitions). The text is a dialogue, in which Anuš ʿUtra speaks in the first person and narrates.

JB 76 (Lid. text: 273-77; transl.: 242-44)

In the name of the great Life be honored the Most High Light.

I come with sandals of diamonds and in my hands are chosen stones and pearls. In my left a weapon[24] lies and a great axe, that dissolves solutions before me (it opens the road up before me). I destroy and rebuild, I throw down and reconstruct the foundations of my building.[25] The figures that were painted on the walls, I have always erased by going from left to right. They placed crowns on my head.

I roamed about for generations and worlds, for generations and worlds I roamed, until I reached the door of Jerusalem. I prepared my throne, I sat down and spoke in the mysteries of my wisdom, that in Jerusalem, whose doors were closed and where latches and bolts were locked shut, through my voice and utterance, its doors, that were closed, opened up, and bolts and latches pulled themselves to one side.[26] Jerusalem was radiant in my splendor, all my perfumes spread fragrance abroad. They, whose smell was a stench, obtained perfume from the fragrance of my perfumes. To the blind I opened their eyes and the lepers healed; to the mute and the deaf I placed speeches in their mouths. The cripples and the lame, I made them walk again on their feet.[27]

Mšiha raises his eyes, his look becomes confused, he changes his colors, his tongue is contorted, and he speaks to me in every color.[28] . . . He

24. This is a club, a stick, or something similar.

25. The exact sense of this metaphor escapes us. Some think that it is a polemical reply to Jesus' pronouncement on the destruction and reconstruction of the temple-body (John 2:19).

26. The syntactic variation is in the original.

27. The resurrection of the dead (a miracle quite decidedly un-Mandaean in that death is liberation from the body) has now disappeared, while in the more archaic versions of the story (and therefore nearer to the Gospel texts, such as Luke 7:22-27, that interpreted the prophecy of Isaiah 35 and 61) it had been preserved.

28. The presence of "colors," compared with Mandaean whiteness, is always the mark of impiety and sin.

says: "Who are you of the First Life and from that Most High Being? Show me your miracles in Jerusalem." I stamped my foot on the ground, and shook; . . . (gap) the heaven and [the stars?] were shaken; I wrote a letter to the water of life, and he did not despise my letter; I showed my mark to fire, and fire did not sin against me, Anuš ʿUtra.[29] . . .

Whoever listens to me, Anuš ʿUtra, and believes, for him a place is prepared in the place of light. He who does not listen to me, Anuš ʿUtra, his place will be erased from the place of light. His name will be erased from my leaf; his figure becomes darkness and is shining no more.[30]

According to the Mandaeans, Jesus, after his ignominious death, returns to his heaven (Mercury's) where, given that he is a demoniacal reality, he carries out his allotted task of guarding the house of punishment *(maṭarta)* entrusted to him. This is mentioned in some accounts of journeys into the next world, of which two examples follow here. In the first (GL 1.4 [Pet. 26-38; Lid. 443-52]), the soul of the Mandaean, having left the body, rises from *maṭarta* to *maṭarta*. As soon as it sees each one, with the atrocious sufferings taking place there, it is seized with terror, invokes the Life, is answered, shows to the guardians its name and marks of its Mandaean faith (baptism, radiance . . .), and is left free to continue to rise. Then it asks whose the *maṭarta* is, and who is punished there. In this text there are eight *maṭarta,* and the eighth, of Abatur, is a place of punishment for hypocritical Naṣuraiia. The place of beatitude, with the water of Life, Radiance, the celestial Vine, and so forth, is to be found beyond the heavens. Below is a synthesis concerning the fifth and sixth *maṭarta*.

5. "This *maṭarta* is that of the sorcerer Mšiha, the son of the spirit (Ruha) of deceit, who introduced himself as god of the Naṣuraiia. . . . In this *maṭarta* the saints are punished, men and women, the virgins of both sexes, the celibate and the nubile, the men who did not desire women and the women who did not desire men, those who kill children so as not to have them, those who destroy the children in their bodies, those who cut away their living seed, despite the fact that it had reached them from the house of the Life."[31] They will be tortured or burned until the end of time.

29. Asked to show miracles in Jerusalem, Anuš shows his universal lordship, declaring his own power over the world, the heavens, water, and fire.

30. Here the passage ends with a final formula of no interest.

31. This is the usual concept, according to which the human seed derives directly from the water of Life.

6. It is the *maṭarta* of Euat, or Ruha d-Qudša. There find punishment the "fasters, male and female, that fast a sacrilegious fast and pray a lying prayer; they are hungry for bread and do not eat, they are thirsty for water and do not drink. They sit in mourning and lamentation, they hold their head straight and do not respond to a greeting." The punishments are always the same.

The passage we have seen does not go beyond expressing a generic anti-Christian acrimony, finding in the Christian ethic, or, more specifically, the monastic ethic, the object of its polemic. The next passage, called "My measure in the world was full" (GR 5.3 [Pet. 180-88; Lid. 183-90]), however, goes a good deal further, primarily thanks to a more elaborate description of the *maṭarta* of Mšiha. The literary framework and the structure of the passage are similar to those of the previous passage. Here follows a synthesis concerning the second, the sixth, and the eighth *maṭarta*.

2. This is the *maṭarta* of the "Virgin, daughter of her Father. Before her are her 67 daughters. Her breast is uncovered to dishonor and their side is open to perdition. They take the hearts of the gods and capture the spirits of the sons of men." The soul is then asked for its permission to pass; when it is recognized to be the soul of a Mandaean, those creatures are terrified; they make threats against the prospect that another will follow its example, but the soul replies boldly: "To you, Ruha, splinters will be stuck in your eyes, and the eyes of your head will be darkened" (i.e., she will not even see the Naṣuraiia that pass?). The Virgin of seduction (Venus) is therefore interpreted as Ruha herself.

6. This is the *maṭarta* of Išu Mšiha, called "a nullity." Imprisoned in it are "all those who deny the Life and confess to faith in Mšiha." As in the previous scenes, the soul asks what the souls of those are similar to, but here the description is developed differently, including material from a story of the return to heaven of Manda d-Hiia.

Those souls are like a large and numerous flock before Mšiha. Mšiha takes them (the sheep) to the seaside and places them by the sea. They ask for water, but the beaches above the sea are high and the water of the sea deep. They would like to drink water, but they have none. The souls say to Mšiha: "Mšiha, our Lord, when we were still in the world, we clothed with garments [our neighbors] and wrapped them with cloaks, we ransomed prisoners and gave alms and did good works. Why, now that we require water, is there none?" And Mšiha says to the souls: "In the name of whom have you . . . carried out good works?" And the souls reply to Mšiha: "In the name of the higher being, and in the name of the lower being, in the name of Išu Mšiha, in the name of Ruha d-Qudša, in the name of the God of the Naṣuraiia and in the name of the Virgin, the Daughter of her Father." And Mšiha says to the souls: "The higher being is the heavens, the lower being is the earth, Išu Mšiha am I and the Holy Spirit is here."

Then "the man of proven righteousness," the synonym of Manda d-Hiia, appears, who escorts "all the stock of souls" — that is, he liberates all the dead Mandaeans. Christ then asks him "his name and his marks of identity," that is, the usual permission to pass by. As soon as Manda d-Hiia utters his name, Mšiha bows down before him "four times."

Then the souls say to Mšiha: "Mšiha, our Lord, did you not say, when we were in the world: 'There is no one greater or stronger than I; I am the God of Gods, the Lord of Lords, I am the king of all the worlds, I am the chief of all works'? And now there is this man, who has passed before you, and you have bowed down four times with the deepest of bows before him. Who is this man?"

Jesus replies that he is one who has never named any of the entities recorded above. Then the souls ask to be sent back for three days into the world: "We wish to sell all our goods, go up the Jordan, and have ourselves baptized in the name of the man who passed beyond you." And Christ says:

"O deceived ones, you who have been deceived! Did you ever see, when you were in your bodies, that a child, once it left its mother's body, was then put back again inside its mother? . . . Do you not know, O you deceived, that you have been deceived? I am a good for nothing messiah (*mšiha*), flayed for my torment,[32] wise for evil, he who modifies the doors of sleep, utterly distorts the works of the spirit, leads pious men astray and throws them down into the powerful clouds of darkness. When I showed

---

32. This detail, absolutely anomalous, leads us to think of the way it would seem Mani was martyred, flayed alive in a public square. This could therefore be a feature of the polemic against Manichaean, reutilized once more in an anti-Christian context.

you bolts and keys [to enter into heaven], I beguiled you and created longing in you. I gave you gold and silver so that you would keep me company
in the darkness, in this place in which we now find ourselves." . . .

8. This is the *maṭarta* of Ruha d-Qudša, who "sits on the mouth of
Karafiun, the swallower."

The harp of the pleasures of the flesh is to be found on her shoulder, and
she laments with the company of her 360 scions. A viper is stretched out
around her. With [the sound of] citharas she speaks and calls the Twelve,
the traders that recognize themselves in her.[33] They say to her: "Our Lady,
why have you called us and why did you desire us?" And she says to them:
"I have called you and you have been desired by me like the tar and pitch
on the mouth of Karafiun the swallower." She has a dulcimer in her hand
and sits on the mouth of Karafiun the swallower. She plays the dulcimer
for the twelve Doors[34] who believe in her, and she throws them inside. She
says to them: "Go, go, my children, I shall close the door and follow you."
And they wander around inside the jaws of Karafiun and cannot even
gropingly find how to enter and to lean on her.

Manda d-Hiia continues rapidly on his ascent, and Karafiun reproaches
Ruha d-Qudša for not having handed him over to him, but she replies: "Your
mouth at that moment was like the little opening of an ant-heap; a little wind
comes up, a leaf falls on top of it and it is blocked." Finally, once beatitude has
been reached, the man of proven righteousness answers the Life, who has
asked him: "Ruha, Mšiha and the planets are like flies on the edge of a vase;
their wings get drenched in the steam that reaches them and they fall down
into the vase."

Another Mandaean way of explaining Jesus consists in identifying him
with evil mythological figures. Here is one example.

33. Called "traders" because of their journeyings across the celestial sphere, they may
be the signs of the zodiac, or else, identified with these, the apostles (also wanderers since
they were sent to preach throughout the world).
34. Each sign-cum-apostle is considered to be the head of a religious sect.

GR 12.1.158-59 (Pet. 58-59; Lid. 52-53)

158. My chosen ones! I say to you, the perfect that are and will be born in that time, when the Roman appears: do not stray away — I say to you — from true wisdom. . . .

159. Do not praise with the song that Nbu Mšiha sings in the world. When he assumes another guise, they call him "lascivious Aurus," he who sings the song of sorcery and lasciviousness.[35] They call him Aurus the lascivious [because] he throws [lasciviousness] into the world. His mother Ruha boasts of him. With his pleasant manner and through sorcery he leads the children of men astray. At his behest brides leave their bridal chamber and those that have just given birth leave the house where they have given birth.[36] He throws lasciviousness over men into the world, a hubbub and lasciviousness on to the women. Men run after women and women run after men. He drags old men and old women out of their houses; he takes married men away from their brides. He tears young men away from their families, and they no longer utter the name of their families.[37] He throws shamelessness, adultery, prostitution, craving and passion on to men and women, on to young men and young girls. They will sing [hymns?][38] to the whoremongers(?).[39] The women dance before the men and the men before the women. He throws lasciviousness and falseness into the world.

35. It is by no means clear who this Aurus is; he was thought to be a deformation of Orpheos, transliterated *aurpius*. In Greek Gnosticism a Christos Horos ("Limit") appears, a divine emanation that extends to the outer borders of the Pleroma, outlining its shape and solidifying it in relation to the outer darkness.

36. They therefore break the most significant Mandaean taboo to satisfy their own unbridled sexual desire.

37. Conversion means abandoning the family clan.

38. A gap in the text?

39. The word is unclear; are they the planets?

THE TRUE MANDAEAN REPLY
TO CHRISTIAN PROPAGANDA

GR 2.4 (Pet. 67; Lid. 61-62)

The next excerpt is from a short and at times poetical passage devoted entirely to the polemic against celibacy and virginity. Praš is the Mandaean name of the Euphrates.

Come up on to the sea's beach and watch the fish in the sea: they go in the sea in couples and they do not die out. Look at the birds that fly in the heavens: they fly in couples and do not die out. Now then, look, why do you wish to ruin yourself? Come up on to the bank of the great Praš and look at the trees that stand erect on the banks of the great Praš: they drink water and bear fruit and do not die out.

Look on the other hand at a dried up river, where water does not flow. As it dries up the trees on its banks lose their leaves and die. Thus the souls of both male and female virgins dry up and die, of those men that do not seek women and those women that do not seek men. When they leave their bodies, they obtain their place in a dark cloud. For they are fertilized by their own bellies and [what is conceived] comes out of them from their mouths, since they have done what I did not impose upon them to do. . . . In the world in which you live make weddings for your sons, the males, and for your daughters, the females, and believe in your lord, the Most High King of the light. For this world has an end and will pass.

Two chapters of the "Book of John" (11 and 12) present the messenger of the Mandaean divinity in the guise of a shepherd. This immediately brought to mind the Christian Good Shepherd, but, as will readily be seen, this is a Mesopotamian shepherd and a fully Mandaean one. The passages are centered on the importance of water and on the observance of Mandaean rituals. I conclude here with passages from the beginning and end of the first of the above-mentioned chapters.

JB 11 (Lid. text: 40-55; transl.: 44-51)

In the name of the great Life honored be the sublime Light.

A shepherd am I, who loves his sheep, and sheep and lambs I protect. On my neck [I carry] *ribna*,[40] and from the village the sheep do not stray. I do not take them to the edge of the sea, so that they may not see the whirl-pools of the waters and not be afraid of the water, and when they are thirsty they do not drink that water. I carry it (the *ribna?*) and they drink the water from the palm of my hand, until they have drunk their fill. I guide them to the good sheepfold and they graze near me. From the mouth of Praš, from the mouth of Praš Ziua I bestowed upon them things of marvelous goodness. I brought them myrtle and white sesame and I brought them luminous *drapšia*. I brush them and clean them and make them smell the perfume of the Life. . . .[41]

Of a thousand, I find one again. . . . It is a good thing for him that he escaped from the Seven and the Twelve, who steal the sheep. . . . It is a good thing for the young girls that they free themselves from the bonds of Ruha, they free themselves from the grime and scandal and chains without end. My chosen ones! Whoever will live at the end of the time of Nirig, may his own conscience defend him. He will come and will rise up into the luminous dwelling place, into the place where the sun does not set and the rays of light do not go dark.[42]

40. This is probably a skin bag or jar full of water. The word is otherwise unknown, and translators, under the influence of Christian iconography and stories of the Good Shepherd, translate "sheep," "little ewe," but by doing this they make the rest of the passage incomprehensible.

41. Afterward the shepherd saves the sheep from a flood (persecution or apostasy) and puts them on board a boat, but many drown.

42. Perhaps these last words, with the mention of Nirig (Mars), the planet of the last days, are of the Islamic era.

8. The "Son of the Arab Butcher"

For Mandaeanism, Islam is an ever-present threat, with the essential danger of Moslem domination being felt to lie in apostasy. Its founder (called Ahmaṭ, Mhamaṭ, M(u)habaṭ and Abdala/Abdula) is continuously covered in insults relating both to him and to his origins. In actual fact, this is the only way an oppressed people can try to release a part of the inevitable tension it is made to feel.

GR 1.203 (Pet. 29; Lid. 30)

Then came Ahmaṭ, son of the sorcerer Bizbaṭ. He propagates a shout that is not a shout, he does much evil in the world and leads the stock of souls (the Mandaeans) astray, into error.

GR 2.1.164 (Pet. 61; Lid. 54)

After that I explain to you, perfect and faithful: After all the prophets a prophet will rise up from the earth. The Arab prophet comes and rules over all the peoples. Thus wretchedness is great in the world. After that dominion the world will be in confusion. After the Arab Mhamaṭ, son of Bizbaṭ, no prophet will come into the world, and the faith will disappear from the earth.

The "Son of the Arab Butcher"

Haran Gauaita (cf. Drower, *The Haran Gawaita and the Baptism of Hibil Ziwa*, p. 12)[1]

I shall say to you, *tarmidia* who live in the Arab era, before the son of the Arab butcher (or, perhaps, "the son of the butcher, the Arab"), came and prophesied like a prophet in the world, so that they performed circumcision like the Jews and changed the speeches — for he is the most degenerate among the false prophets. Nirig accompanied him, for he is the seal of the prophets of lies, and Mšiha [will come] after him at the end of the era. I warn you, O Naṣuraiia, that before the son of the Arab butcher (see above) arose and was called the prophet in the world and Nirig came down with him, he took out his sword and converted people to his own faith with the sword.

The sense of belonging to a besieged community is very much present in several texts. Especially bitter is chapter 22 of the "Book of John," which contains a prophecy, voiced by John the Baptist, concerning the disappearance of Mandaeanism following on the arrival of Muhammad.

JB 22 (Lid. text: 83-86; transl.: 87-90)

"The men of proven religious faith disappear and the voice of the Life is no longer called in the world. The *masqata* (plural of *masiqta*) disappear and a pure *burzinqa* (turban) is no longer worn. The baptism of life disappears and the marvelous sign disappears."

When Iahia said this, Iaqip, Bnia Amin and Miriai spoke in this way to Iahia in Jerusalem: "[We beseech you], O Iahia, for the Life that you invoke, and again we beseech you, Iahia, for the evening of the Day, whose name is dear to us: Must they really disappear, the men of proven religious faith? . . ."

When Iaqip and Bnia Amin and Miriai spoke thus, Iahia said to them in Jerusalem: "When all the *kahnia* have been massacred and are no longer, [when] the Jews have been killed, Muhammad will be born, the son of a female slave of ʿAbdallāh.[2] He rallies all the world around him, eliminates all

---

1. The text is full of gaps, and at times the parts do not fit together.
2. The arrival of Islam in Mesopotamia was therefore prophesied at the time of the

the houses devoted to the Mandaean cult, and mosques rise up in great numbers in the world. He eliminates justice and salvation; trickery and crime dominate the world. He eliminates the faith. Images for the women giving birth are no longer painted and the little bells are no longer rung in Tibil.[3] And not even do all the children of crime sound the rattles, they who bring into the world a wisdom of crime. They reject prostitution, but go with prostitutes; they reject theft, but steal; they reject simple and compound interest, but give one and take nine. They alter their scales with trickery and increase their weights. Some get rid of the fleas of their heads, others let their hair grow, others dye their beards with henna. Some dye their beards with henna and then they go and pray in their mosques. When they see a man who is wearing a (Mandaean) sash, an attack of violent anger takes possession of their entire body. They surround (them) and interrogate (them) and say to them, 'Who is your prophet? Tell us who is your prophet; tell us what is your holy book; tell us who you pray to.' The cursed and the brazen do not know and do not understand, they do not know and do not understand, that our Lord is the King of the light on high, He, the Only One."

JB 24 (Lid. text: 88-89; transl.: 92)

Choose a wife and take a wife but do not take a wife that [is a] daughter of the Godless. Do not take a wife from the house of the Godless, so that the flaming fire may not consume you. She who is impure and does not keep herself as she should, the flaming fire will consume her. She who is impure and does not keep herself as she should, will have her sex empty (she will not give birth). She who is impure and does not keep herself as she should, will give birth to dead children. She who is impure and does not keep her-

---

destruction of the Judaic priesthood (the *kahnia* are the priests) and the Jews' political power. It does not seem to make sense to think here, as some do, of the destruction of Jerusalem in A.D. 70 (more likely the text refers to the seizing of Jerusalem by Chosroes in A.D. 614). I believe the text is alluding to the breakup and dispersal that the Babylonian Judaic hierarchies must have suffered at the time of the Islamic occupation. Before this, the head of the Jews in exile (the Exilarch) was considered a prince of the court, with hereditary rights recognized in his title.

   3. This is alluding to apotropaic practices during labor; it means that no more children are born (among the practicing Mandaeans).

self as she should, heaven and earth curse her. For she has contaminated the deep water, she has unveiled the hidden secrets and has gone and thrown [her abortion] in the manure. The sun and the moon have risen and have uttered a solemn curse upon her.

JB 54 (Lid. text: 199-200; transl.: 193-94)

From the Torah come their writings, but they do not wish to recognize the Torah. They circumcise themselves like the Jews, but curse the Jews. They do not know that Ruha has brought confusion upon the Jews and has thrown confusion into their midst. They quarrel endlessly among themselves and they [no longer] know who they are praying to.

My chosen ones! From the day in which Jerusalem was built until the coming of the demon Bizbaṭ,[4] I (Manda d-Hiia) could not dwell in the world among you; my garment, in fact, was not corporeal, to enable me to live in the world among you. I rose up on to the heights and I journeyed to Mšunia Kušta; there I placed myself and said: ". . . What sorrow I experience for my *tarmidia* who live at this time. They inflict bad treatment on the pearls, they do wrong and they offend me. What sorrow I feel for my *tarmidia* who live at this time. Ruha freed and brought against them filth and menstrual discharge and makes them collapse at the doors of darkness."[5]

At a religious level, the explanation of the success of Islam is relatively simple. Muhammad is Nirig (Mars), the planet of violence, the Lord of the times of the end. Like Jesus, he is hence a son of Ruha; like Jesus, he is the head of a "door" of his own and has his own subject demons *(humria)*. Evidence of this is a drawing of a *Diuan Abatur,* representing a planetary or demoniacal entity, whose caption is *mhamat bra d-ruha,* that is, "Muhammad son of Ruha." Thus literary material similar to that used to describe Jesus, insofar as he is guardian of his own *maṭarta,* can be reutilized to describe Muhammad.

---

4. Here it is Muhammad himself who is demonized, not his father.

5. The passage also contains praises for those who manage to preserve their faith "at the time of the demon Bizbaṭ."

GR 3 (Pet. 122; Lid. 137)

The door that Nirig fashioned was fashioned completely in lies. Completely in lies was it fashioned and in the world they wander in the desert. In the desert they wander through the world and show their violence in the world. The *humria* that come from him *(sic)* are settled here in Tibil for their rage. They procure murders and spill blood. He who calls them to the rally, marches at the head of the army. At the head of the army he marches to spill blood in the world. On the day he commits a murder he is more pleased about the murder than about a good action. On the day he commits a murder he talks and laughs to himself. On the day on which he does not commit any murder, his body is painted with bitter grass. The door that fashioned Nirig will end on the day of the end of time.[6]

GR 9.1 (Pet. 231-34; Lid. 232-34)

Now I wish to teach you about the door founded by Nirig who is called ʿAbdallāh the Arab, from which the seven figures of rage come.[7] The stock of souls is killed by him and the whole Tibil bends under his throne. From him comes the whip. They devour sovereignty and exercise royal power. They draw sword and saber and spill the blood of the children of Adam. They loot and take prisoners; [they sell] what they have not purchased with their gold, what they have not purchased with their silver, what they have not acquired with their goods. They seize the son from his mother, the husband from the bride, the father from the son, and take from them strength and iron. Men are unable to save themselves from them; they weep, they lament, and burst into tears. Day after day they make war and spill blood and their persecution reaches the entire stock of souls and the great race of the Life. They oppress them in unheard of ways and say: "We want to erase them from the world." They eat bread with the sword. . . .

6. Here the text seems to refer to Islamicized Arab tribes. Like the Muntafiq, they controlled southern Mesopotamia. The "lies" refer to Muhammad, prophet of lies.

7. The reference would seem to be to the planets, but it sounds rather strange that all seven derive from Mars. It is perhaps alluding to the first seven Imam, the Prophet's successors (according to the so-called Seveners among the Shi'ites); the Mandaean redactor of this passage would then seem to have been in contact with Imamist Islamic tendencies of that kind.

Nirig speaks to them: "There is no god that is more powerful and greater than I." Without rest he brings sword, saber, war, killing, hunger, sorrow, struggle and persecution against his brothers.[8] In all Tibil he brings the clamor of war every day. All the souls that have opposed (?) the Arab 'Abdallāh, they fight with sword, flame and fire. Every day Ruha moves to do battle and make war on Nirig.[9] She says to him: "I have given you the book and the discourse and I have revealed to you the mystery of death! I have entrusted the whip to you, and (political) power, and speech, and the capacity to grant. I said to you that every light would be put out for you.[10] You explain to your worshippers: 'Now then, I shall make you rise up into paradise, to the place your eyes look up to full of hope,' and with this you throw them down into the deepest hell. You deceive them with the whip and lordship, gold and silver, then you sink them down into the deepest hell and you oppress them with an instrument [of torture], shackles on their feet, various tortures, imprisonment and martyrdom (sufferings). I spoke to you; did You not say, 'I am the powerful god; I shall show you the light, I shall give you oil and honey to eat, I shall clothe you in splendid garments, I shall procure you every pleasure and you will find [your] good. There is no god that is stronger than I; I shall give you beautiful women'?[11] Why now do you oppress them with instruments [of torture], shackles, tortures, chains and sufferings, and judge them with a judgment without justice? The servants of the alien man, against whom we have brandished our swords, now have ascended into the world of the higher light, while we are separated here in the darkness, and in the black water, and we do not find either relief or beatitude."[12]

The Arab 'Abdallāh speaks to his servants and to all the doors that have adhered to him: "When I deceived you with the great invasion, I sub-

8. I believe that what is meant is that Muhammad ('Abdallāh), in that he is Nirig, and all the Moslems believe themselves to be superior to the planets and therefore combat "against the brothers."

9. Here Ruha is Byzantine Christianity: The allusion is to the constant state of war between Christians and Moslems.

10. Islam, therefore, is a deviation of Christianity.

11. In the polemic against Islam it is usual to refer to the promise of otherworldly glory for those who fall fighting for the faith.

12. At this point Muhammad-Nirig is considered the otherworldly judge, responsible for his own damned (his own followers) in his *maṭarta*. The last phrase is placed on the lips of the latter.

dued the entire Tibil to you, I lent you the whip and lordship, I subdued every divinity to you and sacked every people, borders and languages, then I and my mother Ruha together deceived you. I said to myself: 'Thus at the last day for me, for the great Qaduš, my father, from whom I was generated, and for my father Leviathan,[13] a dinner will be made ready.' Now then, you see how all the planets together did not have the strength to match your strength, and the servants of the planets, my brothers, were not up to your height and did not have the power to match yours. Now in the great day of judgment, you cannot find any information (any help) from me. Since I have nourished you with . . .[14] and honey, you have been softened up with perfumed crowns, flowers and aromas, I have had you strut in rich raiment, journeying between heaven and earth in the chariots of anger, I have transformed you into fat rams;[15] no one now will free you from my hands and loose you and lead you up to the light."

13. *Qaduš*, a term connected to "saint" or "holiness" in other texts, indicates the divinity of the Jews. Leviathan *(l'uiatan)* is here probably 'Ur, the monster of the abyss.

14. An unknown word.

15. Ready, therefore, to be sacrificed and thus to become the "dinner" of which the text speaks.

Glossary

Ab father; *Aba Saba* white-haired father (a reverential address); *Abatur* divine name (Third Life, Father of Ptahil and the *'utria*); *Abahatan Qadmaiia* "Our First Fathers" (among the commonest of prayers, in the form of a litany).

Adam Abu l-Farağ a proper noun (a human figure who arrives to help the Mandaeans).

Adiaura (divine) helper.

Ahl al-kitāb a people of the book (an Arab term that indicates a population enjoying a special status of religious tolerance).

'Aina spring; proper noun of divine hypostasis.

Alma (pl. *almia*) world.

Andiruna ritual hut (built for weddings and the ordination of priests).

Anhar female proper noun (wife of *Šum*; wife of *Iahia Iuhana*).

Anuš Enos; *Anuš 'Utra* the name of a revealer; *Anuš bar Danqa* the name of a Mandaean dignitary at the time of the Islamic invasion.

Ašganda, šganda (pl. *-ia*) acolyte; proper name (an ancient scribe).

Asut Malkia "Greetings to the kings" or "Greetings of the kings" (prayer).

Bar, br son.

Bimandia see *manda*.

Bnia Iamin sons of *Iamin* (proper noun of a Jew and of a male convert).

Daiua (pl. *daiuia*) demon.

Diuan (pl. *diuanan*) scroll; explanation.

Dmuta image; proper noun of a divine hypostasis.

GLOSSARY

Drapša, drabša (pl. *-ia*) ceremonial standard with a support in the form of a cross.

Draša (pl. *drašia*) book; words.

Dukrana commemoration (for the dead).

Ganzibra (pl. *ganzibria*) great priest; "bishop."

Gap monstrous divinity of the abyss, brother of Ruha.

Ginza treasure; library; the name of a holy book.

Habšaba Sunday; proper name of a divine hypostasis.

Halala (pl. *halalia*) a man in the state of purity.

Hamra a surrogate for wine.

Haran Gauaita "Inner Harran" (the title of a written text).

Hibil Abel; *Hibil Ziua* Abel Radiance (the proper noun of a celestial revealer).

Hiia life (literally, "the living," plural).

Hšuka darkness.

Humarta (pl. *humria*) demon.

Iahia John (from the Arabic).

Ialupa (pl. *ialupia*) cultured secular layman.

Iam the name of a son of Nu.

Iamin a proper noun (the ancestor of the Jews?).

Iapit Japheth.

Iardna (pl. *iardnia*) free-flowing water; the Jordan.

Iauar Radiant One (?); the proper name of a celestial figure.

Išu Jesus.

Iuhana John.

Iurba (Iao rba?) divine name (Iao the Great?).

Iušamin (Iao haš-šammaym?) a divine name (Iao of the heavens?).

Kana (d-zidqa) the whole (of the offerings); celestial hypostasis.

Kanta cultic edifice of the *Kantaiia* Kantaeans.

Kasia (pl. *kasiia*) hidden; secret; mystical.

Kenoma lack; emptiness (Greek).

Kibša submission; conquest.

Klila (pl. *klilia*) a small crown of myrtle.

Krun, Akrun a monster of the darkness.

Kušṭa right; truth; celestial hypostasis.

Laupa (pl. *laupania*) community; in the plural, communion; sacred meal.

Lilita (pl. *liliata*) female demon.

'Lizar Eleazar.

Madda knowledge.

Malaka (pl. *malakia*) angel.

Malka (pl. *malkia*) king; celestial spirit.

Maluaša (pl. *maluašia*) sign of the zodiac; in the plural, zodiac.

Mambuha holy water used for ceremonies.

Mana (pl. *mania*) receptacle; spirit; primordial highest spirit.

Manda knowledge; dwelling place; cultic hut (*bimanda, bit manda* "house of manda"); *Manda d-Hiia* Knowledge/Dwelling Place of the Life (the name of the principal celestial revealer).

Mandaia (pl. *mandaiia*) Mandaean (he of the *manda*).

Mandi holy area, where the *manda* is found, together with the pool for ablutions.

Mar Toma Nazrani Christians of St. Thomas.

Mara lord; *Mara d-Rabuta* Lord of Greatness (divine epithet).

Margna a priestly staff made of olive wood.

Markabta celestial chariot.

Maṣbuta (pl. *maṣbutiata*) solemn baptism.

Masiqta elevation (a ceremony that helps a soul).

Maškna ceremonial hut.

Mašknaia (pl. *mašknaiia*) synonym of Mandaean (he of the *maškna*).

Maṭarta (pl. *maṭarata*) heavenly house of punishment.

Mdudia a plural term of unknown meaning; *Mdudia d-Qudša* m. of the sacrament (particles of the catholic communion?).

Miša oil; unguent; Moses.

Mšiha Messiah, Anointed One; Christ (proper noun of Jesus).

Mšunia Kušṭa the chosen ones of the Truth (collective plural, it indicates a kind of earthly paradise).

Nahra (pl. *nahrauata*) river.

Namusa, nimusa law (Syriac translation loan of the Greek *nomos*), Mandaean or Judaic (Torah).

Napaqa someone departing (the definition of someone dying in the ceremony called *'ngirta*).

Naṣiruta knowledge of the Nasureans.

Naṣuraia (pl. *naṣuraiia*) Nasurean.

'Ngirta (pl. *'ngiriata*) the ceremony of the ordination of the *ganzibra*.

Nhura light.

'Nisbai Elizabeth.

Nišimta (pl. *nišmata*) soul.

GLOSSARY

Niska (pl. *niskia*) a unit of measurement.

Nitupta drop; sperm (epithet of good female personages).

Nu Noah.

Nuraita (Nhuraita, Anhuraita) wife of Noah or of Šum.

Pagra (pl. *pagria*) body; *(d-)pagria* bodily, physical (adjectival locution; e.g., *Adam pagria*).

Paisaq declassed priest.

Panǧa the "five" days that are supernumerary in the calendar; the feast on the occasion of their recurrence.

Paruanaiia see *Panǧa*.

Paṭira (pl. *paṭiria*) a kind of tiny loaf or tiny biscuits (usually sixty-six in number) prepared in certain ceremonies.

Pihta holy bread.

Piriauis a name of the celestial Iardna.

Pleroma Fullness (Greek); the world of the divinity.

Praš the Euphrates (earthly or celestial); *Praš Ziua* the Euphrates Radiance (a name of the celestial Iardna).

Ptahil demiurge creator (son of *Abatur*), Fourth Life.

Qadmaia (pl. *qadmaiia*) first.

Qaptān commander (Arabic, from the Spanish *capitán*); any European (in Turkish).

Rabuta greatness.

Ram the name of the first male ancestor of the second age of the world.

Rasta ceremonial garment made up of seven parts.

Raṭna neo-Mandaic dialect.

Rba (pl. *rbia*) great.

Riš head; *riš ama* (pl. *riš amia*) Mandaean ethnarch.

Rišaia the first.

Rišama, rušuma complete ablution.

Rud the name of the first female ancestor of the second age of the world.

Ruha spirit; *Ruha d-Qudša* female Holy Spirit (of the Christians).

Ṣa (pl. *ṣaia*) a little flat bread roll in use in the nuptial ceremonies.

Ṣābi'un, Ṣābi'ah Sabei (Arabic).

Šarh explanation, commentary.

Šaṭṭ al-'Urdunn (Arabic) name of the Jordan.

Šayḫ Sheik; the title of the Mandaean priest.

Šganda see *ašganda*.

Sidra book; synonym of *Ginza* the "Book" par excellence.

Simat, simta treasure; *Simat Hiia* Treasure of Life, epithet of female celestial entity.

Sindirka date palm; the proper noun for a divine hypostasis.

Šitil Seth; his celestial hypostasis.

Skandula a powerful talisman, made up of a knife joined by a little chain to a ring with apotropaic images engraved on it (the whole of it in iron).

Škinta (pl. *škinata*) house, dwelling place, temple; celestial house; celestial world; this world; divine hypostasis.

Spar book; *Spar Maluašia* Book of the Zodiac.

Šualia, ašualia disciple, candidate for the priesthood.

Ṣubbi (pl. *Ṣubba*) Mandaean (Arabic name).

Šum (bar Nu) Shem (the son of Noah); *Šum Iauar Ziua* name (Shem-Iauar-Radiance) of the priestly ring.

Sup Zaba Sea of Reeds (the biblical Red Sea); the Euphrates; infernal waters.

Šurbai name of the first male ancestor of the third age of the world.

Šurhab'il name of the first female ancestor of the third age of the world.

Ṣurta ritual isolation (especially on the occasions of childbirth, menstruation, and weddings).

Taga ritual priestly crown.

Ṭamaša, ṭumušta baptismal immersion (without a priest).

Tan(n)a vapor, cosmic cloud; female celestial entity; container; primordial or original spiritual reality.

Tarmida (pl. *tarmidia*) priest, disciple.

Tibil the created world.

Ṭura d-Madai Mount of the Media, a mountain of the Mandaeans.

'Ur monster of the abyss, a son of Ruha.

'Utra (pl. *'utria*) wealth; name by which the entities of the world of Light are defined.

Zahr'il negative spiritual entity, the sister of Ruha.

Zakria Zacharias.

Zidqa (brika) offerings (blessed); the name of a ceremony.

Ziua radiance; epithet of celestial personages.

Zuṭa small.

Index

266

Index

Hussein, Saddam, 4

Iahia, 96, 115-18, 228-32. *See also* John the Baptist
Iam, 52, 200
Iapit, 50, 200
Iaqip, 146, 149, 152, 153
iardna, 13-14, 22, 39, 176-77, 182n.20
Ignatius of Jesus, 11n.10, 13, 17n.16, 25, 26n.28, 57, 83, 89n.60, 94-103, 113, 114, 120n.132, 122, 144, 160, 182n.20
illness, 42-43
incense, 25
India, 99, 163
Innocent X, 99
Iran, 3-4
Iraq, 4, 6, 62
Islam, 3-4, 35, 51, 52, 103, 104, 122, 127-28, 165, 203, 254-60
Išu Mšiha, 96, 203, 206-9, 224, 232-33, 241. *See also* Jesus
Iuhana, 224-25. *See also* John the Baptist
Iurba, 216
Iušamin, 39, 175

Jacobites, 72n.20
Jerusalem, 58, 61, 136, 144-50, 151-53, 169, 213, 215-20, 231, 246, 257; destruction, 147, 147-48, 170
Jesuits, 69-70, 70, 72, 80, 83, 90
Jesus, 37, 52, 116, 162, 164, 208, 240-53; baptism, 232-33; virgin birth, 121
Jews, 36, 52, 140-41, 147-48, 203, 205-6, 210, 213-15, 218-19, 242, 257
Joam de Lucena, 75
John the Baptist, 12, 26n.28, 52, 65, 66, 69, 75, 88, 95, 96-97, 111-12, 119-21, 153-55, 224-39; baptism of Jesus, 232-33; birth and education, 225-32; death, 125, 148, 234-38; in Jerusalem, 145; preaching, 154; significance in

Mandaeanism, 162-65; and *tarmidia*, 157-58
John the Evangelist, 75
Jordan River, 14, 39, 235
Judaea, 145
Judaism, 44, 47, 123, 144-45, 160n.54
Juliano de Noronha, 99

Kantaeans, 9
Karun, 5
King of darkness, 179-81
King of Light, 178-79
Kiuan, 203, 204-5
knowledge, 8-9, 34
Koran, 3, 43, 101
Krun, 47
Kuzistan, 5

Labrosse, Joseph, 106n.97
language, 53-54
laupa, 10, 32
Left Ginza, 55
Leonelli, Carlo, 94n.74
Libat, 203, 206
Lidsbarski, Mark, 123
Light, 37-38, 39, 47, 178-79
Lilith, 120-21
liturgies, 54
love, 38
Luther, Martin, 63n.5, 164

Macuch, Rudolf, 124-25, 159
magic texts, 58
malakia, 175
Malka d-Nhura, 39
malkia, 10, 175, 178
Mameluke, 67
Mana, 39, 176, 191
manda, 14-15, 19
Manda d-Hiia, 9, 45, 52, 116, 120, 136, 145-46, 150, 188n.8, 189, 234-38
"Mandaean question," 123-25
Mandaeans: as "apes," 101; as Christians, 71, 74-75, 95, 96; conversion to

269

INDEX

Christianity, 106-10, 144; diaspora, 5; extinguished, 135, 159; flight from Palestine, 97-98, 144; heretical, 158; hostility to Christianity and Judaism, 164-65; interaction with missionaries, 95-98; in Iran, 3-4, 7n.7; as Jewish sect, 125; linear history, 49-50; kingdom, 128; meaning of term, 8-9; Mesopotamian origins, 165; origins in Palestine, 114, 122-23, 125-26, 144, 158, 160; origins in Ṭura d-Madai, 157, 159; persecution in Jerusalem, 129, 147-50, 152-56, 160; Ricoldo description, 65-67

mandi, 14

Mani, 37, 172n.74, 249n.32

Manichaeism, 172, 209-10, 249n.32

Mara d-Rabuta, 39, 119, 136

margna, 10

Maronites, 111n.104

marriage, 17, 56

Mary, 74, 79, 108, 120-21

maṣbuta, 15-16, 17-18, 20, 22

Mascarenhas, Geronimo, 76n.32

masiqta, 28, 32, 57

maṭarata, 57

Matthew of Saint Joseph, 101-4

Matthias of the Holy Spirit, 77

Melchizedek, 47

Melkites, 73n.21

Messiah, 162n.58

meteorological events, 44

miracles, 147, 154

Miriai, 146, 149, 150-53, 219, 220-24. *See also* Mary

missionaries, 69-78, 81, 84, 94n.75, 102-4, 160

monasticism, 209n.24, 248

Mongols, 62, 128

Monophysites, 72n.20

monotheism, 41

moon, 209-10

Mormonism, 161

Moses, 47, 136, 137, 140, 141, 155, 159, 162, 164, 203

"Mount of the Mandaeans, The," 128

"Mount of Media, The," 128

Mšiha. *See* Išu Mšiha

Mšunia Kušta, 45-46, 127, 128, 159, 162

Mubārak, 76-78, 81, 83

Muhammad, 63n.5, 66-67, 153, 154, 158n.46, 162-63, 164, 203, 255, 258n.6

Musa, 133, 134

myrtle, 114

mystery, 190n.17

myth, 38, 130

names, 17

Namrus, 218

napaqa, 29-30

naṣuraiia, 9-10

Nazoraeans, 9

Nbu, 203, 240

Nebuchadnezzar, 147

Negroes, 51, 52

Negus, 67, 69

Nestorians, 72n.20, 112

Nhur Hai, 237

Nhuraita, 202

Nicola Peretti, 88n.54

Nirig, 203, 206, 210-11, 257-59

Nisbai, 224, 226, 228-29. *See also* Elizabeth

Noah, 45n.51, 50-51, 52, 165

Norberg, Matthias, 114-15, 122

Nu, 50, 200-202

Nuraita, 200

Nusairs, 114-15, 116

Old Testament, 36

Oman, 91-92

oral childbirth, 120-21

oral traditions, 128, 134

Oriental Aramaic, 51

Origen, 241n.2

Ottoman Empire, 8, 51, 67-69, 83-84

19994954R00182

Made in the USA
San Bernardino, CA
22 March 2015